Jossey-Bass Teacher

Jossey-Bass Teacher provides educators with practical knowledge and tools to create a positive and lifelong impact on student learning. We offer classroom-tested and research-based teaching resources for a variety of grade levels and subject areas. Whether you are an aspiring, new, or veteran teacher, we want to help you make every teaching day your best.

From ready-to-use classroom activities to the latest teaching framework, our value-packed books provide insightful, practical, and comprehensive materials on the topics that matter most to K–12 teachers. We hope to become your trusted source for the best ideas from the most experienced and respected experts in the field.

Whole Novels
for the
Whole Class

Whole Novels for the Whole Class

A Student-Centered Approach

Ariel Sacks

JB JOSSEY-BASS™

A Wiley Brand

About the Author

Ariel Sacks has been teaching middle school English in New York City public schools for nine years. She studied progressive pedagogy at Bank Street College of Education and is committed to implementing student-centered methods successfully in public schools. After teaching seventh- and eighth-grade transitional English Language Learners in a bilingual school in East Harlem and serving as eighth-grade English teacher, team leader, and department chair at a middle school in Crown Heights, Brooklyn, she currently teaches eighth-grade English and coordinates the grade's advisory program at Brooklyn Prospect Charter School. A coauthor of *Teaching 2030: What We Must Do for Our Students and Our Public Schools—Now and in the Future*, Ariel has published articles in *Education Week Teacher, Educational Leadership*, the *New York Daily News*, and Bank Street's *Occasional Papers Series*, and has presented on innovative teaching methods and education policy issues at conferences across the country. She writes regularly about teaching practice and educational issues on her CTQ-featured blog, On the Shoulders of Giants.

■ ■ ■

The illustrations at the start of each chapter were drawn by Renata Robinson-Glenn, who teaches middle school social studies at the Young Women's Leadership

Academy of Queens, New York. She and Ariel both studied middle school education at Bank Street College, where Madeleine Ray was their advisor. Renata first worked with Ariel as a student teacher, leading a whole novel study, and then began teaching social studies at the same school. Renata and Ariel worked together on the same grade team for four years and collaborated in their teaching of literacy, critical thinking, and social skills to their students. When the opportunity to create illustrations for this book arose, Renata brought together her passions for art and student-centered teaching practice to create rich visual representations of concepts from the whole novels method.

Acknowledgments

Years ago, I named my blog "On the Shoulders of Giants." Though it may not be the most original name, I could not think of a better one, because I truly believe that any success I have as a teacher and writer is standing on the shoulders of giants. Here I acknowledge some of the giants who helped me write this book.

Madeleine Ray, for sharing your genius, for your incredible persistence, and for your mentorship in helping me become a teacher who takes risks and stands by principles; Kate Gagnon, who saw the potential in this book, took a chance on me, and offered thoughtful support along the way; Robin Lloyd, Tracy Gallagher, and everyone else at Jossey-Bass who helped me through this process and made this book look great and real well; John Norton, for being my writing mentor and encouraging me (and so many others) to find my voice as a teacher writer; Barnett Berry and Jon Snyder, for believing I had important things to say and helping me grow into a teacher leader; Dan Rubenstein, LaNolia Omowanile, Penny Marzulli, and Craig Cetrulo at Brooklyn Prospect Charter School, for providing me a wonderful, flexible educational environment to continue developing and sharing the methods in this book; Marcia Stiman-Lavian, Daniel Brink-Washington, and Yusuf Ali, the wonderful learning specialists who have cotaught with me and contributed over the past several years to the development of whole novels methods; the families of my students at Brooklyn Prospect Charter School, for supporting me on this project; Nancy Toes Tangel, for your thought partnership, your belief and innovations in the whole novels approach; Anthony Rebora, for helping me first get the idea out there in an article in *Education Week Teacher*; Renata Robinson-Glenn, for being an amazing teacher, colleague, friend, and artist; Meredith Byers and Liliana Richter, for your courageous work with whole novels and for keeping up a dialogue with me about it; Makaira Casey, for understanding the method and lending generous help as I was writing the manuscript; Juliana Garofalo, for helping to lead discussions this year and sharing your reflections with me; my husband, Samuel Cruz, for keeping on me to make this book happen and for supporting me during the countless long nights of writing; my parents, for advice, moral support, and your roles as teachers in my life; Baba, for guiding me into the world of literature when I was a child; and all of my students, past and present, for developing whole novels with me, helping me see what's working, and always showing me how it can be better.

Contents

■   ■   ■

For Madeleine Ray, a true teacher

Whole Novels
for the
Whole Class

Introduction

When I began my teacher training at Bank Street College ten years ago, my faculty advisor, Madeleine Ray, who founded the middle school education program there, encouraged me to try an unusual approach to teaching a novel I had chosen: *Scorpions*, by Walter Dean Myers. I was a student teacher at Bank Street's own School for Children, a private lab school for progressive teaching on the Upper West Side of Manhattan. "Instead of having them read sections and making them answer questions about each one," she said, "let them read the whole thing. Then have them talk about it, like adults would do in a real book club." I was not sure why she thought this was going to be a better way at that point, but I trusted her enough to give it a try. That was one of the benefits of student teaching: I got to try things out.

My students at the School for Children easily read the 210-page book in the week I gave them to complete it, recorded their thoughts on sticky notes as they read as I asked them to do, and brought their responses to share. We had a fascinating time discussing and taking apart the novel, finding evidence for our assertions, acting out sections, and writing about the big issues it brought up. The process seemed to bring a lot of the students out of their shells, out of the usual roles they

1

assumed in the classroom, and into a multidimensional literary world. I was intrigued.

The next year I got a full-time position teaching seventh- and eighth-grade English in a public Title I middle school in East Harlem, working with a diverse group of students, many of whom were transitional English Language Learners (they were fluent in conversational English but still very much acquiring the language). I carefully chose an engaging, developmentally appropriate novel for my new students to read. I gave them a daily reading schedule and a due date on which they were to have completed the book and begin discussions and activities.

On the date the book was due, we gathered together for discussions. It quickly became apparent that exactly half the class had read the book and the other half had not gotten past the first few pages. Some students did not even seem to know there had been a deadline. I realized I had some problem solving to do if I wanted to use this approach with students of such varying levels of reading experience and study habits. And yet I was impressed that half of my students had completed the entire book on their own and were speaking their minds and analyzing the story. We had incredible discussions with the half who had finished, driven by their authentic responses to the novel and propelled by rereading sections they chose for closer analysis. They seemed intellectually and socially energized by their experience and were hungry for more. I wanted to help all my students rise to the challenge.

For the past nine years, I've been developing a dynamic student-centered structure for reading and studying whole novels as a whole class. I've continued to work with Madeleine Ray, sharing my practice with her and learning from her unwavering commitment to teaching methods that are in sync with both children's needs and the nature of literature. I've also had the chance to collaborate with other students of Madeleine, like Nancy Toes Tangel, who taught whole novels in Newark, New Jersey, for years, as well as great special education coteachers, all of whom have influenced and cocreated the program. I've worked in three different New York City public schools—in East Harlem, in Crown Heights in Brooklyn, and now at Brooklyn Prospect Charter School, which serves a diverse population of students integrated across race, ethnicity, and socioeconomic status. I've continued to develop the method in response to the unique needs of each group of children and the lessons I glean from each whole novel study.

I've seen my students go from struggling to decode simple texts to literally plowing through three-hundred-page eighth-grade-level novels independently. I've seen shy and reluctant students become avid discussers of literature, powerfully arguing their points, and outspoken students find new channels for their voices in writing. Most of all, I've seen my students develop a genuine love of reading and a community in which to practice it.

I've also come to understand the theoretical basis behind the approach Madeleine Ray has been advocating for years in her Children's Literature course. Teachers must protect their students' subjective experience of reading fiction if we want them to truly read and love books, study and think critically about them, and explore original ideas in their writing. We must step out of the role of the chief thinker in the classroom and create space and support for a classroom full of critical thinkers.

THE WHOLE NOVELS APPROACH

Rather than using novels simply to teach basic literacy skills and comprehension strategies, the whole novels program approaches literature as art. Theorists such as Louise Rosenblatt have long argued that reading literature is a subjective experience, whereby an author compels a reader to enter a virtual world, live in it, and respond to it.

So often in school, we steal that experience away from students by attempting to control it in one way or another. We usually do this with the good intention of accomplishing our short-term learning objectives more quickly. In so doing, however, we bypass the natural affinity children of all ages have for stories. Ironically, we find ourselves on a much more arduous route to creating literate students and critical thinkers, one that often loses learners along the way.

Whole novels is built on the idea that students must first read and experience a work of literature wholly and authentically. After reading the entire story—with layers of support from teachers and classmates—students begin the process of analyzing the work and their reactions to it through student-driven, seminar-style discussions. In multiple rounds of these discussions, students construct deeper levels of understanding and analysis of the work. They make the shift away from their own personal responses to consider the author's perspective and investigate the decisions the author has made in creating the text.

In the whole novels program, we try to build up readers' literary repertoire— not by quickly touring genres but by selecting a series of works that build on common, developmentally relevant themes. Students begin to recognize similar themes and structural elements as they appear in increasingly difficult texts, a process that builds their confidence and understanding. The focal point of the program is the novel, but within each novel study, we include other forms that build a rich, well-rounded experience for readers. I include nonfiction texts, poetry, folktales, and films to facilitate deep examination of the themes and forms over the course of a year.

Authentic reading experiences and student-driven discussions lead organically to stronger writing. Students develop their own ideas for writing based on the content of discussions. Intellectual arguments lead to literary essays, and critiques of plot and the writer's style lead to inspired experimentation in fiction writing.

Whole novel studies serve as a foundational piece of my overall English language arts (ELA) curriculum—and much of the writing and vocabulary work we do revolves around our literature studies. However, as English teachers know well, the curricular demands of our subject are heavy. The whole novels program does not encompass my entire English language arts curriculum. Writing units and lessons may not always connect explicitly to our novel studies, and I strive to balance whole-class novel studies with independent reading cycles, where students have the opportunity to read books they've chosen for themselves. Weaving together these multiple threads is a challenge, but I'm increasingly happy with the balance I've found among them, with whole novel studies at the center propelling the group forward.

AN INVITATION TO READERS

This book sets out my own journey working with students on whole novels—the methods, understandings, and issues. I do this partly for the humbling opportunity it affords me to take apart the practices, look at them, and understand them further. It's my hope that my experiences with whole novels will inspire other educators to engage with the ideas and methods with students in their own classrooms and school communities. I invite readers—adopters and skeptics alike—to join a dialogue about the work at www.arielsacks.com.

The whole novels structures are practical and classroom tested, but flexible enough to allow other practitioners to make their own discoveries, adaptations, and extensions of the basic model in their own contexts. The book presents a guide to implementing a full-fledged whole novels program, but it includes many single lessons, activities, and teaching strategies that teachers can adopt right away in their classrooms. Teachers can also try out a whole novel study to widen the range of experiences students have in their course without abandoning other methods with which they have found success.

My teaching experience has always been in middle school, and the materials and stories I share are primarily from my own classroom. The whole novels methodology, however, is applicable to any age group that reads novels. Madeleine Ray, Nancy Toes Tangel, and I have worked with teachers ranging from third through twelfth grades on implementing whole novel studies, and I draw from those experiences, too.

I write this today, knowing that the method is still growing, and even my own writing cannot keep up with it! I don't want readers to interpret the practices in this book as fixed or absolute. I view the whole novels method as very much alive and responsive to different teachers, situations, and groups of students. I hope this book offers a balance of big ideas about teaching literature, practical lessons and materials, and inspiration to ask questions, take risks, and innovate.

ALIGNING WITH COMMON CORE STANDARDS

I'm pleasantly surprised at how well the whole novels program aligns to the new Common Core State Standards. For example, the program has been especially successful in developing students' ability to critically analyze literary texts, including the author's craft and structure—a skill heavily emphasized in the Common Core Reading standards. Whole novels also allows for plenty of nonfiction reading without decreasing the amount of fiction read in a Common Core–aligned ELA classroom. To make it easier for educators to find lessons that help students develop the skills and understandings the standards require, I've tagged sections of the book that highlight teaching practices that support specific Common Core English

Language Arts Standards. These sections can be found by searching specific standards through the index. (I've used the ELA Anchor Standards for College and Career Readiness, which apply to all secondary grade levels, and I've focused primarily on reading standards, although speaking, listening, and writing factor prominently into the whole novels program.)

LOGISTICS OF MY TEACHING CONTEXTS

In order for you to assess how whole novels might work in your class, I offer some information on the three contexts in which I've taught whole novels:

- *Rafael Cordero Bilingual Academy:* A bilingual program in a large Title I middle school in East Harlem. This was a neighborhood school, and nearly all of the students receive free or reduced-price lunch.
  - I taught two ninety-minute classes daily—one seventh grade and one eighth grade. Class sizes were small just for ELA, with about twenty students in each class for a total of forty students. Most of my seventh-grade students looped up and became my eighth-grade students the following year.
  - I taught transitional ELLs, who had stepped up from bilingual classes to general education classes most of the day but were grouped together with me for ELA. My students were mostly Latino, with some students from West Africa and the Middle East. Most were immigrants or long-term ELLs— young people born in the United States but with home languages other than English. However, I always had a few students who were native English speakers and were placed in my class to separate them from certain other students to minimize conflict.
  - Another curriculum was mandated for English teachers while I was there, but I found ways to take the best from the mandated curriculum and still teach whole novels. I had support from Bank Street faculty advisors through a partnership between Bank Street and my school. I was provided a good classroom library, but the only class sets were old and dusty from the last mandated curriculum. Because my class sizes were so small, I ended up buying class sets of paperbacks with my own money and using the Barnes & Noble's educator discount. I spent about $110 for a set for one class.

- *School for Democracy and Leadership:* A small, public Title I secondary school, serving grades 6 to 12 in Crown Heights, Brooklyn. This is a neighborhood school, and nearly all of the students receive free or reduced-price lunch.
  - I taught three fifty-seven-minute classes daily. Each class had an average of twenty-three students, for a total of about seventy students. This was the entire eighth grade, and classes were heterogeneously grouped.
  - The majority of my students were from West Indian households; some were new immigrants from the islands, including Haiti, and others had been born in the United States. A smaller number of students were African American. There was a significant special education population at the school, and I cotaught one inclusion class with a special education teacher.
  - The school has no mandated curriculum to contend with, but also no classroom library provided. I was able to bring many books I'd purchased over the years from my previous school and ordered some books at the beginning of the year. It was often difficult to know when there was funding for books and when book orders would arrive, so often I ended up investing my own money in class sets or to populate my classroom lending library.
- *Brooklyn Prospect Charter School:* A new, midsized, public charter school, serving students of mixed income levels, building up to serve grades 6 through 12. Approximately 45 percent of students receive free or reduced-price lunch.
  - I teach four fifty-two-minute English classes daily. Class sizes are between 24 and 28, for a total of 106 students in the eighth grade. I first taught seventh grade, and then looped up to eighth grade for a second year with the same students. Classes are heterogeneously grouped.
  - My students are highly diverse in terms of race, ethnicity, socioeconomics, and learning needs. My eighth graders' reading levels span from second grade through college. There is a large special education population, and I have cotaught inclusion classes with three different learning specialists.
  - There is no mandated curriculum for ELA, though there are demands around collecting data on student progress. There are funds, as well as a simple and reliable system for ordering books, so I no longer spend my own money on class sets. My colleagues, administration, and parents are supportive of whole novel studies.

I include many anecdotes about my own students in this book. The details of these stories are real, though I have sometimes created composite students. Student work samples are included, all of them unedited. I have changed the names of students to protect their identities.

HOW THE BOOK IS ORGANIZED

This book is divided into two main parts. The chapters in Part 1 set out the big ideas and essential practices of the whole novels program. The chapters in Part 2 are about making whole novels work in real-world contexts. They explore how my colleagues and I have developed the whole novels program in order to support students in their participation and growth.

Two other features of this book are unique. Between several of the chapters are short sections, called Parts of the Whole, that provide important context or tools that support elements of the program or keep it moving in the right direction. In addition, I provide links for video clips from my classroom to illustrate practices I describe throughout the book.

The appendices at the end of the book include more examples of materials I use and samples of student work.

In Chapter 1, I explain just what I mean by "whole novels" and explain why this method is meaningful and appropriate for students, helping them develop a love of literature and prepare for college-level work. I make the case for student-centered pedagogy, for whole class novel studies in general, and for students to read the entire work before having analytical discussions. Following this chapter, the first Parts of the Whole section shows my annual curriculum map, illustrating how whole novel studies fit within my entire ELA course.

In Chapter 2, I discuss the five dimensions I consider when selecting literature for whole novel studies. I carefully create a year-long trajectory in which the texts as well as the ideas build in complexity.

Chapter 3 turns to the lessons I use to teach students to respond to literature using literal, inferential, and critical thinking and record their thoughts on sticky notes as they read. I explain my reasons for this approach and how it fuels the students' reading of whole novels. The Parts of the Whole section after this chapter presents a view of whole novel study from start to finish.

Chapter 4 explains how I structure the discussions that take place after students have finished reading the entire novel and my role in these discussions. I illustrate the tools of rereading and finding evidence to support claims, the role of student-generated homework assignments, and how to keep the seminars going for multiple rounds. I describe the patterns I've noticed in the shape the discussions take over three days and the kinds of discoveries students make by the second and third days. The Parts of the Whole that follows addresses lessons from beginning teachers on leading whole novel studies.

Chapter 5 outlines the ways in which the whole novels program fuels my students' writing. I provide examples of expository and creative writing opportunities that emerge from whole novel studies.

In Chapter 6, the opening chapter of Part 2, I describe the preparation and ritual I've developed for beginning a novel study, as well as the organization and accountability structures I set up that support student participation and success through the reading portion of the whole novel study. The Parts of the Whole section that follows Chapter 6 explains my classroom setup, which I've designed to support my routines and rituals.

Chapter 7 describes the group miniprojects and supplemental experiences my students engage in during the reading portion of a whole novel study. These speak to how I ensure that students are acquiring specific ELA skills and literary concepts across the year. The final Parts of the Whole, following this chapter, addresses the role of technology in the program.

Chapter 8 addresses the crucial question of how to support the appropriate growth of all students, struggling and advanced readers alike, in the whole novels program.

I end the book in Chapter 9 by sharing some data on the impact of the whole novels program on student learning. I reflect as well on why this program prepares students for the lives ahead of them and share some of the new directions my colleagues and I are exploring within the program.

PART 1

Essential Practices

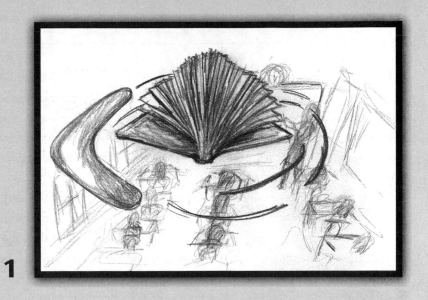

1

A Case for Whole Novels for the Whole Class

"That carefully prepared leap of faith my students and I take . . ."

I n our second whole novel study of the year, one of my most struggling readers, Hector, had a breakthrough. He is not literate in his native language of Spanish and has major difficulty decoding multisyllabic words in English. He has a bright mind and lots of potential but had resisted putting in the immense effort it would take for him to make progress. He had often dismissed learning opportunities with phrases like "I don't know" and "It's boring." But when he borrowed a classroom MP3 player with the audio tracks of the book, Hector began to follow along in the grade-appropriate novel the class was reading together, *When You Reach Me* by Rebecca Stead.

At the end of the period, the students had a five-minute social break, but Hector did not want to stop listening to and reading the book. Whereas his attitude toward education seemed to have revolved around what he couldn't do and how much he hated reading, he was suddenly saying to me and the other students, "Don't bother me! This book is really *interesting*!" It was the choice of the word *interesting* that especially called my attention. To be sure, he was happy to be able to read what everyone else was reading and share in the experience; more important, he was experiencing a feeling that was totally new to him in relation to the written word—a feeling of genuine interest.

In this chapter, I make a theoretical and practical case for why I believe the whole novels approach provides a natural and compelling way into reading for all kinds of learners. Struggling readers like Hector, who've been through the gamut of reading interventions, have woken up to literature in the whole novels program, and advanced readers, who often feel marginalized in reading classes that don't challenge them, have found belonging and new directions through this approach. Why this method works and why it's not currently a norm in schools—but could be—are the questions I begin to answer here.

LET THEM HAVE STORIES

Stories are interesting; there's no question about it. We are "the story-telling animals," Jonathan Gottschall shows us in his fascinating book, *The Storytelling Animal: How Stories Make Us Human* (2012). We live for the stuff of stories! We have an innate drive to experience and tell stories; they are part of how we think and relate to the world every moment of our lives. Stories are also an important piece of how our brains learn and remember. Dan Willingham, author of *Why Don't Students Like School? A Cognitive Scientist Answers Questions about How the Mind Works and What It Means for the Classroom* (2010), explains, "The human mind seems exquisitely tuned to understand and remember stories—so much so that psychologists sometimes refer to them as 'psychologically privileged,' meaning that they are treated differently in the memory than other types of material" (66–67). Later Willingham notes that in psychological experiments, stories were consistently rated more interesting than any other presentation format, even if the information was the same.

And yet we also have a widespread problem across the United States of students not wanting to read—not even stories. Kelly Gallagher, author of *Readicide* (2009), believes the problem has reached a point of "systemic killing of the love of reading" (2), and I can't say he's wrong. The coexistence of these two opposite realities suggests one thing to me: when students are asked to read fiction, and this mostly happens for them in school, they aren't really experiencing the stories.

Over the past ten years, it seems as though the whole country has fixed its eyes on the noble goal of teaching all children to read but gotten horribly distracted by its questionably motivated doppelganger: the goal of raising all students' literacy levels a requisite amount each year, as measured on a standardized test. Under the pressure and threats of raising scores, it is easy to lose sight of the reasons we even chose to devote our careers to teaching children to read and the reasons we love to read in the first place.

Even the strongest among us have probably found ourselves on occasion telling students they must read a particular story or random excerpt because someone with greater authority than ourselves told us that we had to do it. Or how many of us, in a moment of weakness, have caught ourselves telling students they won't pass their standardized exam or move to the next grade if they don't sit down and read *right now*?

These scenarios are part of the reality of teaching in the current test-driven educational climate, and they shape our students' school realities even more. Most of us know that students don't learn because they are told to and that standardized test scores do not motivate most of our students on a day-to-day basis. Furthermore, the mental frameworks of the testing culture become damaging when we build our practices on them.

To combat this pressure, we need to consciously seek out the deeper motivations, realities, and needs that exist for our students and ourselves. Then we must build our curriculum practices and the language we use with students around these deeper goals.

Humans inherently love and need stories. Why is this hard to see in schools today?

A LOVE SUBVERTED: MY OWN STORY OF READING

Strangely, I don't remember reading a single novel for any middle school English class I took in the early 1990s. I can recall the names of some of the books I pretended to read and can still picture the teacher talking about the important points of last night's chapter in front of the class. I remember one of my English teachers talking to us about *To Kill a Mockingbird*—a truly great book, I discovered later. I guess I found her lecture irrelevant to my life and whatever occupied my mind at that point. It didn't even occur to me to want to read it. With the information she gave in lectures and assignment sheets that allowed me to search through a chapter I never read for the answers, I was able to do well on the tests, or whatever else was required, without more than reading a chapter here or there. And this was before the days of finding book reviews and summaries on the Internet in seconds flat!

Secretly, however, I was a big reader. My grandmother, Baba, an educator herself, always gave me gifts of the latest and best adolescent fiction. These novels appealed to my own interests. I remember *The Mozart Season*, by Virginia Euwer Wolff, about a girl my age who was practicing Mozart for a big violin audition. I instantly connected with this book because I, too, studied violin seriously and battled the challenge of practicing. I also remember staying up late into the night reading *The Devil's Arithmetic*, by Jane Yolen, about a Jewish American girl, like myself, who asks at Passover why we have to remember the past and is transported to an alternate reality in which she is a prisoner in a Nazi concentration camp.

I didn't stay up reading these books because someone would be checking the next day to see if I had read. Nor was I motivated by some abstract notion that I had to improve my reading skills. In fact, no one at school even knew what I read at home. Had I shared more with them, my teachers might have known me better; however, as a middle school student, I was concerned primarily with what my friends and classmates thought. Sadly, I perceived that reading was not a socially acceptable hobby in my 'tween social circle, so I read privately. I talked to Baba on the phone about the books, but I never let them see the light of day in school.

My experience may not resonate with everyone, but the disengagement I felt is no stranger to English classrooms today. Many adolescents don't see their interests represented in the assigned reading they do for school and the tasks tacked on to check their understanding and teach skills with no discernable application. Gallagher (2009) argues that the limiting of authentic reading experiences is one of the key causes of "readicide" (4).

BREAKING FREE OF THE CHIEF THINKER ROLE: PUTTING STUDENTS' INTERESTS FIRST

One of the barriers to authentic reading experiences for kids is what I call "the chief thinker" role, which is when teachers privilege their own questions and interpretations over those of their students. It can be tempting to do, because adults do know more about the world than children do, and part of our job is to impart some of our knowledge to students. Also, many of our own teachers positioned themselves as chief thinkers, and it can be difficult to find models who truly depart from this one.

However, we can't teach by doing the thinking for the students. If we do, we discourage them from connecting authentically with the world the author has created, effectively robbing them of this experience. Under these conditions, students become insecure about their own thinking (perhaps asking themselves, *Why can't I understand this book the way my teacher does?*), especially if they don't have people like my grandmother in their lives to validate their thinking behind the scenes. For a child's interpretation of a work of literature to be measured against that of an adult is not only unfair, but also misunderstands what the act of reading fiction actually involves.

At its core, a literature program must answer and be propelled by the desire humans have to experience stories of all forms, the nature of which changes over the course of a reader's life. (More on this in Chapter 2.) Often teachers' efforts to improve students' technical skills in reading seem to stray from this crucial aspect of a reader's development.

When we read fiction, our intention goes beyond comprehension. It is a deeper, highly personal process. In *Fiction and the Unconscious* (1962), Simon Lesser, a psychologist and literary critic who studied and wrote extensively on the psychological impact of literature, explains the phenomenon:

> Fiction accomplishes something more miraculous than [a formulated understanding]. It *involves* us in the events it puts before us, without permitting us to become aware of the nature and extent, or usually even the fact, of our involvement. The emotions fiction arouses in us are evidence of this: they are too powerful to be explained solely on the basis of our cognitive reactions, conscious and even unconscious. (189)

If we read only to comprehend, we would read every text with equal interest and with little or no response. But as both teachers and readers, we know this is hardly the case. On the contrary, we read fiction to gain experience. Under the right conditions, we take great pleasure in the process, which allows us to inhabit the lives of others: we can journey to foreign lands, solve murder cases, get swept up in great love affairs, and confront our worst fears. Much like the compelling virtual worlds of games (though there are key differences in the use of imagination during reading versus video games), these opportunities provide a powerful incentive for children and adolescents to read fiction.

Without student motivation to experience a story, our efforts at teaching comprehension through fiction are dull, and our attempts to engage students in literary analysis lack purpose and context.

Back to Hector, and his comment, "Don't bother me! This book is really interesting!" The feeling he had at that moment is more compelling than any achievement goal we can set for kids. We must keep that reality front and center in the literature classroom, no matter what other priorities we have for our students.

WHY STUDY WHOLE NOVELS AS A WHOLE CLASS?

Independent reading programs, where students select their own reading materials, have done a lot to connect students with developmentally appropriate books and create classrooms full of readers. I'm compelled by the richness of Donalyn Miller's practices as a teacher of reading, revealed in *The Book Whisperer* (2009), and I've learned from her classroom, especially when it comes to my own practices around students' independent reading. If I were a parent, I would be thrilled for my child to be in her sixth-grade English language arts class.

At the same time, I would not want my child's entire English language arts education to be structured around independent reading, as some proponents of reading workshop models suggest. The main argument against whole class novel studies has been that one book will never meet all the needs of a whole class of students and that the traditional methods of teaching whole class novels are flawed. While it is a challenge to select books and work with them in ways that benefit all students, I believe there are needs that whole class novels can serve, which pure independent reading models don't.

Even Miller writes at the end of *The Book Whisperer*, "Yes, students benefit from the deep analysis of literature that a thorough look at one book provides." She adds, "You create a common literacy experience to which you can make future connections, and reading a book together fosters community among your students and you." But, she qualifies, "There needs to be a balance between picking a book apart to examine its insides and experiencing the totality of what a book offers" (127). In her suggestions for alternatives to traditional practices, she calls for a rethinking of the whole class novel.

The whole novels program, which I have been developing over the past ten years with Madeleine Ray of Bank Street College of Education, is a radical rethinking of how to engage students with works of literature using the novel as the primary literary form. In the whole novels program, we honor the nature of the literary art by having students look at the whole work, not breaking the experience into little pieces. Through the work, we create an intellectual community that is socially relevant for students and gives them opportunities to build the critical-thinking skills, creativity, and habits of mind they need in the twenty-first century. The shared experience capitalizes on the drive of adolescents to connect to their peers and construct knowledge together.

 To hear from students about their experience in the program, visit https://vimeo.com/61677466 for video 1.1: Student Voices in Whole Novels.

Madeleine Ray distinguishes between a literature program and a reading program in her Children's Literature course at Bank Street College of Education. She writes the following in a course handout:

> A literature program focuses on the reader's response to the literary work and not on reading skills per se . . . In reading we emphasize code breaking; the specific meaning of words in sentences . . . these are denotative activities and skills . . . Literary "skills" . . . are mainly connotative. The reader, through experiences with various fictional works, builds awareness of varying levels of quality in writing; of imaginative power in the author's ability to tell a story that [continuously] engages the reader; of uniqueness in style through the use of language, and

the unity of the world of literature as old plots are reimagined and permutated into new stories.

We build on the human desire to enter a virtual world by structuring a literature program in a way that protects the reader's experience of the story. Children should experience compelling works of literature that in their conflicts and themes are relevant to their development, and in their use of language and other craft elements are aesthetic works of art. The experience becomes intellectual when students can share their varied responses in a community forum and begin to study the ways in which authors are able to use language to provoke certain responses in their readers. We look at the ways in which those responses differ for each reader and what those differences mean.

These critical analysis skills are central in the Common Core State Standards, but teachers are struggling to figure out how to achieve them in ways that engage students at their level. Whole novels provides a way to bring about critical analysis quite naturally. Perhaps ironically, I've found that the key to helping students take a work apart for close analysis is letting them read the whole thing first. Figure 1.1 shows how the interaction between student and text works in the whole novels program, leading to critical analysis of the work.

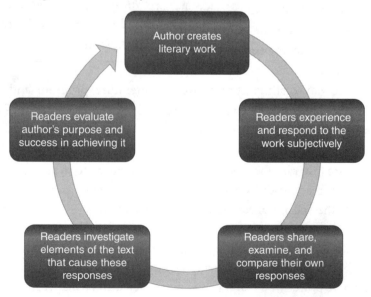

Figure 1.1 Whole Novels Reader Response and Analysis Cycle

WHY WE READ THE WHOLE BOOK FIRST

Imagine going to see a movie in the theater. You've heard good things about this movie, and you feel that special movie theater excitement when the lights go down and the movie begins.

After the second scene, the movie stops. The lights come on, and someone at the front of the theater with a microphone starts asking people what they think about the movie. Why do you think the director made this movie? What is motivating the characters? How will it end? The person in the front then begins taking people's comments about the movie so far.

You try to listen, but you were much more interested in the movie itself than in what random people in the theater think about it. The person at the microphone starts talking about how one of the characters in the movie reminds her of herself when she was young. Someone next to you whispers, "I don't care what these people think about this right now. I came to see the movie!" The two of you begin chatting about other things in an effort to kill time until the movie resumes. Finally, the person in front says, "Well, that's all the time we have for today. Come back tomorrow, same time, same place, to see the next scene!"

Would you come back?

Now consider another scenario. You've just seen a really interesting movie in the theater. When it finishes, the lights come up, and someone in front of the theater with a microphone explains that there will be a brief break during which people are encouraged to visit the concession stands. Then people are invited to discuss the film in special rooms in small groups. The theater will even have the ability to rerun certain scenes, such as the opening scene, to spark discussion. You happen to have an hour to kill until you need to move to your next commitment.

Would you consider participating in such a discussion?

The whole novels method builds on the reader's interest in experiencing the story by allowing students to read the entire book before formal discussions of the work begin. This may seem logical, as in the movie analogy. Adult book clubs use the same structure: members usually take a month or so to read on their own time and then come together to discuss the entire book. College seminars work the same way, using a faster pace of about a week to read a book.

In my experience, however, having spent time in many different English language arts classrooms in public, private, and charter schools in New York City, I have very rarely seen students read an entire novel before being asked to speak or write analytically about it. The standard for whole class novel studies in both traditional and progressive classrooms seems to be that students read and discuss the books chapter by chapter.

WHY NOT DISCUSS CHAPTER BY CHAPTER?

The chapter-by-chapter model parses up the reader's experience in a way that takes a lot of the pleasure out of the process and can even interfere with comprehension. The story is a piece of art that is intended to be experienced as a whole. If we were reading a collection of short stories or poems, we could naturally discuss each story or poem. But a novel is a longer form created to allow readers to more deeply enter an elaborate world the author has developed. The power of the novel comes from the time we spend in these worlds with the characters, experiencing the conflicts, the symbols, and the author's unique style of prose. In the classroom, we can build a social experience of living in the literary world without discussing each chapter.

The prolonged experience in the literary world of the novel is crucial to understanding and appreciating the form. Lesser (1962) explains that in order for a reader to become captivated by the world of a story, "the indispensable condition of such an experience, and the first stage of the experience itself, is a relaxation of the vigilance usually exercised by the ego. A willing suspension of disbelief, a receptive attitude, is essential not only to the enjoyment but even the understanding of comprehension" (192). Reading fiction is a highly personal experience, in which the reader is actively participating. In her article, "Literature: The Reader's Role" (1960), Louise Rosenblatt describes it this way:

> In reading a poem or novel, we are preoccupied with the experience we are living through in the actual reading. We are intimately involved in what we are recreating under the guidance of the text . . . We live through the suspense, the foreboding, the ultimate resolution. The structure of the work for us is the structure of our experience while under its spell . . . No one else can read—i.e., experience—a literary work of art for us. (39)

What happens to a student's experience of a work of fiction—to the student's state of receptive relaxation—when, with the best of intentions, we constantly interrupt with formal requests to evaluate, predict, and express their thoughts about the story while they are busy reading? Are they able to remain receptive to the world the author is creating, when, like overbearing parents, we try to control their experience? When adults read, we allow the author to guide us with nothing but the work of art he or she created. We need to help students develop that special relationship with a text rather than trying to be a third member of the relationship—especially since we are authority figures for students, and they are conditioned to look to us for answers and interpretations. This reality makes it far more difficult for students to relax their egos while they read. We need to step away to allow genuine interaction between our students and novels.

As adult readers, we have a tendency to want our students to "get everything" in the novel, so we don't want to let them read too much without us. When we try to direct a student to discover all of the features of a text during a first reading, Lesser (1962) reminds us that we "may require him to read with a strained alertness, which is inimical to enjoyment" (193). That state of pleasure and relaxation is necessary not only for a student to like a book, but also for a reader to be able to understand the work of fiction. Kelly Gallagher identifies this problem as "overteaching books," citing it as one of the four causes of "readicide."

We also have to understand that our reading of a story is colored by our own imaginations and therefore is different for each reader. Contrasting writers with painters, Gottschall (2012) explains that writers "give us expert line drawings with hints on filling them in. Our minds provide most of the information in the scene, most of the color, shading, and texture. When we read stories, this massive creative effort is going on all the time, chugging away beneath our awareness" (5). If we push our own interpretations of fiction on our students, we also push our own imaginations on them, which can shut down their imaginative process of reading the novel. If their imaginative process shuts down, they will lose the ability to comprehend the story. Thus, teachers can easily shoot themselves in the foot as they try to help their students "get the story"!

When we allow students to read an entire novel, they can experience it fully and truly themselves, even though this understanding may be limited to their relatively few years on the planet, as compared with our own.

STUDENT-DRIVEN DISCUSSIONS: MAKING MEANING OF THE WHOLE EXPERIENCE

Armed with their story experience, students bubble over with things to say in a discussion, often surprising even themselves. Though I play a key role as facilitator, students decide what gets discussed and they can say anything they want about the book. I find that they are eager to listen to other students' reactions to characters and issues in the book and use evidence to argue their points. (For more on how I structure whole novel discussions, see Chapter 5.)

In whole novel discussions, students are motivated to reread sections that caused confusion, or were particularly intense, for deeper meaning and alternative interpretations. In the second and third readings of passages during discussions, students naturally become more analytical in a way that does not happen in a first reading. At that point, the work of critical analysis that many teachers labor at doing with students along the way can be done much more efficiently, powered by intense student motivation.

The practice of having students read an entire novel before holding discussions does present some challenges for us, but in teaching, we constantly face challenges and choose which ones to address. This, I believe, is worth taking on

---

Student Comments about Discussions from End-of-Year Survey, 2011–2012

- "It's good and helpful to share your ideas, and work off of the ideas of others."
- "Even if the literature sucks, it's always nice to discuss with others about the good parts and bad parts. You also find different things within the literature when discussing it."
- "It's interesting to read something and hear new perspectives on it, and also be able to share your own thoughts."
- "I like hearing other people's perspectives."
- "I have always liked debating big ideas with others."
- "It's interesting to hear other people's opinions and let it alter your own."

---

because it provides meaningful, pleasurable experiences for students and leads to high levels of critical thinking and creativity. When I prioritize the innate drive children have to experience a story, I find that they are willing to work hard to develop the reading skills they need to sustain the work.

It's sort of like my friend who has just fallen in love with someone who speaks only Japanese. Whereas before, he had only marginal interest in learning Japanese, he is now receiving regular love letters in Japanese. He has figured out how to translate them. He seeks help from tutors and spends the time it takes to learn the meaning in the words and to be able to respond. Love of story and membership in a novel community can create the same phenomenon for struggling readers, as it is doing for Hector and others in my classes. In order to create such conditions, we need to believe in the power of the stories we select and allow students to experience them the way their authors intended for them to be read.

BUT WILL THEY READ IT?

In conversations with teachers about the whole novels program, a common concern is that they fear, or expect, that students simply won't read the book. I understand the worry; however, I've spent years devising ways to make sure all my students are able and motivated to do the reading. Here are the keys I have found to making this happen:

1. *A positive expectation.* If we don't believe they will read a book we've asked them to read, then it is doubtful that they will. But if we do believe they will, students will most likely try their best. Conditions 2 through 4 will help you to feel more confident that they will be able to meet the challenge and help them believe you when you tell them they can do it. When students experience the discussion seminars once, there is added motivation to complete the books and participate.
2. *Strategic book selection.* In Chapter 2, I discuss the criteria I have for choosing books for a whole or half class that appeal to students' developmental, cultural, and social interests and appropriately match their reading levels.
3. *A habit of free-form authentic response to stories as they read rather than depending on teacher questioning.* In the next chapter, I share my method for teaching this habit.

4. *A system for holding students accountable for reading.* Although no teacher can force any student to do anything, we use the business of routines, grades, and outreach to encourage students to keep up with assignments. I discuss my system in Chapter 7.

5. *Support for students along the way.* In Chapters 7 and 8, I share the ways I support individual students while they are reading a novel, as well as the whole class, using group activities, supplemental stories, films, picture books, and assistive technology such as audio recordings.

LETTING GO OF PRECONCEPTIONS: THROWING THE BOOMERANG

Another concern I hear from teachers is that their students might read the novel but won't understand all of the subtleties the author has written into it or master the specific standards the teacher has chosen to address in the study of this novel. I have some practices that help ensure students reach certain standards, which I share in subsequent chapters. However, in my own practice, I've come to believe in what I think of as the boomerang phenomenon.

Part of launching a whole novel study is letting go of the preconceptions I have of what I want my students to "get" from a work of literature. I have to let go even of the things I love most about the novel and surrender to the power of the author's craft and my students' abilities to experience the work of fiction for themselves.

This process is like throwing a boomerang. If I throw it well, I can be fairly certain the boomerang will return to me on its own. In my classroom, this translates into my having faith that the students will get what they need or what they are ready to learn at that moment out of the study. I can be artful in how I select the novel, set up the context and conditions for the study, and support my students along the journey, but the real work happens between them and the text.

This may seem to run counter to the basic idea of objective-driven teaching. Don't I need to begin knowing what I want the outcomes to be? I do need to have objectives for the study and for individual students, but when the students begin reading, I need to let those expectations go and focus on working with them wherever they are. I need to stay open to new ideas and routes. I have found over and over that through the process of reading and discussing the work authentically, students come back around to almost everything I would have set out for them to discover anyway. It's not always in the way I imagine it, but the group is much better when it's not just my thinking fueling the direction. In fact, they usually exceed my expectations in what they discover in the text and the depths they are able to go to in their writing. Of course there have been difficult times where something doesn't go well with a particular student or class, but these difficulties have led to creative inventions that end up serving all of the students in subsequent novel studies.

It's the boomerang phenomenon—that carefully prepared leap of faith my students and I take (because they have to trust me, too)—that keeps teaching literature fresh every year. It keeps me from becoming my own middle school English teacher, who talked about *To Kill a Mockingbird* day after day and never tried to get me to read it myself. It keeps me interested and invested in my students and what they will bring to the work, year after year.

HELPING STUDENTS PREPARE FOR THEIR FUTURE

Another reason I believe it's important to allow students to read whole novels themselves has to do with our role in preparing them for the next steps in their education, whether that is high school- or college-level work. Most teachers I've spoken to agree that the goal is for students to be able to read and analyze complete novels on their own at high levels—and in college, students need to be able to do large amounts of reading in short amounts of time. The Common Core Standards, too, are pointing us toward this in College and Career Readiness Anchor Standard 10 for reading: "Read and comprehend complex literary and informational texts independently and proficiently." Students also need to be able to share their ideas in discussion seminars in high school and college. Yet even by the end of twelfth grade, many students have never had the experience of reading a whole novel themselves and then participating in sustained discussions about it.

What I have found is that if we select developmentally meaningful books and create the right conditions in our classrooms, we don't need to wait until college or even high school to help students reach this goal. In the whole novels program, not only do the students know from firsthand experience that they can read a whole book, but they also gain a method for reading, recording responses, and pacing themselves; they know how long it takes them to finish. Ideally, with years of experience and practice reading and analyzing whole novels in a classroom community, we can send students off to college with more certainty that they are prepared for the work ahead.

Beyond college readiness, we want our students to become confident readers, writers, and thinkers. We send a message to them that we believe in them when we demonstrate that they are not dependent on a teacher to cut a novel into bite-size chunks and interpret it for them. Rather, they discover that they can do the work themselves and that what they have to say about it is valuable to the classroom community. Students are aware of the subtle messaging in this approach, and the positivity builds on itself.

Over the school year, students recognize their own growth and specific strengths and needs, and they see that there is room to share their novel ideas in the classroom community. I take a lot of feedback from students throughout the year about the work we do. Once they understand the basic structure of whole novels, there are opportunities for them to influence the curriculum and adjust structures to better fit their needs and interests. Whole novels is a flexible framework, and teachers and students alike can make it their own.

WHOLE NOVELS HAVE REACH

Whole novel studies create a robust thematic framework for my English language arts curriculum, which includes four strands: reading, writing, language study (vocabulary, mechanics and conventions), and classroom life (routines and how we function as a group). Content from the novel studies becomes fuel for reading related nonfiction, as well as poetry, short stories, plays, and graphic novels. Novel studies inspire much of the writing we do, both creative and analytical, which I discuss in Chapter 6. Some writing units don't connect directly to a novel study, such as essays students write about community in September, or a journalism project on the neighborhood we do in December and January— but they build on themes from stories we read and foreshadow ideas that we'll see later in our literature studies.

Whole novel studies create many occasions to integrate technology into our processes, from Google Docs journals shared between reading partners and online discussion forums, to students who research authors' lives online or make film spin-offs of books. I also collaborate with colleagues to create interdisciplinary connections between our novels and content from history, art, and science classes. Skills we practice in relation to novel studies in English transfer to tasks that students encounter in other subjects.

In these ways, students are always moving in and out of the literary and real worlds, responding to the various experiences, drawing comparisons, and discovering patterns. In *Becoming a Reader: The Experience of Fiction from Childhood to Adulthood* (1991), J. A. Appleyard of Boston College describes the act of reading as "primarily an encounter between a particular reader and a particular text in a particular time and place, an encounter that brings to life the story, poem or work in question . . . the story is an event that has roots both in the text and in the personality and history that the reader brings to the reading" (9). By extending "the roots and branches" of the novels we study to interact with our students' life experiences, history, other texts, other disciplines, and the world around us, students can have stories—and much more.

PARTS OF THE WHOLE

My Annual Curriculum Map

A map follows of my annual curriculum for my current eighth-grade English language arts classes; it shows the books that we read throughout the year and how I balance reading and writing while working with whole novels. All novel studies lead to writing, but not all the writing we do derives from a novel study. The year-long thematic content, however, builds through all units, whether they are focused on whole novel studies or something else.

This map is an example, not a prescription. It has elements that I think would work for other eighth-grade classes, but it has been designed with my current population of students in mind. I've had to make significant changes to my own curriculum choices to respond to the strengths, needs, and interests of populations I've taught at each of three schools and from one year to the next within the same school. It wouldn't be a good idea to apply this curriculum to another population without first considering the needs and strengths of the students there.

Finally, in this big picture map, I've focused on some aspects of my curriculum over others. I've articulated the reading and writing skills of my curriculum partly because they seem most relevant to this book, partly to conserve space, and also because they more easily align with language in the Common Core English and literacy standards. There are other important pieces of my curriculum that are not well represented in this map. One aspect is the large amount of listening and speaking students do in my class and as part of whole novel studies. Two other underrepresented pieces are the explicit teaching of writing mechanics and the study of vocabulary through Latin roots. The map therefore includes many, but not all, of the content and skills I teach in a year.

Annual Eighth-Grade English Language Arts Curriculum Map

1. Classroom Community (September)	2. Language of Setting (October)	3. Four Types of Conflict (November)	4. Journalism Study (December–January)
Thematic Focus	**Thematic Focus**	**Thematic Focus**	**Thematic Focus**
Class community	Home/environment	Home/environment	Environment
Difference/belonging	Identity/dreams	Cultural identity	Community
Balance: give and take	Sexism	Conflicting worlds	Diverse perspectives
Self-awareness	Writing as freedom	Discrimination	Journalism
Texts (read aloud)	**Whole Novel #1**	**Whole Novel #2**	**Texts**
The Hundred Dresses	*The House on Mango Street*	*The Absolutely True*	*Our America*
"Harrison Bergeron"	**Literary Focus**	*Diary of a Part-Time*	Articles and reviews
The Giving Tree	Theme	*Indian*	Survey data
Student survey data	Setting	**Literary Focus**	Interviews
Skills	Symbolism	Setting	Independent reading
Classroom routines	**Other Materials**	Four types of conflict	cycle 2
Authentic response	*Martian Chronicles*	Character development	**Literary Focus**
Three kinds of thinking	Documentary: *The Latino*	**Other Materials**	Nonfiction structure,
Discussion protocol	*Project* (HBO)	Film: *Smoke Signals*	purpose, audience
Reflecting on work	**Skills**	*American Born Chinese*	**Reading/Research**
Independent Reading	Analyze descriptive and	*Flight*	**Skills**
Cycle 1	figurative language	Articles on reservation	Problem-solve
Selecting books	Identify themes	life	vocabulary words
Literal, inferential, and	Write L, I, C notes	**Skills**	Identify structure and
critical (L, I, C) sticky	Discussion habits	Identify and analyze a	purpose in nonfiction
notes	Analyze author's purpose in	conflict	Ask questions
Reading habits	narrative structure	Make connections	Read for information
Writing	**Writing**	across texts	Identify bias
Community principles	Vignettes project	Close reading	Do an Internet search
essay	**Writing Skills**	**Writing**	Evaluate sources
Weekly reflections	Word choice	Conflict miniproject	Conduct interviews
Writing Skills	Descriptive language	Conflict story	Conduct surveys
Improvisational drama	Figurative language	In-class essay	Analyze data
to brainstorm	Develop a theme		Identify multiple
Narrative versus	Peer feedback		perspectives
argument essay			**Writing**
Select the form that best			Feature article
supports your content			Vocabulary miniproject
Paragraphing			

Annual Eighth-Grade English Language Arts Curriculum Map (*Continued*)

1. Classroom Community (September)	2. Language of Setting (October)	3. Four Types of Conflict (November)	4. Journalism Study (December–January)
Assessments	**Assessments**	**Writing Skills**	**Writing Skills**
Reading levels	Sticky notes (L, I, C	Support claims with	Write a hook
Quiz on three kinds of	response, theme	textual evidence	Show multiple
thinking	identification, close	Organize essay	perspectives on issue
Assess sticky note	reading of language)	Develop an original	Provide background
responses in	Participation in	character and conflict	information
independent reading	discussions	Write dialogue	Quote from sources
Essay: assess content/	Vignettes (description,	Choose point of view	Structure logically
diagnose writing skills	figurative language,	**Assessments**	Revise for flow
New York State	theme development)	Sticky notes: L, I, C	**Assessments**
Common Core	**New York State**	response, conflict notes,	Feature article: content,
Reading Standards	**Common Core**	connections	organization, style and
1, 2, 3	Reading Standards	Conflict analysis	mechanics
Writing Standards	1, 2, 3, 4, 5, 6	In-class essay: structure	**New York State**
1, 3, 9	Writing Standards	and evidence	**Common Core**
	3, 5, 10, 11	Story: dialogue, conflict,	Reading Standards
		point of view	1, 2, 5, 6, 7, 9
		New York State	Writing Standards
		Common Core	2, 4, 5, 6, 7, 8, 10
		Reading Standards	
		1, 2, 3, 4, 6, 9	
		Writing Standards	
		1, 3, 4, 9	

Annual Eighth-Grade English Language Arts Curriculum Map

5. Family Influence (February	6. Power Structures (March–April)	7. Poetry of Resistance (April)	8. The Hero's Journey (May–June)
Thematic Focus	**Thematic Focus**	**Thematic Focus**	**Thematic Focus**
Family	Oppression	Resistance	Journey
Independence	Resistance	Heroism	Trials
Culture	Counterculture	Self-expression	Transformation
African American history	Sacrifice	Fantasy/reality	Home
Whole Novel #3	**Whole Novel #4**	**Materials**	**Whole Novel #5**
Nobody's Family Is	*The Chocolate War*	Film: *Pan's Labyrinth*	Journey book clubs (in this
Going to Change	**Other Materials**	Selected poems	final unit, students lead their
Literary Focus	Film: *Swing Kids*	*The Life of Poetry*	own whole novel studies, and
Character	"The Lottery"	(Muriel Rukeyser)	have their choice of among
Point of view	*The Book Thief*	**Literary Focus**	several journey-themed
Other Materials	"The Love Song of J.	Poetic devices	novels):
The Rock and the River	Alfred Prufrock"	Poetic forms	*The Ear, the Eye, and the Arm*
The Dream Bearer	**Literary Focus**	**Skills**	*Parable of the Sower*
Like Sisters on the	Protagonist	Read poetry aloud	*The Alchemist*
Homefront	Antagonist	Recognize poetic	*Somewhere in the Darkness*
Anya's Ghost	Archetypes	devices	*Ship Breaker*
Essays by Amy Tan	Moral dilemma	Recognize poetic	*Where the Wild Things Are*
Assorted poems	Tone	forms	*Sylvester and the Magic Pebble*
Skills	**Skills**	Analyze figurative	Interview with Joseph
Strategies for challenging	Infer plot	language	Campbell
text	Reread	Take notes on	**Literary Focus**
Identify complex versus	Identify shifting point	challenging texts	Plot structure
flat characters	of view	**Independent Reading**	Setting
Point of view	Recognize allusions	**Cycle 3**	Character
Analyze character	Identify archetypes	Note new interests	Theme
Analyze author's purpose	Make connections	Increase stamina	**Skills**
Identify mood	across texts	**Writing**	Recognize plot arch
Writing	**Writing**	Original poems	Recognize stages of the
Fictional scenes	Moral dilemma	Book reviews	journey
In-class essay	monologue		Critique author's use of
"I Am From" Poem	Critical essay on		literary elements
	multiple texts		Lead discussions
			Writing
			Journey stories

Annual Eighth-Grade English Language Arts Curriculum Map (*Continued*)

5. Family Influence (February	6. Power Structures (March–April)	7. Poetry of Resistance (April)	8. The Hero's Journey (May–June)
Writing Skills	Assessments	**Writing Skills**	**Writing Skills**
Organize essay around an argument	Sticky notes	Find inspiration for poetry writing	Outline journey
Quote from text	Formal paragraphs	Write metaphors	Use dialogue, description of actions, interior monologue
Use line breaks	Monologue	Revise for rhythm	Develop hero
Revise poem	Critical essay	and line breaks	Develop settings
Assessments	**New York State**	Revise for economy	Develop conflicts
Sticky notes: L, I, C, mood, say "what?" notes	**Common Core**	of language	Choose point of view
Discussions	**Reading Standards**	**Assessments**	**Assessments**
Literary essay	1, 2, 3, 4, 7, 9	Reading-level assessments	Student-led whole novel discussions
"I Am from" Poem	**Writing Standards**	Book review	Journey stories
New York State Common	1, 4, 5, 9, 10	Poetry discussions	**New York State**
Core		Poetic devices quiz	**Common Core**
Reading Standards		Collection of original	Reading Standards
1, 2, 3, 4, 6		poems	1, 2, 4, 5, 9, 10,
Writing Standards		**New York State**	Writing Standards
1, 4, 5		**Common Core**	3, 5, 6, 10, 1
		Reading Standards	
		1, 2, 4, 5, 9, 10,	
		Writing Standards	
		3, 5, 6, 10, 11	

2

Selecting the Right Books
Five Dimensions of Good Chemistry

"But this book is different! This is *good*!"

One day, as I was approaching the art room door at the Fox Point Boys and Girls Club in Providence, Rhode Island, I noticed Taiye, a sixteen-year-old girl, crouched (almost hidden) in a corner of the hall with her nose in a book. I walked over to her and startled her out of her literary daze. "I thought you didn't like to read!" I exclaimed.

"Oh, this?" she said pointing to the book. It was *The Coldest Winter Ever* by Sister Souljah, a best-selling novel I had read. It is a drama about an African American girl from Brooklyn who loses her family to incarceration and drug addiction and has to make it on her own. It is a gritty, well-written 413-page saga with developed characters and a thoughtfully woven message to teens about the realities of sex, drugs, and violence.

"This is different," Taiye said. "This is *good*!"

Interesting, I thought. *So this book doesn't count as "reading," because it is* good.

35

Fox Point is a poor neighborhood located blocks from Brown University, where I was an undergraduate English major. I had worked as the arts and crafts counselor there for three years and had gotten to know children of all ages. That semester, as part of an independent study, I organized a poetry group at The Club for teen girls and their mothers. Some girls were still in high school; others had dropped out of school. The girls agreed to participate because they knew me and were curious. However, they told me upfront, "We don't like to read." When I probed their response, they shared stories about their negative experiences with school, certain teachers, and books that all seemed to add up to a general disdain for the written word (though they had enjoyed spoken language activities like debate and improvisational theater).

There was truth in what the girls had told me about their relationships to reading, but the whole picture turned out to be more complex. Taiye, as I had been as an adolescent, was what Jo Worthy calls a "renegade reader" in her wonderfully titled article "'On Every Page Someone Gets Killed!' Book Discussions You Don't Hear in School" (1998). Renegade readers, she says, do not like the reading they are assigned in school. Their teachers may see them as disengaged readers, but in fact they are avid readers on their own.

Selecting books for the whole class takes a great deal of thought. We need to invite students like Taiye in by getting to know their interests and finding materials that won't "feel like reading." For whole novel studies to work, students need to be able and willing to read the books more or less on their own. My beginning-of-the-year selections must be highly engaging and readable for a wide range of students and allow a high degree of identification with characters, especially for struggling readers. However, as I begin to gain my students' trust and their reading maturity and confidence increase over time, my criteria for selecting books changes.

In this chapter, I share my thinking behind selecting books for whole novel studies and outline the process I go through to choose reading materials for my classes.

CHOOSING FOR THE WHOLE CLASS: THINKING IN FIVE DIMENSIONS

Making good book selections for whole novel studies, like the rest of teaching, requires a combination of intuition and calculation. Each whole novel study has a profound impact on the academic development of the class, as well as the group culture. The world of the novel becomes an almost tangible layer of our classroom environment for the weeks that we're reading, discussing, and writing about it. When we complete the study, as individuals and as a group we are not in the same territory we started in. Each novel study creates a group journey of sorts, and the journey of each book fits into the larger trajectory of our entire year of reading.

In order for a novel to be appropriate for an entire class to live in for a length of time, it must have strengths that on some level transcend the realm of personal taste. Each book selection must be meaningful for students, connected to their interests, and accessible for my heterogeneously grouped classes. It also must be connected in some way to what came before it and what will come after it, so that the reading trajectory builds momentum and complexity across the year and students do not want to miss out on any piece of it.

When I search for books for whole novel studies, I consider the merits of each title in five key dimensions by asking myself these questions:

1. *Development.* How does the content of the novel connect to my students' developmental stage? Why do I think this book is appropriate for my age group?
2. *Identification level.* How do the book's content and setting relate to the life experiences of my students? Are they mirrors (familiar) or windows (unfamiliar)? Directly or indirectly connected?
3. *Reading level.* What is the reading level of this book in relation to the reading levels of my students? Is this book accessible for all, half, or just some of my students? Is it good for the beginning, middle, or end of the year?
4. *Thematic connections.* How does this book connect thematically or structurally to what came before it and what will come later in our annual curriculum?
5. *Literary strengths.* Which literary elements are strongest in this work? What opportunities does it provide to focus on the author's craft?

This may seem like an overwhelming list of considerations, but once I got used to thinking about each dimension of a single book, it became much easier to see the multiple dimensions at once and determine whether they combine to make a good whole novel choice. There is always an element of experimentation in teaching—and a bit of a gamble in the choices we make—but the clearer I am on the theory

Are you looking to try out just one whole novel study? Are you planning an annual course curriculum? Are you selecting novels for book clubs or another approach? These five dimensions for selecting books will be useful in any of these situations.

behind my decisions, including anticipating weak points, the better prepared I am for what may come and the better the outcomes will be.

Finally, my own assessment of any book is only part of the equation, since I'm not its primary audience in the whole novel study. A young adult book has to earn its respect from me personally, as well as from my students, in order to be accepted into the classroom canon. The classroom canon has nothing to do with the traditional literary canon out there, though. It's made up of books that my students widely love and, perhaps more important, are respected for their craft by those who don't love them.

SELECTING BOOKS THAT TRANSCEND PERSONAL TASTE: TAPPING INTO DEVELOPMENTAL THEORY

In my graduate studies in education at Bank Street, I learned about the college's signature developmental-interaction approach. The approach, which permeated every course I took at Bank Street, asserted that a child's academic and social-emotional development do not occur along two separate continuums; rather, they constantly interact with each other as the child interacts with the world, peers, and adults (and physical development, too). At Bank Street, teachers learned that "cognition and emotion are always interconnected in any teaching situation . . . Meaningful content (provided by a teacher) and active relationships and collaborations with student peers and teachers provide the basis for learning. By closely observing the reactions, reflections, and interactions of students; by guiding with her own comments and questions; and by encouraging every ounce of student curiosity, the educator teaches her students" (as stated at www.bankstreet.edu).

Part of our task as students at Bank Street was to learn as much as we could about the students we worked with, and developmental research was a major resource for us in this pursuit. Before every curriculum piece, I was required to write a development statement—a profile of the age group for which I was designing the lessons. Among the many theorists and researchers, I especially appreciated the writing of David Elkind who, in his book *A Sympathetic Understanding of the Child: Birth to Sixteen* (1995), describes the patterns of behaviors, needs, interests, and conflicts of children at each year.

It's well worth checking into the specific developmental patterns of children in the years you teach. I've been surprised how clarifying it is to revisit adolescent development as a more experienced teacher, as well as how many teachers missed out on in-depth study of developmental theory in their teacher preparation. We naturally glean a lot about our students' developmental stage through experience, but the research helps name and categorize common interests and behaviors in helpful ways.

Using Developmental Characteristics to Guide Book Selection

As an example, here is a description of many of the developmental attributes of early adolescents, as seen through my work with twelve- through fifteen-year-olds and in reading Elkind's work. Based on each attribute, I've given examples of themes and texts that speak to the age group. I've indicated the grade levels for which I believe these make ideal choices to read with the whole class. The designations are based on content more than reading level. Students outside these grade levels can certainly read these books, but my attempt here is to pinpoint the developmental sweet spot for each text.

Developmental Attributes, Themes, and Titles for Early Adolescents

- *Attribute:* Negotiating distance from their parents. They begin to see their parents as people and think critically about them while still being quite dependent on them for basic needs, approval, and affection.
  Theme: "Parents are people, too," identity, independence
  Book titles:

  Nobody's Family Is Going to Change, by Louise Fitzhugh (6–8)
  The Dream Bearer, by Walter Dean Myers (6–8)
  The Rock and the River, by Kekla Magoon (7–9)
  The Ear, the Eye and the Arm, by Nancy Farmer (7–8)
  Somewhere in the Darkness, by Walter Dean Myers (6–8)

- *Attribute:* Developing strong identification with peer groups, generally of the same gender.
  Theme: Friendship, adventure, trust
  Book titles:
  I Hadn't Meant to Tell You This, by Jacqueline Woodson (6–8)
  The Outsiders, by S. E. Hinton (7–8)
  When You Reach Me, by Rebecca Stead (6–7)

- *Attribute:* Developing secondary sex characteristics and beginning to negotiate sexual desire. Many are concerned with the issue of homosexuality, whether or not they experience desire for those of their same sex.
  Theme: Sexuality, dating
  Book titles:
  From the Notebooks of Melanin Sun, by Jacqueline Woodson (7)
  My Heartbeat, by Garret Freymann-Weyr (8–9)
  Aristotle and Dante Discover the Secrets of the Universe,
      by Benjamin Alire Sáenz (8–9)
  Same Difference, by Siobhan Vivian (7–9)
  Story of a Girl, by Sara Zarr (9–10)

- *Attribute:* Becoming (often painfully) aware of the existence of social hierarchy.
  Theme: Popularity, difference
  Book titles:
  The Skin I'm In, by Sharon Flake (6–7)
  Stargirl, by Jerry Spinelli (5–6)
  Wonder, by R. J. Palacio (4–7)
  Thirteen Reasons Why, by Jay Asher (8–9)

- *Attribute:* Developing the ability to think critically and self-consciously about themselves, others, and, to some degree, systems. They are learning to see the consequences of their own choices and imagine themselves in another person's position.
  Themes: Choices, forgiveness, identity, discrimination
  Book titles:
  Scorpions, by Walter Dean Myers (7–8)
  The Hundred Dresses, by Eleanor Estes (3–12)
  The Absolutely True Diary of a Part-Time Indian, by Sherman Alexie (8–9)
  Taking Sides, by Gary Soto (5–7)

Feed, by M. T. Anderson (8–10)

Ship Breaker, by Paulo Bacigalupi (8–9)

- *Attribute:* Beginning to grasp the concept of a system or a society: a world of interconnected people, things, rules, and norms. They also question the workings of such systems and of whole societies.

  Themes: Justice, power, oppression, resistance

  Book titles:

  The Chocolate War, by Robert Cormier (7–9)

  The Hunger Games, by Suzanne Collins (6–8)

  The House on Mango Street, by Sandra Cisneros (8–12)

  The Book Thief, by Marcus Zusak (8–11)

  The Giver, by Lois Lowry (6–8)

  Before We Were Free, by Julia Alvarez (7–8)

  The Parable of the Sower, by Octavia Butler *(9–11)*

  "Harrison Bergeron," by Kurt Vonnegut Jr. (7–10)

- *Attribute:* Developing an awareness of one's cultural background and how this relates to the development of an individual identity. Often involves separating from one's parents and constructing a new identity.

  Themes: Culture, identity, tradition, independence, loss

  Book titles:

  How the García Girls Lost Their Accents, by Julia Alvarez (9–11)

  American-Born Chinese, by Gene Luan Yang (7–9)

  A Step from Heaven, by An Na (8–9)

  Mexican Whiteboy, by Matt de la Peña (8–9)

  Like Sisters on the Homefront, by Rita Williams-Garcia (8–10)

  Anya's Ghost, by Vera Brosgol (8–10)

- *Attribute:* Discovering that the transition from childhood to adulthood often involves a painful awakening to the harsh realities of the world, including depression, illness, and death. These titles discuss mature subjects and offer a safe avenue for students to discuss challenging topics.

  Themes: Loss, loss of innocence, ambivalence, risk

  Book titles:

  The Perks of Being a Wallflower, by Stephen Chbosky (8–11)

  It's Kind of a Funny Story, by Ned Vizzini (8–10)

Go Ask Alice, by Anonymous (9–10)
Speak, by Laurie Halse Anderson (8–11)
Wintergirls, by Laurie Halse Anderson (8–10)
The Fault in Our Stars, by John Green (8–10)
Looking for Alaska, by John Green (9–11)
The Alchemist, by Paulo Coelho (8–11)

It's key that whole novels speak to the developmental interests of the students. This is a way in which a great book can transcend the realm of personal taste and appeal to a wide range of students. It's worth mentioning that developmentally appropriate books are generally not going to be classics, because most of those canonical works were not written with the child or adolescent reader in mind. Instead, they are going to be works of young adult literature, the best of which deals with developmentally meaningful topics and has literary merit. Teri Lesesne, author of *Reading Ladders* (2010), makes this argument to skeptics: "From its earlier incarnations, YA literature has suffered from a misconception that it is somehow less literary than *real* literature . . . I am willing to bet that you have encountered this apparent prejudice against using contemporary literature in the classroom, particularly for classroom study. I think those that would denigrate using YA literature fail to see that it has structure, style, and substance. It *is* worthy of study in the classroom" (4). Lesesne goes on to show that quality young adult literature is not only relevant to students today but is also rigorous.

Whole novel selections must be quality works of young adult literature, because, as with any other genre, all books are not written equally well. Just because a book has an appropriate theme for an age group doesn't make it a book worthy of study. Complex characters and well-crafted plots and themes do.

As we get into adolescent literature, many of the best titles include content and language that are mature and may seem questionably appropriate for the classroom. I have gotten comfortable leading eighth-grade students in reading books with profanity, some sexual content (though not with "on-screen" full sexual acts), and other mature topics. There are two practices that make this possible. First, I always consult other teachers about these book choices to make sure I'm not off in my determination that the book is appropriate for my group. Second, I set some ground rules about how we deal with this content and language. In the letter I write to my classes when I launch the novel, I tell students that they are mature enough to understand that the language and content are in the book because the author wanted these to

 Visit https://vimeo.com/61678477 for video 2.1: Prefacing Mature Language in Literature

be part of the characters' world, but not because they are appropriate to say or do in our school community. We go over the letter in class and parents see it, too. If the book is, in fact, appropriate for the age group, I've found students rise to the occasion.

A Theory of How Readers Develop

Literary themes speak more or less to readers, depending on their developmental stages. Readers also have different purposes for reading fiction as they mature. In *Becoming a Reader: The Experience of Fiction from Childhood to Adulthood* (1991), psychologist J. A. Appleyard shares a helpful theory of the major stages children go through in becoming mature readers. Initially he planned to investigate patterns among high school readers in public schools in the Boston area, but he found that in order to understand what he was seeing at the older levels, he needed to go back to study earlier stages of development. What Appleyard puts forth is a fascinating progression of roles that readers take on that correspond loosely to age ranges. Each of the roles, which are meant to be successive, seek different experiences in reading fiction. I'm providing a rough summary of each role here, though I highly recommend reading the chapter in Appleyard's book that corresponds to your age group.

The *preschool child*, says Appleyard, listens to stories and takes on the role of a player in the fictional world, captivated by the vivid images of the story, without distinguishing between reality and fantasy. According to Appleyard, the crucial question for these young children is how much they can trust the fictional world, which can be pleasurable as well as scary, as they play imaginatively within it. Eventually they learn to distinguish between fantasy and reality and progress from this role.

Appleyard names the *school-age child* "Reader as Hero or Heroine." At this stage, the reader's purpose is to gather information about the wider world and how it works, while building a sense of his or her own competence within it. Elementary school readers are fixated on the archetype of the hero, who is clever, resourceful, and "can solve the problems of a disordered world" (59–60). The reader unconsciously identifies with the main character's story as an extension of his or her own experience.

Like school-age children, *adolescent readers* love to get wrapped up in a compelling story, but what they seek to take away from the experience is different. Appleyard names the adolescent reader "Thinker," because he or she looks to stories to discover insights into the meaning of life. Adolescent readers "seek authentic role models for imitation" (14), and on a deeper level, stories help them evaluate the "claims of competing truths in their own lives" (101).

Appleyard categorizes the role of the *college readers*, namely, English majors and those who go on to study literature, as the "Interpreters." In this role, the reader "studies literature systematically as an organized body of knowledge with its own principles of inquiry and rules of evidence . . . learns to talk analytically about it, acquires a sense of its history, and perhaps even a critical theory of how it works" (15).

Finally, in *adulthood*, the majority of readers become what Appleyard calls "Pragmatic" readers. Having had some experience in each of these roles, adults become free to choose from among them to suit their interests and specific occasions.

Appleyard's theory is helpful in identifying our students' deeper, developmentally related motivations for reading stories, which are essential in selecting books that will draw them in. The classes we teach include wide ranges of students, grouped together only because of their common age. One way we can meet their needs as developing readers is to make sure we're offering opportunities for them to take on the roles that their age group desires to inhabit.

FROM IDENTIFICATION TO EXPLORATION: SELECTING TEXTS THAT OFFER MIRRORS AND WINDOWS

I want all of the literature in my classroom to be developmentally meaningful for my students. However, though two stories may deal with similar themes, they can be easier or more difficult for students to identify with depending on the familiarity of the character, setting, and language use. The ability of a reader to easily identify with the main characters of a story (the main focus of the school-aged Reader as Hero role) makes for a less demanding process than reading that requires exploration of unfamiliar territory. I want to include both types of reading experiences in my curriculum, but ideally my text selections begin with many familiar elements and gradually move in the direction of texts with less familiar elements.

While individual students in a class are different, I find that the group often develops a unique personality or flavor of its own. It's possible to interact with and influence the culture of the group through the careful selection of novels using the constructs of mirrors and windows. Teacher Emily Style (1988) makes the case that strong curriculum should provide students with both "mirrors and windows."

Reflecting Students' Worlds in Mirror Texts

Style uses mirrors as a metaphor for aspects of the curriculum in which students can see themselves, to which they relate directly. In terms of literature, it is important that at least some of the time, students read books with characters that live in places like the ones they know, walk the streets with the same color skin as they do, and have similar struggles.

Students should feel welcome in their own classrooms, and the curriculum needs to be inviting. This idea serves more than an ideological purpose; it's a practical one, too. For reluctant readers, giving them something of the familiar to read eliminates obstacles between the reader and text. If you have renegade readers like Taiye in your classroom, who have concluded that the reading assigned in school has no relevance to their lives, a novel with characters and conflicts with direct connection to their life experiences can draw such readers out of hiding.

It's important to begin the year with a novel that will have mirror qualities for as many students as possible.

Expanding Students' Worldviews with Window Texts

At the same time, a strong literature curriculum provides students with windows into the lives of people, time periods, and places in the world that are starkly different from the ones they intimately know. In doing so, literature often reveals that the trials and tribulations of humans are universal on many levels. We surprise ourselves by relating to characters and situations that at first appear totally foreign to us.

Window reading is challenging, because there's a great deal of information to assimilate at once. With a familiar setting, the storyline alone presents the main puzzle for comprehension. With an unfamiliar setting and characters, the reader must connect these foreign elements along with the storyline to enter the virtual world. Though rewarding, this is a lot more work. It's important that students have already developed some confidence in their reading and in the whole novels process before opening a window into an unfamiliar literary world.

Seeing Our Reflection in the Window

For my seventh-grade ELL students, *The Hundred Dresses*, by Eleanor Estes, started out as a window into an unfamiliar world. This book, written over fifty years ago, takes place in a white suburban town in Connecticut. In it, a group of students tease their classmate Wanda, who comes from Poland and wears the same dress every day. And then one day, Wanda is gone. Many of my students expected not to like this book. Its cover and language were unfamiliar and didn't seem relevant to their lives.

In fact, they were quickly drawn into it. In discussions, they connected events and behaviors from the book to things that had taken place at our school. By coincidence, a few months earlier, many students had witnessed or participated in the teasing of a new girl (not a member of our English class), the only white student in the entire building. One day she was gone, and we heard that she had transferred to another school. Here is the part of the discussion, where students made this connection:

MARI: There's an example in this school—Racquel. She left because people used to make fun of her.

ADAM: And Pedro, too.

MARI: I used to make fun of him calling him *perro* [dog]. This book is like you [Ms. Sacks] telling us why he left. I remember the white girl, too.

LILIANA: But they was both bad, too. They did things to make it happen.

RASHIK: Wanda didn't. She was by herself.

MARI: It's a difference, Wanda and our kids.

What began as a window into a foreign world became a mirror held up to our own world, inspiring critical thinking and reflection. This example illustrates the timeless quality of great literature. The novella also worked for this group of students because they were ready for it. By that point in the year, they trusted me to choose well for them, and they were confident in their ability to enter and analyze literary worlds.

A Mirror for One, a Window for Another

When any class is matched with any one text, some elements of it are mirrors for some students and windows for others. If we're reading one novel, the gender of the main character, for example, will never be a mirror for an entire coeducational classroom. When I choose whole novels, I try to alternate between studies with female and male protagonists, and I make sure my year-long curriculum has a good balance when it comes to gender. I can also balance the gender of the main character with supplemental texts within one whole novel study. Finally, I have found it useful to split the group once a year by gender, and have students read two different texts with common themes, each with a protagonist of their own gender.

In order to know whether a text will serve as more of a mirror or a window for my students for factors less obvious than gender, I have to get to know my students as people, beyond our academic context. What are their neighborhoods like? What do they do outside school? What cultural backgrounds do they come from? Sometimes it's easy to find something that will be familiar for the whole group: a young adult novel set in Brooklyn for my current students or a novel about a recent immigrant for a class of ELLs. Other times, it may be difficult because of the diversity of the population. However, it's still a factor to consider. Which of my students will identify easily with this character? For whom will this be a challenging aspect of reading this novel? When weighing these factors, I consider the struggling readers in my class and try to give them the advantage of direct identification with the main characters at the beginning of the year.

Mirrors and Windows in an Integrated School

In my current school, the movement from windows to mirrors is complicated by the fact that students come from a wide range of backgrounds, both cultural and socioeconomic. Within the same city, what is a mirror for some of my students is a window for others. *The House on Mango Street*, for example, is familiar to my students from Sunset Park, Brooklyn, a mostly Latino neighborhood. It almost seems to be set in their neighborhood. (Students at my first school in East Harlem felt the same way about this book.) But for my students from Park Slope and Carroll Gardens, wealthier, whiter areas of Brooklyn, this text provides a window into another reality that is mere blocks away. We reconciled this in a few ways.

First, a big part of the literary journey of eighth-grade English language arts is developing understandings across the differences among my students, and so this book gives us an occasion to recognize these differences in discussion and through creative writing (see the vignettes project in Chapter 7). Second, we can all relate around the urban setting of this book, so on some level, it is a mirror for everyone. By contrast, when we read *The Chocolate War* later, which takes place in a boys' Catholic prep school in Connecticut, we are all experiencing a window text.

Finally, the content and structure of *The House on Mango Street* posed a challenge for everyone; however, students from Sunset Park had the advantage of a greater understanding of the perspective of the author. It's not often that students from Sunset Park have an advantage over students from Park Slope, so this created a subtle but positive balancing effect in the classroom.

These complicated dynamics shift throughout the year along with the balance of all five dimensions of each whole novel.

UNDERSTANDING STUDENTS' READING LEVELS: BUILDING CONFIDENCE, INCREASING COMPLEXITY

In the three different contexts in which I've taught, the wide range of reading skill levels has always been the greatest challenge in teaching whole novels. The first step is to know what reading skills my individual students have and what they struggle with in their reading. I want to preface this section by saying that there are educators far more expert than I on the subject of literacy assessment. I offer my own lens for understanding my students' reading levels, which draws from some of the wisdom in the field but is heavily filtered through my experience developing the whole novel approach.

Piece Together a Story of Each Reader

I gather information about my students' reading through a combination of formal and informal assessments. What I'm looking for in these assessments is much more than just a reading level designation for each student, however. A reading level tells me something about the way a student might respond to a given text, but as I learned with Taiye, the whole story is more complex. Especially with older students who read below grade level, there is a history to uncover. Students have built up reading identities, including fears and beliefs about what they can and can't do and defenses against the feeling of failure or being misunderstood. Understanding these stories, as well as the specific skills students need to acquire, is often key to unlocking their potential.

Use Formal Assessments as a Starting Place

I've used a variety of methods to formally assess my students' reading levels toward the beginning of the year, including running records, Qualitative Reading Inventory (QRI) assessments, Leveled Reading Assessments from Teachers College Reading and Writing Project (which correlate with Fountas and Pinnell reading levels), and Diagnostic Reading Assessments (DRA). All of these methods provide data that paint a picture of each student and a class as a whole and can inform my text selections.

However, for me, the most helpful part of conducting the formal assessment is just that: the experience of conducting the assessment. These methods require my sitting down with an individual student for up to twenty minutes, recording observations as he or she reads aloud, asking a series of leveled questions, and analyzing the responses. I learn a great deal about each student, especially struggling readers, through these interactions. The assessments prompt me to ask questions I might not think to ask myself in an informal assessment. The individual attention I'm giving and the vulnerability the student must show during the assessment help build trust between us. It's important that I maintain a supportive tone that makes it clear I know that the student's intelligence is not defined by her ability to read. I avoid anything even close to condescension and, while looking for clues as to how I can help, keep a look of interest and care about what's happening for her while she reads.

The data from these assessments are more useful than those from standardized reading tests, because they help find the level at which the student can read independently and the level at which the student can read with instructional supports in specific areas. Standardized testing data are far less detailed and throw in the wild cards of multiple choice and time. Selecting answers to multiple-choice questions in a timed environment is not a reading skill. Unless the questions and answer choices are very straightforward, we are testing a combination of reading skills and reasoning skills in an inauthentic context. Those two processes are not at all the same, and I don't want to mix them up in one assessment.

For ideas on managing the assessment process with a large load of students, see Chapter 1 of Maddie Witter's *Reading without Limits: Teaching Strategies to Build Independent Reading for Life* (2013).

The downside of the formal assessments is that they are quite time-consuming. Unless you have a very long class period or a small overall number of students, it's difficult to manage assessing all students during class time. In some schools, I've been able to arrange slowly pulling students out of other classes or advisory or study hall periods, and even after school, to conduct assessments. Sometimes a team of teachers works together to assess an entire grade of students; this way I get the data more efficiently, but I don't sit down and go through the process with all of my students individually. If you are a new teacher or have never done this type of assessment with a whole group of students before, I recommend trying to carve out the time to do it at least once. That experience has helped me know what to look for and what kinds of questions to ask individual students in informal assessments and conversations in subsequent years without using the full formal process. A less time-consuming option is to use diagnostic data from standardized or classroom assessments to identify readers with the highest needs and conduct formal assessments for them only.

Investigate Students' Reading Interests

To put together the story of each student's strengths and needs, I pair the formal skills assessment with knowledge of my students' reading interests and habits. A student's apparent reading level can vary a fair amount based on his or her level of interest in the text. When students are interested, their motivations and positive expectations are higher. This eliminates the sense of burden that comes with an uninteresting challenge and makes the work feel easier to them.

For insight and techniques for getting to know students' reading interests and developing relationships with them around their and your reading lives, consult *The Book Whisperer* (2009) by Donalyn Miller.

Knowing what kinds of reading a student is interested in and familiar with helps me better predict how a reader will respond to a text that challenges his or her abilities. By beginning the year with independent reading,

Figure 2.1 Talking to Students about Their Reading

surveying students about their reading interests, and lots of conversations with students, I find out about my students' likes and dislikes when it comes to reading (Figure 2.1).

Monitor Students' Reading Behaviors through Informal Assessments

I do a lot of informal assessing of students' reading throughout the year. While students read independently during class, I talk to individuals quietly, casually asking them to tell me about what they're reading—what's going on and what they think of it. I have students read a section aloud to me, and we talk about it. I listen for their fluency and assess their comprehension and critical thinking through conversation.

At the beginning of the year, I also read and tell stories aloud to the class. I take note of students' critical-thinking skills in response to hearing text and keep that in mind as I look for this same skill in relation to their independent reading. My pet peeve is hearing teachers say in a general way that a student "lacks critical-thinking skills" when they are really talking about a specific reading context, in which there is probably also a lack of engagement or comprehension of the text. Sometimes I do find that students are not accustomed to thinking critically about stories, whether they are reading or listening. In Chapters 3, 5, and 7, I share some of the ways I build my students' habits of critical thinking.

I observe students' conversations with classmates about their books through in-class activities and around the school. I look out for students who "sneak-read" in the hallway or under their desk during class and follow up with conversations. I also look for clues about students' reading habits at home and ask questions through surveys and conversations. I learn a lot about students this way!

This year, I've started allowing students who have their own iPads or e-readers to use them to read independently. This led me to learn about a genre new to me—"fan-fic," fiction written by unknown Internet users about celebrities. In this case, a group of my students obsessively read fan-fic about the boy band One Direction. The writing quality varies wildly, the students tell me: "Some are bad, but some are really good when the writers use big words and lots of detail." This piques my interest. Could fan-fic be an authentic way to engage students in critiquing various authors' craft?

For a wealth of help in diagnosing individual students' reading needs and strategies for responding, I strongly recommend *When Kids Can't Read: What Teachers Can Do* (2002), by Kylene Beers.

I also watched two students from dramatically different social circles discover that they both loved graphic novels. Now they trade and compare notes on the latest graphic novels daily at the beginning of class.

Respond to Data from Authentic Assessments

Authentic assessments are my favorite, because they help me form a multidimensional picture of each student as a reader while still zooming in to assess specific skills in context. Most of the activities described in subsequent chapters of this book serve as formative assessments, providing me a great deal of information about my students' reading through multiple modalities that I use to inform instructional decisions.

In the next chapter, I share my method for teaching students to respond on sticky notes, using literal, inferential, and critical thinking. Stickies are an essential component of my ongoing assessment of students' reading skills across the year. I share my criteria for assessing sticky notes and the way I provide feedback to students on their progress. I use my observations of students' notes to design group miniprojects, which I describe in Chapter 7. These projects are also used as formative assessments of their thinking about the novel, but the work has a collaborative, social level, too. Finally, I assess my students' reading through their participation in whole novel discussions by transcribing their comments and studying the notes. I use those to generate essay questions. Essay writing provides an opportunity for me to assess their literal, inferential, and critical thinking about the whole text in written form.

All of these authentic assessments help me monitor my students' progress and predict how each one will respond to the next novel I choose. I reflect on the skills they're becoming adept at, how their interests are expanding, and which aspects of texts challenge them most. Who is ready for a greater challenge, and who needs additional experience reading and responding at a similar level?

Build Up Students' Missing Story Experience

Before we move on from the dimension of reading levels, let's return to Appleyard's theory on how people develop as readers. The roles he's discovered provide another way of looking at students' reading levels because of the progressive nature of the stages.

According to Appleyard, the ability to assume each role—from Player to Hero to Thinker to Interpreter to Pragmatic Reader—depends on the understandings gained through the experiences of the previous role. This raises a few questions for English teachers because our education system asks students to take on the role of interpreter well before college. What is the impact of that on their development as readers? Appleyard cautions teachers against rushing children into "higher" roles before they arrive at them on their own.

As a teacher who does see her eighth-grade students beginning to develop interpretations of literature and take on aspects of adult pragmatic readers, I take this theory as a strong reminder that the other roles (Player, Hero, and Thinker) are still very important and, in fact, necessary for students to experience if we are to guide them toward higher levels of reading and analysis.

So what happens when a student has missed out on the experience of taking on a particular role as a reader in an earlier stage? I believe that many students, especially those who can decode words but struggle to comprehend what they read, find themselves in that position because they are missing important story experiences. This includes the experience of being read to or told stories. It also includes exposure to the basic plots of literature found in the myths, folktales, and fairy tales from any culture that are repeated in various ways in all new works of literature. Story experience includes imagining oneself inside a story world and identifying with the heroes and heroines. Without having played these roles as listeners and readers, some students lack reference points for interacting with the narratives they encounter. No amount of explicit skill instruction can replace the experience of hearing, reading, learning, and living in a great number of stories.

Nevertheless, in my experience, older children who are missing story experience can catch up. Their cognitive, social, and emotional stages are ahead of the reading roles they've missed—in other words, they know the difference between fantasy and reality, and if they are adolescents, they are aware of complexities and contradictions in the world around them. They need to rewind and catch up in the literary world to where they are in the real world, so that they can connect the understanding gained from their life experiences (including stories gained through film and television) to the act of reading and the world of literature.

To help students make these connections, I include folktales and picture books in my curriculum no matter their age, and I read them aloud to my classes. I watch my students have an immersive experience that takes them back to childhood. I have students dramatize scenes from folktales, inventing dialogue and new twists—learning to play with the story as young children (and also fiction writers) do. As we discuss the stories, the students naturally transition into the role of adolescent thinker.

Depending on the needs of my students, I sometimes spend a few months at the beginning of the year on independent reading and folklore. By looking at a series of folktales with similar plot structures or themes from around the world, students can compare elements of each version and build reference points for patterns that exist throughout literature. With ELLs or struggling readers, I recommend this at any age. Their progress can be astounding.

When I have wide variance in the needs of students in a single class, which is common, I can choose to modify the general curriculum for struggling students or increase the level of support for them, or I can create parallel programs for them within the same curriculum. I explain these options in Chapter 8.

Prepare to See Nonincremental Growth

I've come to believe that a student's general skill level in reading is much more flexible and less predictable than we often think. Skills and feelings can be incubating inside a reader, and the right chemistry in a classroom environment or set of texts can be a game changer for a struggling reader. A huge influence in this process is the motivation a child has to engage with the desired work and exert effort. Another huge factor is time. Just as a baby doesn't transition from crawling to walking in prescribed increments over a set amount of time, a struggling reader doesn't become fluent in predictable intervals across a year either.

I remember Josephine, who came from Haiti when she was seven, having gone to school only sometimes in her country. She had never learned to read in her native Creole language. One of my most struggling readers, she came to me as a seventh grader, repeating the year. She had made slow progress in my seventh-grade class, mostly visible in the effort she put into her work. As an eighth grader, she began to blossom as a reader. By writing several sticky notes on every page, she monitored and recorded her understanding along the way. Through pullout sessions in Wilson reading instruction (a highly effective program designed to help older struggling readers catch up on their phonemic awareness and reading fluency) with a resource room teacher twice a week, she was learning to recognize new words every day.

She was still a slow reader and didn't understand every word she read, but she had figured out that she could follow the story of almost any novel I put in front of her. I remember the day her best friend, who was not in our class, came up to me and said, "Ms. Sacks, what happened to Josephine? She came over to my house to watch a movie last night, and she wouldn't put that book with those sticky notes down the whole time!" Josephine finished the three-hundred-page book and participated strongly in the discussions with everyone else. It cost her more effort to read through that book than it did the other students in the class, but she wanted to be part of the group. Motivation, support, and time to grow were all key factors in the increases in Josephine's reading skills.

As teachers, we need to set our sights high and, with our book selections, allow for the possibility at any moment of rapid growth as well as incremental or invisible growth.

CREATING CONNECTED READING EXPERIENCES: ASSEMBLING COMMON THEMES AND STRUCTURAL ELEMENTS

Choosing a series of novels that build on common themes is another way I try to transcend the confines of personal taste in my text selections while helping to increase my students' story experience and reading maturity at the same time.

In her Children's Literature course at Bank Street, Madeleine Ray (2003) recommends that teachers design a curriculum to build on a theme or organizing principle that students can recognize in different forms in each work they read. She writes this to students in her course:

> A major program goal is to provide an opportunity for your students
> to encounter the same thematic ideas, such as fairness, and/or structural
> ideas, such as repetition, in each work. They should gradually begin to see
> that a literary theme or idea can be used over and over again in new contexts
> and with new story twists. Thus you are building a repertoire of story
> awareness that they will bring to any new story experience. They then are
> able to relate that knowledge to new items that are randomly presented,
> reinforcing the awareness that there has been a permutation of the basic
> plot or form that they already know. This recognition is part of a
> constructivist process that gives children power over the story they are
> hearing or reading and future stories that they encounter in all media. (1–2)

Madeleine points out that mature readers—what we want all our students to become—have a range of experiences with stories and have spent time reading deeply in a particular genre of their liking. She writes, however, "The child who has read little or no fiction has not had the opportunity to build the kind of experience that complex texts require. The repetition of theme and structure provide a simulation of what mature or experienced readers create for themselves through their reading history" (3).

Choose a Series of Thematically Related Novels

I plan my annual curriculum to have a narrative quality to it, so that students feel that they are part of a unified experience, where each piece has meaning by itself but also within the whole curriculum. For each novel, I ask myself, How does this text connect to the other books, stories, films, poems, and articles the students have read this year? How does it build on what's come before it, and what new themes or context does it bring to students?

 Visit https://vimeo.com/61678466 for video 2.2: Student Voices on Connections.

When I taught seventh-grade transitional ELLs, my students began the year studying a series of Cinderella tales from around the world, starting with Grimm's Ashputtle. The crux of an Ashputtle-type story is that a protagonist loses a parent, and, with that loss, her place in the world becomes unclear (at best). Over the course of the story, the character must overcome trials and maintain integrity to regain his or her proper place in the world. Then we read three novels, each featuring a character who loses a parent in one form or another (literally or metaphorically) and struggles to develop and maintain connection to the world despite it.

We read Roald Dahl's *The Witches*, in which an orphaned boy raised by his grandmother gets turned into a mouse by witches who are bent on eating children. He has to outsmart the witches to get his life back. In *The Jacob Ladder*, by Gerald Hausman and Uton Hinds, which takes place in rural Jamaica, the main character's father gets put under a spell by an "obeah" woman and leaves the family. (*Obeah* is a term used in the West Indies for magic or voodoo spells.) Tall T has to come of age on his own, without his father's guidance. In *The Skin I'm In*, by Sharon Flake, the main character's father has died and her mother is not quite herself in her grief. She throws her grief into sewing Maleeka all her clothes, to Maleeka's chagrin. Maleeka borrows outfits from the school bully in order not to be teased. The students notice the twist on the clothing switch from Cinderella. Maleeka has to find her way back to who she really is by standing up to the bully and connecting to the memory of her father. Finally, in *From the Notebooks of Melanin Sun*, by Jacqueline Woodson, Melanin feels that he has lost his mother when she reveals that she's in a relationship with a woman. He has to come to terms with who his mother is, what others think, and what matters most in order to regain his place in the world.

The novels are not consciously based on the story of Ashputtle, or Cinderella, but all of literature is connected, and the same patterns come up in stories over and over again. Each story we look at is somewhat more complex than the previous one, and students' previous experience supports their assimilation of the new pieces and ambiguities. At the end of the year, students identify the key elements of an Ashputtle story and write their versions.

My eighth-grade curriculum in my current school focuses on the theme of identity in various settings and under various conditions and the structural motif of the journey. The first half of the year focuses on identity within a particular setting. The second half focuses on oppression and resistance and their impact on identity. These two pieces come together in the final study of the hero's journey.

Here's how it unfolds, from one novel to the next. Note that it has taken me years to develop this trajectory. I am describing here what it has become in my current school context through experimentation with my students, collaboration with colleagues, and revisions. I'm including only the main text for each study, though there are additional materials for each:

- Identity within the classroom community, the setting of *The Hundred Dresses*. The notion of leaving the community comes up, but not for the main character yet. Wanda, the outcast, leaves, and the community is left to respond. I introduce the roles of oppressor, victim, resister, bystander, and martyr in this context.
- Identity and its relationship to home and neighborhood in *The House on Mango Street*. Esperanza longs for a home of her own, unlike Mango Street. The end suggests that she has left Mango Street to find a new home, but returned by writing the book.
- Developing an identity in two different worlds in *The Absolutely True Diary of a Part-Time Indian*. Junior lives on the Indian reservation where he grew up but attends an all-white school off the reservation and must reconcile the two worlds.
- Nonfiction journalism study: Students investigate the neighborhoods surrounding our school. They conduct interviews and surveys, looking for a story with multiple perspectives. They read and study the form of a feature article and write their own feature articles. Many of the themes we see in the novels come up in the issues students identify for their articles.

- Identity and family, and the extent to which family, race, and culture versus personal choices have an impact on identity. In *Nobody's Family Is Going to Change*, Emma wants to be a lawyer and Willie wants to be a dancer, but their parents, and to some extent, society, deny them support and opportunity to do so. Oppression and resistance are also themes in the book.

> An amazing resource for finding great books and great series (or reading ladders) of related books for grades 4 through 12 is *Reading Ladders*, by Teri Lesesne.

- Identity within oppressive power structures in *The Chocolate War*. Jerry attends a boys' prep school, where a secret society, the Vigils, manipulates and controls students. Jerry decides to quietly rebel and faces the consequences.
- Identity and the hero's journey in book club groups, including *The Ear, the Eye and the Arm*; *The Alchemist*; *The Parable of the Sower*; *Somewhere in Darkness*; and *Shipbreaker*.

Add Depth and Breadth to the Novel Study with Supplemental Materials

The sequence of novels has a connected quality. Within each novel study, I select additional texts to build on themes, topics, allusions, or structural elements within the novel. The purpose is to help students gain a wealth of connected experiences, which allow them to do any of the following:

- Broaden their understanding of ideas in the novel
- Connect aspects of the novel to real life or history
- Compare different authors' perspectives on the same ideas
- See how different writers use the same tools or structural elements in different ways and with different levels of quality
- Find out about the author's life and context
- Read critics' reviews of the novel or genre and compare with their own perspectives

These materials may include articles, poems, speeches, short stories, interviews, graphic novels, and films. I also select additional books for students who finish the whole novel early. These become what I call seeker opportunities, offered for credit (not extra credit) for students who choose to read them. (See Chapter 8 for more about seeker opportunities.) Students who don't finish early can still opt to read the seeker books in their next independent reading cycle, and often they do.

Within each novel study, I consider how the novel connects to students' learning in other subjects and try to make this happen where possible—without anything becoming too forced. Usually these connections happen with the social studies. For example, when we read *The Absolutely True Diary of a Part-Time Indian*, which takes place on an Indian reservation, students are studying westward expansion and the Trail of Tears in social studies.

The other day, though, we were discussing *Nobody's Family Is Going to Change*, about a brother and sister who have a strong passion for dance and law, respectively. Students brought up the idea of whether these talents were innate or not—the nature–versus-nurture debate. Students happen to be studying genetic traits in science and were able to bring their knowledge to the discussion. This was an unplanned but exciting connection, and I'm following up with an article for them to read on nature versus nurture.

Common Core Connection

By connecting whole novels with a range of ancillary texts, teachers can help students excel in CCRA.R.7: "Analyze how two or more texts address similar themes or topics in order to build knowledge or to compare the approaches the authors take."

Let the Students Discover the Connections

I select the texts to allow students to make connections and build conceptual understanding, but I want them to discover these connections through their experiences rather than my presenting to them. One day, my eighth graders were discussing *The House on Mango Street*. It was round 2 of discussions, and students had been grappling with the idea of Cisneros's purpose in writing this book. We had also been working on a creative writing piece in which students were describing a place, real or imagined, in vivid detail. Here's a piece of their discussion in which some connections became clear:

KANDICE: I think the moral of the book is, "Never say never" or never say you'll never get a house if you're poor, because maybe you could get it.

JOFREY: You should dream.

VICTOR: Maybe she wanted to write it about her family also.

ASUNCIÓN: I think maybe she wrote this when she was a child. She gives so many details it makes you feel like you're there.

JOFREY: Hey, this is related to what we were writing in class! You said, "make a setting that I can imagine I'm there"!

ASUNCIÓN: I agree with Jofrey.

MANUEL: I think you planned all this.

ASUNCIÓN: Usually setting comes in every book we read.

My students become accustomed to making connections across texts and between their reading and writing. That's because, as Manuel suspected, I plan it that way! In my eighth-grade program, we look at the ways in which authors develop the literary element of setting. However, I allow the students to draw out these connections. I don't post them as essential questions at the beginning of the year or unit, because I want the students to have these moments where they figure it out. I select books and create assignments to maximize the potential for students to make connections across the variety of literary experiences. This moment in discussion led Asunción to the realization that "setting comes in every book," evidence of her emerging conceptual thinking about literature.

In their discussion comments, sticky notes, and writing pieces, I see evidence of my students' abstract thinking and a growing awareness of the connectedness of literature. They seem to find great satisfaction in making connections. The more I can create conditions that help students to do so without doing the work for them by prescribing the connections, the better.

Selecting books that deal with common themes in increasing complexity over the year also helps students appreciate a book they might not choose to read on their own. In this way, they gain enjoyment from both the novel and from the mental work of connecting and comparing it to what came before it and assimilating it into their broadened understanding of the theme and the world of literature.

ASSESSING THE STRENGTHS OF A NOVEL: FINDING A LITERARY FOCUS FOR THE STUDY

The last question I ask myself when selecting a novel for the whole class is about the quality of the writing. If I'm considering a work of literature for a whole novel study, it must have merit. Beyond that, I ask these questions:

- What's strong in the writing of this novel?
- Which literary elements does the author draw really well?
- What opportunities does this novel offer students to study formal elements of literature?

The House on Mango Street is composed of short vignettes told in the first person. The way Cisneros uses language to create a sense of setting in this work is strong and worthy of study. The book also presents an opportunity to identify themes and symbolism, because they are what hold the vignettes together to create a progressively structured narrative. The book does not, however, provide an opportunity to study plot or character development. *Nobody's Family Is Going to Change*, by contrast, is excellent for looking at character development, plot structure, and point of view, but setting and symbolism are not as strong.

I assess each whole novel selection for its formal strengths, so that I can anticipate an appropriate literary focus of the study. In a whole novel study, students bring up the content, based on their responses to the text; however, my assessment of the novel can help me anticipate those responses. I can also point students to pay extra attention to the element through special formats for sticky notes, accompanying minilessons, and collaborative miniprojects. (See Chapters 3 and 7 for more on these.)

The same literary elements exist in every novel, and we don't forget the ones that are not the focus. For example, we focus on setting in our first whole novel study, and students continue to bring up setting in subsequent novel studies. Assessing each novel's strengths and choosing a focus helps me make sure I'm providing students an array of literary experiences across the year. By the end of the year, I want students to become adept at making observations and comments about a range of literary elements in a text. They need some in-depth exposure to each element and subsequent opportunities to interact with them across the year.

A PROCESS FOR BOOK SELECTION THROUGHOUT THE YEAR

The process I use to select texts across the year takes into account all five dimensions: development, identification level, reading level, thematic connections, and literary focus. These concepts and tips can be helpful whether you are hoping to try out a single whole novel study or plan a year-long whole novels curriculum. They can be equally helpful for selecting titles for a literature curriculum using any approach.

Before School Starts—or At Any Point You Decide to Try Whole Novels

- *Review the developmental theory on your age group, and choose a developmentally meaningful theme.* It should be one that is broad enough to be visible in a variety of contexts and works of literature. For eighth grade, I choose identity. Among the many possibilities, for seventh grade, I recommend belonging or difference; for sixth, I might recommend friendship or trust, and for ninth, coming of age.
- *Get to know the literature for your age group.* Search for titles for your classroom library and for whole novel studies. I've spent a great deal of time in the Bank Street Children's Book Store over the years, where the staff is knowledgeable and the selection of adolescent literature is extensive. I wander around YA sections of other bookstores and surf Amazon and blogs, hunting down interesting reading materials for my students. A wealth of quality literature exists for children and young adults that often doesn't make its way into schools. The genre is growing fast, but it takes some time to find the best works.
- *Find books that connect to your theme.* Look for a range of reading levels, a balance of male and female protagonists, and mirror and window opportunities for your students. Make sure to read any whole novel candidate before making your decision. Not every young adult book is a good one for an individual or as a selection for a specific group of students. You don't want to disappoint your students or yourself by discovering after it's too late that a book does not meet your expectations.
- *Find out what means you have of acquiring books.* Talk to your school about the process for ordering books. Some schools don't have a clear process, but this doesn't mean there aren't funds for books. By asking and following up with the right personnel, things can happen. Make sure to have a good explanation for

why you need a classroom library to support students' independent reading and class sets of novels for whole class study. Ample research shows a strong correlation between time spent reading and academic success. If you have special education students, you can make a case for certain titles being an appropriate use of funds for special education students.

- *If your school is unable to purchase books, prioritize acquiring class sets for whole novel studies.* For class sets of novels, DonorsChoose.org matches donors with classrooms in need. Funding for simple requests like class sets of novels are almost guaranteed there. Research organizations like First Book. You can even talk to your local banks, which all have funds set aside for giving back to the community. If you approach them, you are doing some of their outreach work for them. You can promise some good photo opportunities of your students with books.

- *Rely on other means for donations to your classroom lending library: friends, organizations, and garage sales, for example.* You can also encourage students to acquire books for themselves. If your community has a good library, make friends with a librarian. Take your students on a trip there; for older students, a homework assignment can be to get a card and check out a book.

Beginning of the School Year

- *Start the year with an independent reading cycle*, allowing students to select books for themselves. During this time, get to know your students' reading interests, reading habits, and reading levels. Ask them to fill out a survey about what they like to read and how they feel about reading. Share what you're reading. Give them structured chances to talk to each other about their reading. (Consult other resources recommended in this chapter on independent reading programs.)

- *Assess your students' reading levels.* Choose a method that works for you. At the least, sit down with each student individually sometime in the first few weeks of school—in class while other students are reading or at another time during the day. Have the student read aloud to you from his independent reading book. Then ask him to tell you about what he just read. Ask a few literal, inferential, and critical questions. Have a few other books on hand of varying reading levels. If the student's book is clearly too hard, pass him an easier book. Ask him to read the first half-page, and repeat the process. If his book is too easy, ask him to read from a harder book and repeat the process. Take notes.

- *Tell a story or read aloud to your students.* Select a folktale or series of similar folktales, a very short novel, or a series of high-quality picture books to read aloud to your students during the independent reading cycle. These texts should be thematically or structurally connected to your first novel or the theme for the year. Let students respond to these stories. Don't prescribe questions. (See Chapter 3 for more on this.)

The First Whole Novel Study

- *Select an engaging, accessible novel.* If the content is developmentally appropriate and the writing quality is strong, it's fine if the book is "too easy" for some readers. Ideally this book has characters with whom the majority of your students can personally relate. It should have a compelling beginning that will draw in reluctant readers and motivate them to put in the effort. It's best for the first whole novel study to focus on one novel for the whole class (as opposed to dividing the class into two or more book groups).
- *Determine a literary focus* for the whole novel study by assessing the strengths of the book (ask yourself what the author does especially well in this work) and the knowledge of your students. It's often good to start the year with a focus on character, a primary and easily engaging element. If students have a lot of prior experience looking at character traits, relationships, and development, it can be good to challenge students by looking at a different element or device. Plan a few activities to help students engage with the literary element during the reading process. (See Chapter 7 for ideas.)
- *Plan supports, including audio recordings, in advance for students who will need them.* Talk to colleagues who can offer support to struggling readers. If your school has any after-school tutoring program, talk to the adults there about the novel study. (See Chapter 8 for more ways to accommodate diverse learners.)
- *If possible, select an additional book to offer as a seeker opportunity for students who finish reading the first book early.* (Estimate the number of students who read more quickly than your schedule.) This could be another work by the same

author or a text that is thematically or structurally related to your whole novel. (See Chapter 9 for more on this practice.)

- *Select supplemental materials for in-class work during the study.* Include a nonfiction article or excerpt that connects to the novel. Try to include something visual—a film, a graphic novel, or even a photograph, painting, or political cartoon. Try to include a poem or short story.

- *After the whole novel study, begin another independent reading cycle.* Take note of students' book choices for themselves now and throughout the rest of the year. Reassess reading levels for students you might be wondering about.

Building the Whole Novels Sequence

- *The next whole novel should be a step more complex or challenging than the first.* It might be longer, have a less straightforward plot structure, or have more unfamiliar words, but it should not be such a huge jump up in reading level as to overwhelm students. It should build on themes present in the first novel and bring some new themes or context to the fore.

- *Depending on the range of reading levels, there can be two whole novel groups, reading thematically related novels of differing reading levels.* Students must read one and may also read both. I generally have students preview both and choose which book to read (unless I am splitting by gender). Students usually choose the more appropriate book on their own. If I disagree with a student's choice, I may privately counsel her to rethink it or allow the student to try it out anyway. Sometimes I'm surprised by a positive outcome; other times, the student learns from the consequences of making the choice.

- *If possible, follow a split study with a book that the whole class can read to bring the group back together.* If finding one novel for the whole class is going to be tough and uncomfortable, try a graphic novel. Perhaps pair a graphic novel with a related film to build up the common story experience of the class.

Taking Time to Reflect

- *Pay attention to how students respond to the novels in terms of content and reading challenges.* Reflect on what's working and what needs work in each novel study. Consider how the choice of novel related to the strengths or weaknesses of the study. Consider whether you would teach this novel again with a similar group. Talk to colleagues about your thinking. Review the five dimensions again for each text: development, identification, reading level, thematic connections, and literary strength.

- *Look for ways to adjust the text choices moving forward to serve the group.* Perhaps it's time to challenge students with a novel or a short story with a less straightforward narrative or an unfamiliar setting. Maybe you want to try the whole novel approach with a work of narrative nonfiction. Or maybe you moved too quickly into a challenging novel or something that students couldn't relate to; in this case, you may need to find something more accessible to reengage them or cushion the challenge with a related film that can be an anchor for students.

- *Celebrate student growth!* When the class succeeds in a whole novel study, highlight the accomplishment. When individual students begin reading more challenging texts than they could in September, point out their growth. Make sure they understand that they are the ones who did all the work and deserve all the credit.

3

Authentic Note Taking
Three Levels of Thinking, Three Levels of Response

"And what will they do while they read?"

I remember a conversation I had during my first year of teaching with a fellow English teacher who was serving as a literacy coach. I was telling her about my plan for a lesson she was going to observe the next day.

"Then I will give them reading time," I told her, after describing the lesson.

"Great," she said. "And what will they do while they're reading?"

Confusion. Wasn't it obvious?

"Well, they will read their books," I said tentatively, knowing that would not sound like an adequate answer.

"Yes, but what will you tell them to look for when they read?" she rephrased.

"Um . . ." I didn't know how to answer this question. I hadn't planned to tell them to look for anything in particular. I wanted them to find for themselves whatever brilliance or mystery or horror awaited them in the story. I wanted my students to let the story perform its magic on them. Giving this more thought, I knew that I wanted them to note points of interest, points of confusion, ask questions, and formulate opinions. But I didn't want to direct students to do something that was going to be unnatural to their reading process and put a damper on the experience. I just wanted them to read!

The conversation with my colleague didn't go much further than that. I took her advice for the observation and directed students to "write down characters' motivations" in their notebooks as they read, or something to that effect. But I didn't especially believe in what I was doing. It felt like canned, superimposed "school stuff" on top of the child's experience of a work of literature.

To this day, I don't want my students to think that reading and responding to literature is some kind of trick. Throughout their schooling, students learn endless acronyms and strategies designed to help them be better readers. Some of these tools can be effective, but their sum total often leads kids to the perception that reading and responding to literature are overly complicated tasks and that they are incapable of doing these right (or at all) without the help of a teacher's directions and questions. Already avid readers may conclude that real reading doesn't happen in school.

At the same time, I've also come to realize—and it took me a while to admit this—that all students can gain from being guided toward conscious habits of reading, which is what my colleague was trying to help me to do. I've devised ways of doing this that honor the intrinsic motivation kids have to experience and respond to stories and are flexible enough to benefit all students' critical-thinking skills, regardless of their individual reading levels.

MADELEINE'S FAMOUS THREE-WAYS-OF-THINKING LESSON

On the first day of her Children's Literature course at Bank Street College, Madeleine Ray tells a story, a favorite folktale of hers. She instructs students to just relax and listen, which creates a novel experience for her graduate students. When she's done, the story becomes the focal point for a brilliant, constructivist lesson that she calls the three ways of thinking. In it, students learn to distinguish their own literal, inferential, and critical responses to a story. This lesson has been an instant success in elementary, middle and high schools throughout New York City, in demo lessons and observations by many teachers, and has even been transferred to the social studies classroom by some of my colleagues. It has also become the foundation for the reading habits I teach my students to use throughout the year in the whole novels program. What follows is a description of how I teach this same lesson in my middle school classroom. I've taught this lesson with several different folktales, but for a while now, I've settled on one called "Isaac and the Treasure." It is a Jewish folktale about a peasant man who has a recurring dream of a treasure in a faraway place. When he follows the dream in search of the treasure, he doesn't find it where he dreamed it would be. However, he gets information from an unexpected source that leads him back to his own home, where he finds the treasure. As the story goes, after becoming a rich man, he uses the treasure to build a temple. It's a classic plot that exists in many cultures and has made its way into novels and movies as well.

"Isaac and the Treasure" serves two purposes in my classroom. First, it gives me an opportunity to share my ethnic background with my students early on, which I feel is an important aspect of my identity to acknowledge in a culturally diverse classroom. Second, the tale of a journey, and I use it to foreshadow the journey theme that recurs throughout the year in the literature we study and that ultimately shapes the end of our year. In all literature, but especially in the classic journey story, beginnings and endings are connected, and I like that I can mirror that effect in the curriculum itself.

Telling the Story

I do this lesson in the permanent meeting area I've set up in my classroom: three benches that form a U-shape around a rug in the front of the room. (See "Parts of the Whole: My Room Setup," after Chapter 6, for room configuration ideas.) When the students are seated, I begin: "I'm going to tell you a story. I learned this story while traveling in Poland after college, where my family lived before immigrating to the United States. It was told to me inside of the temple Isaac, one of few Jewish temples in Poland still standing after World War II."

"You're Jewish?" one student invariably asks me.

"Yes, I am," I say, and pause to allow for more questions. Sometimes there are a lot. I usually answer one or two and then tell them I'll be happy to answer any more questions individually.

"And now for the story. While I tell it, I want you to just relax and enjoy it. And since I'm telling it from memory, which is not easy to do, help me out by holding your comments and questions until the end. We will get a chance to talk about it afterward. Any questions?"

"Can we sit on the floor?" someone often asks.

"Okay," I say, "provided that you sit back on the bench when the story is done." Several students move to the floor.

"Can I close my eyes?" another student asks.

"Yes, provided that you don't fall asleep," I respond. "Can anyone explain why it might be important not to fall asleep?" This line of questioning—the ridiculously obvious one related to classroom behavior—seems to go far with middle school students, who are not above testing the limits of the appropriate. Taking a moment to acknowledge that the ridiculous is always a possibility and asking them to consider the consequences of such possibilities in advance often eliminates their urges to enact such behaviors. This also lets students know I will not be astonished by antics, which is half of their appeal in the first place.

And then I begin: "A long time ago, in a small village at the side of a great forest there lived a man named Isaac." As I tell the story, I see that even the most reluctant students' eyes grow wide with interest as the plot progresses. I notice the adolescents humor me as I repeat certain phrases, like "into the forest, over two hills and around a lake, under a bridge was buried a fabulous treasure, of gold and diamonds and rubies and pearls and all the precious jewels that can be found in the world" numerous times throughout the story. Every student is able to follow the simple narrative through listening, and they always seem to enjoy it quite a bit.

"Can you tell us another one?" someone always asks after I have finished.

> Storytelling is one of the best rainy-day activities for any age group. I've used it when I have to cover someone else's class or have a random one-off extra period with a group of students. The payoff for the time it has taken me to memorize a couple of folktales over the years has been huge.

Drawing Out Students' Natural Response to a Story

When I finish telling the story, I put up some chart paper or project a Word document on my laptop.

"So I'd like to hear your responses now," I say. "What do you think? What do you notice? What do you remember? What stands out to you?"

For the moment, I ask students to refrain from asking questions. We'll get to them later. So students raise their hands and offer responses. I've done this in heterogeneous classes, high-performing groups, transitional ELLs, and with a self-contained class of special education students. With a good folktale, there is never a dearth of response.

"Isaac followed his dream and found the treasure."
"The bridge keeper should have followed his dream!"
"The bridge keeper was selfish."
"I knew something like that would happen at the end."
And so forth.

I copy down each comment verbatim without judgment and without steering the conversation. All comments are valid. I number each response and make sure there are at least ten comments, though usually I have to cut the activity short before the students run out. (So far this lesson has taken about thirty minutes. Depending on the length of the period, I might save the next part for tomorrow. More on timing later in the chapter.)

Categorizing Responses: The Three Kinds of Thinking

Next, the objective is to get the students to classify their own free-form responses into three categories: literal, inferential, and critical). I tell students, "In this lesson we're going to learn about three ways of thinking and how to categorize your own thoughts."

I first ask, "Looking at this list of responses, which ones were stated directly in the story? Which of these is actually, or *literally*, in the text—sort of like a fact?" I reveal just the definition of *literal thinking* on the chart to match my question so students have a visual reference for the term (Exhibit 3.1). I find the poster helps students engage in the moment, and also sends a subtle message that these terms are going to stay relevant. They won't just come and visit for a day and be forgotten. The visual cue helps turn on students' attention and memory muscles.

I read the first response: "'Isaac followed his dream and found the treasure.' Then I ask, "Is this a literal response?"

> ### EXHIBIT 3.1 The Three Ways of Thinking
>
> **Literal:** Your thought was stated directly in the text, like a fact from the text.
> **Inferential:** Your thought was not stated directly, but there is evidence for it in the text; it is hinted at, suggested, or implied.
> **Critical:** Your original thought, opinion, connection, or critical question related to the text.

"Yes," one student says, "because it's stated directly that he went to follow his dream. And it's a fact that he found the treasure. So yes."

"But it's not literal that he found the treasure because of his dream," another student counters.

"Yes, but it doesn't say that's why. It just says that he followed his dream, and that is true, and he found the treasure and that's true. So it's literal, right?" a third student offers.

The debates that arise out of this activity are rich and worthwhile. There often isn't one clear answer, and that doesn't really matter: the opportunity for students to support and clarify their claims is more important.

"Well, what do the rest of you think?" I push. "Is it literal?" The students arrive at agreement that this response is literal, so I put a big red "L" next to the statement, which corresponds to the color-coding on my poster. We go through the rest of the responses, and when students identify other literal responses, I label them with an L.

"Now, which of these thoughts is not stated directly, but it is implied or suggested? In other words, there's strong evidence for it in the story, but it's not exactly a fact. You had to think a little to figure it out," I say. "We call that kind of response *inferential* thinking." I reveal the definition for inferential thinking on the chart (Exhibit 3.1).

I begin to read the responses that have not been labeled with an L. Very often, there is some gray area between inferential and critical responses.

"'The bridge keeper should have followed his dream,'" I read. "Is that inferential?"

"It might be," a student responds. "It is hinted at. The bridge keeper could have become rich if he followed his dream."

A few hands go up. I call on another student.

"It's literal. It's a fact that he would have found the treasure if he followed his dream."

I call on the next student.

"But this was never said in the text. I think that is more like an opinion than a hint, because you're telling the character what he should do," the student offers.

"Yeah," another student chimes in. "You might think the bridge keeper should have followed his dream, but maybe the bridge keeper doesn't want to. That's just your opinion." The first student raises her hand again. I call on her, allowing the argument to unfold a little longer.

"It's an opinion, but if you think about it, the *whole story* sort of hints that the bridge keeper should have followed his dream." At this point, I step in to throw them a line.

"This is a really cool argument! I'm going to show you the third way of thinking, which I think might help you figure this out." I reveal the definition for *critical* response (Exhibit 3.1). "This kind response is your original thought, opinion, connection or critical question about the text. It is not stated in the text, and, though it is about the story, the thinking comes more from the reader than the text. Thoughts?" I ask.

The students mostly agree that the statement about what the bridge keeper should have done is critical, because it is a reader's opinion, but some still argue that it's inferential because the story as a whole seems to imply that the bridge keeper should have followed his dream.

"In inferential thinking," I explain, "there needs to be strong evidence for the statement in the text—in the sense that you could actually point to a specific place in the text where the author leaves a hint. It can't be the entire text." Here I take the opportunity to tell them that a response that makes a claim about what the story as a whole is saying—its message—is called an interpretation. "This type of thinking is really important in the study of literature, and we tend to think of it as critical, because the reader is putting together several thoughts to come up with the conclusion about the whole story." I put a C next to the statement, and we

---

EXHIBIT 3.2 The Categorized Class List of Responses to the Story

1. The man went to the forest to get a treasure because of his dream. **L**
2. The toll guy said to Isaac that he was foolish because he thought there was treasure buried and he had the same dream. **L**
3. Isaac was determined to find the treasure. **I**
4. Isaac had no job, and his wife stayed at home with the kids. **L**
5. Isaac became rich. **L**
6. Something that annoys me about folktales is that they repeat the same thing over and over. **C**
7. I liked the story. It was adventurous and interesting. **C**
8. He had to climb two mountains. **L**
9. He found the treasure not from his dream but the other guy's dream. **L**
10. It was through his dream that he found the guy, who told him where the real treasure was. **L**
11. I think its cool that he built a synagogue with the money. **C**
12. He was thinking of other people, not just himself. **I**
13. I thought it was weird that the bridge keeper had the same dream with the opposite setting. **C**
14. If you think about it, the bridge keeper and Isaac were similar because they were both poor and they both had dreams about finding a treasure. **C**
15. I thought the bridge keeper was lying about the dream. **C**
16. Isaac assumed the "poor man" was him. **I**
17. There was no other poor character in the story. **I/L**

---

keep going, though there are times when the debate is compelling on both sides, and I end up recording an I/C or an L/I. We end up with the list in Exhibit 3.2.

I conclude the lesson by highlighting to students that they came up with all of these responses on their own, with no specific questioning from me. I also point out that they expressed all three kinds of thinking quite naturally in their responses to the story. "In fact," I say, "we use literal, inferential, and critical thinking all the time in response to what we see, hear, and read. We just might not be aware of it." (See Figure 3.1.)

Figure 3.1 Meeting Area Response Session

I am aware that students might be wondering, *Why is it helpful to become aware of our thinking?* I always favor letting kids investigate the concept, even if it's just for a moment, rather than telling them what I think. So I ask them outright: "Why might it be helpful to become more aware of our own thoughts in general? What about while we read?" Students are usually able to provide some great ideas about this. It's worth writing some of these down and posting them in the room near the three-kinds-of-thinking poster as a reminder of the reason for the habit.

This is a rich opportunity to teach students the concept of metacognition, which especially resonates with adolescents because their brains are developing the capacity for this skill. For great resources for this, check out Larry Ferlazzo's Best Posts On Metacognition. My favorite is http://larry-ferlazzo.edublogs.org/2011/10/31/an-effective-five-minute-lesson-on-metacognition/. Students can then read about metacognition, an example of bringing nonfiction reading into the whole novels program.

This opening activity can be done easily with a little preparation:

1. *Choose a folktale.* You may want to choose one that connects with other aspects of your literature program thematically or structurally, one from your cultural background to share with students, or one that connects to another discipline. But any fun story will do the trick!
2. *Learn to tell the story from memory.* Learn it piece by piece; then practice, timing yourself for planning purposes. With folktales, it's okay to vary your wording quite a bit from the version you're studying. These stories get passed down orally and come out differently each time. The storytelling has a different effect on students than a read-aloud does. It's quite a novel event and delivers to children like a gift. After you tell the story, ask them how the storytelling experience felt.
3. *Make a permanent classroom poster* with the definitions of the three ways of thinking.

For a modification with less preparation, read aloud a compelling opening to a novel, such as Roald Dahl's *The Witches* or the opening vignette in Sandra Cisneros's *House on Mango Street*. Poems do not work well for introducing this lesson.

CORE MESSAGES TO STUDENTS ABOUT RESPONDING TO LITERATURE

Following the lesson on the three ways of thinking, I guide students to notice and record their thoughts as they read. There are two big messages I want to send to my students early on to set them up to become critical readers: there is no one right answer, and their real thoughts are important.

Message 1: There Is No One "Right Answer"

Students should feel no external pressure to come up with a particular reaction or idea in response to anything we read. This pressure could come in the form of grades, gold stars, special praise, or any other means I have of influencing their behavior from my position as an authority. Though grades and praise are part of my classroom, I think carefully about the implicit messages my students learn from what may seem like perfectly innocuous practices. As Daniel Pink illustrates in his book, *Drive: The Surprising Truth about What Motivates Us* (2009), when we work under the pressure to comply with external controls, our capacity to think critically actually diminishes, as does our motivation in general. Pink writes, "Control leads to compliance; autonomy leads to engagement." He continues, "For routine tasks . . . gaining compliance usually worked just fine . . . But that was then. For the definitional tasks of the twenty-first century, such a strategy falls short, often woefully short. Solving complex problems requires an inquiring mind and a willingness to experiment one's way to a fresh solution" (107). Students need autonomy in their work space to be themselves and experiment in order to become critical readers. If we prescribe the answers or the structure every time, they rarely get the space they need to think critically and take risks.

Message 2: Your Real Thoughts Are Important

At the same time, students often aren't used to autonomy in their learning, which leads me to the second big message: students need to understand that their own thoughts have value. Their ideas and genuine responses to the text are what matter during the reading experience. These become the fuel for their participation in discourse about the work and the construction of unique interpretations of the work as a whole. But students have to wake up to their own responses to a story. They have to listen and notice and think about these innate reactions in order to build authentic interpretations of text. When students discover the power of their own minds, the effects can be life changing. Socrates famously stated, "The unexamined life is not worth living." By contrast, the examined life can lead to a greater sense of purpose and fulfillment.

> **Common Core Connection**
>
> Becoming aware of one's own responses to literature and using these to expand comprehension and develop interpretations is an important part of becoming an independent reader. The habits of response help students make progress toward CCRA.R.10: "Read and comprehend complex literary and informational texts independently and proficiently."

MY STORY: LEARNING TO LISTEN TO MY OWN THOUGHTS

I recall a key moment in my own education where these two core ideas came together for me. I had been a student of literature at Brown University for two years. I enjoyed reading literature but wasn't a big participator in seminar discussions. I was still reined in by the notion that there were "smart" things to say in class and "right" interpretations, and I was never sure if I had those smart, right ideas. I wrote decent papers, but I was not fully confident in the points I was making, so I meandered around ideas I thought might be important and often fell short. The grade I most often received in my college English courses at that point was a B. Once in a while I'd hit on something really good and get an A, but I never knew what the secret was of how I'd arrived at that better/right idea and how to repeat the process.

In my junior year, something changed. I was growing frustrated with academia, which seemed disconnected from what I thought was "the real world." The real world was a place in which I'd never really lived—having been a suburban kid, taken care of by my parents—but I increasingly wanted to know what it was. My English courses all included a heavy dose of postmodern literary criticism, which was bent on deconstructing the structures of oppression that reside in every aspect of our society, including our language itself.

I don't remember which postmodern critic, alongside which novel, I was reading that week. The ideas were all interesting, but when it came time to write my weekly response paper, I felt aggravated. The article, like many others I had read, insightfully vilified Western society and its literary tradition for weaving narratives that gave voice to elite ruling classes but left out everyone else. Part of me wanted to jump on that high horse with the critic once again, but I couldn't ignore my nagging concern that the language the critic chose for expressing his critique was so specialized that it was nothing short of incomprehensible to anyone but elite literature scholars. He was making an important point but in the quietest way possible: within a tiny corner of academia. This angered me because it would never change anything out in the real world where the children and adults he was talking about, who would likely never write their stories, actually lived.

It wasn't a term paper, so the stakes were only so high, and I decided to take a chance. *Screw it*, I thought, and I wrote what I actually thought. I took apart the critic's argument and the language he used to share it with the world and painted him as a fraudulent coward. I used other critics' ideas about language and power to back up my points, but I did my best to use a natural voice. It was a risky and impassioned move, but I was speaking the truth, and I was sick of hiding.

The next week, I received the paper back with an A+ on the front. Attached to the back was a two-page typed response from my professor. It began, "Finally, a genuine academic response to the course reading!" My professor took up my argument, agreeing with some points and debating others. This attention and validation awakened me to the importance of listening to my own responses to what I read. This time I knew why I earned the good grade and how I might do it again. It was no longer about a right interpretation; it was about an honest one.

I continued speaking my mind for the rest of the semester in papers and in seminar discussions. I learned what it meant to be a real student of literature, not just a hanger-on. I started more actively notating the texts as I read. I starred points that stuck out to me, even if I didn't know why. I argued back to the text in the margins. Then I used these comments to make points in class and in my papers.

The empowerment I experienced in this course stretched beyond school and changed the direction of my life. I began connecting what I was reading and discussing in the class with the experience I was having leading writing workshops with teenage girls and their mothers at the Boys and Girls Club in Fox Point, the poor neighborhood adjacent to the Brown campus. On the last day of class, I brought in the beautiful and searing self-published poetry of an elder from the Fox Point community I'd been introduced to. It shared stories of life working on the docks, of disconnection and longing for his homeland of the Cape Verde Islands. "See?" I said. "There are other narratives if we listen." I not only learned a lesson about how to be a student but also began to get in touch with an emerging sense of what I wanted to do with my life: help people raise their voices and be heard.

I go to the length of telling this story because it informs my approach to teaching literature on many levels. First, it's a reminder that even top students can be alienated from their own critical-thinking skills in school. We must consistently show students that we are open to their ideas and give them the space and attention they need to voice them. We also need to understand that it may take students some time to wake up to the power of their own minds after they've developed other habits. However, I also know that once they do, the study of literature and the practices that support it can help put students in touch with their core beliefs; lead them to follow these notions; make connections with other people, places, and ideas; and take action in their lives. Unlocking this potential requires students' willingness to listen to and communicate their own truth. As teachers, we have the power to point students to their own sets of keys.

STRENGTHENING STUDENT RESPONSE HABITS THROUGH PRACTICE

When I tell my students a story and ask them what they notice and what they think, they offer their free-form responses to the story. If the story is basically engaging and appropriate, kids do not need to be told what to focus on as they experience it. The responses come naturally, in the same way that they might talk in their free time about an exciting or funny episode of a television show they all watched the night before. The lesson helps students develop awareness of their own ideas and responses. Next, I want students to begin to listen to their own thoughts and be able to record them for themselves.

My students use sticky notes to record their responses as they read, which provide a natural and colorful way of talking back to the text without actually writing in the margins (Figure 3.2). In my first year in the classroom, I thought that I would teach my students the lesson on the three ways of thinking once, after which they would forever understand the differences among literal, inferential, and critical thinking and know how to record these thoughts on their sticky notes as they read. Although the first lesson does a lot to accomplish this objective, most kids need practice to get to a place where they both recognize their responses as they have them and establish the habit of writing them down.

Figure 3.2 Classroom Sticky Notes

Figure 3.3 Reading and Responding

I allot about two weeks to teach and reiterate the lesson and give students time to apply the skill to their reading (Figure 3.3). There are different ways to introduce it within a curriculum. As I discussed in Chapter 2, I almost always begin the year with independent reading, meaning students select the books they read. Choosing reading materials is an important habit of reading in itself, and it provides a window of opportunity for

- gauging my students' reading interests and abilities,
- generating excitement around reading by matching students with books they are enthusiastic about reading, and
- focusing on teaching the habits of response.

To couple the habits of response with independent reading, I make sure that students have already chosen books before beginning the lesson. Exhibit 3.3 shows how I organize book selection day.

EXHIBIT 3.3 Organizing Book Selection Day

1. Create a list as a whole class about how we choose books, which I post in the room. It can include, for example, reading the blurb for interest, reading the first page for interest and reading level, getting a recommendation, and looking for an author you know you like.

2. Send students to their tables to complete a survey about reading in general— their interests and struggles, previous experiences, where and when they usually read, and anything else that is relevant to this class. I've made my own reading surveys, but Donalyn Miller her taken this to another level, offering a reproducible one in appendix C of her book *The Book Whisperer* (2009).

3. Position myself by the books so I can make book recommendations.

4. Call up students, table by table, to choose their books while the others work on the survey.

5. Send around a student librarian with a book sign-out page for each student after she or he has chosen a book.

6. Silent reading time!

After the initial lesson on the three-ways-of-thinking lesson, I talk to students about writing on sticky notes the same sorts of thoughts they shared after the story in response to what they read. I demonstrate by reading the first page of a compelling novel aloud and then asking students, "If you were reading this book, what would you write on a sticky note now?" Then I write down one of their suggestions on a sticky note and place it directly on the page I'd just read, so that it sticks out of the book a little bit. Next, I send them to their tables to give it a try. I suggest they try writing a note every few pages, but there is no limit. Some students enjoy writing many notes—putting several on each page—and others prefer to stop less often. (More on expectations for responses in Chapter 6.)

The timing of the first lesson varies. In a single period, we may or may not get to categorize the entire list of responses. This is no problem, though, because completing the activity makes a good homework, warm-up, or group work assignment for the next day. Also, depending on the length of the period, how long it takes to tell the story, and how long I give for responses, I often end up pushing the categorization to the next day.

Table 3.1 Pacing the Three-Kinds-of-Thinking Lesson

Agenda 1: All at Once	Agenda 2: Spread It Out
Day or block 1	**Day or block 1**
• Tell story	• Tell story
• Student responses	• Student responses
• Categorize responses using three ways of thinking	• Independent reading time; students practice recording free-form responses on sticky notes
Day or block 2	**Day or block 2**
• Warm-up (optional): Provide one or two additional responses to the story; have students categorize them; review results	• Categorize responses using three ways of thinking
• Directions: Students try recording the same kinds of responses as we did for the story on sticky notes as they read. Tell them not to worry about the three kinds of thinking for now.	• Reading time—continue free-form responses
• Independent reading time	• Students categorize their own responses
• Students categorize their responses	

Table 3.1 shows two versions of the agenda that incorporate independent reading. Agenda 1 is to do the lesson all at once, which works well with a longer class period, and agenda 2, which works well for a shorter class period.

Over the next two weeks or so, I repeat variations of this basic process:

1. Read aloud. I vary the materials, sometimes using more folktales and often reading excerpts from the beginnings of novels, which also serves to "advertise" the books to readers.
2. Student responses—sometimes just a few.
3. Categorize the responses (or some of them) as literal, inferential, or critical.
4. Independent reading time or practice response individually on sticky notes.

The idea is to give students plenty of group practice responding freely to a story, which helps strengthen their awareness of their own responses and the range of responses readers have and then to give them time to apply this habit to their own reading. I also give students opportunities to share their notes with partners or groups and to categorize their own notes, writing an L, I, or C in the corner. I don't have them code their notes like this while they are reading and writing them, though. I don't want them thinking there is a requisite number of each type of note and staging the responses based on that perceived expectation. At the same time, I encourage students to vary the types of responses they record. When we are truly engaged in the story, responses that show literal understanding of the text, inferential thinking, and critical thinking naturally arise.

In independent reading cycles and in whole novel studies, I expect students to read at home as well as in class. I assign a minimum number of pages and sticky note responses, and I grade the notes. I discuss the assessment and grading of sticky notes in detail in Chapter 6.

During reading time, I circulate around the room, checking in with students about their books and reading their notes. Since we've established that good, natural responses to stories include all three ways of thinking, I can make clear suggestions to students who are not doing this in their individual notes. I've found the majority of students are able to pick up on the three kinds of thinking fairly quickly in their own reading notes. In this independent reading cycle at the beginning of the year, I prioritize building relationships with the struggling readers in my class and making sure they see places to go for themselves and have ways of getting there. That will help them be better prepared for the first whole novel study. I also note students who are particularly voracious readers and try to understand their processes. In Chapter 8, I discuss how I work with individual students of all levels within the whole novels program.

After a few days, I have the class create a list of some of the types of comments they tend to write in their sticky notes. I write these on chart paper and post the list in the room as a visual aid for students during reading time. Kids tend to have a decent toolbox of ideas from elementary school to contribute, in addition to their more recent experiences. Those lists look something like this:

Suggestions for Sticky Notes

- Opinions about characters
- Something about the character's personality

- Questions about characters
- Important things from the story
- Things you're confused about
- Things you wonder about
- Connections to your life/things you relate to
- Connections to other books or to movies
- What you think might happen
- What you hope happens
- Emotions about the story
- Thoughts about the author
- Words you don't know
- Something you like in the story
- Something you don't like

HOW DO WE CATEGORIZE QUESTIONS?

After a week or so, we return to the notion of questions and the three ways of thinking. I used to tell students that questions were always critical. After all, your question about a text is never stated in the text. A question you have cannot really be implied in the text either. We think of questioning as a critical-thinking skill. Yet some questions just don't feel right being classified as critical thinking. "What time is dinner?" you might ask. This might be of critical importance, but no one has to think critically to ask that question. Likewise, "What's the name of the village where Isaac lived?" might be a good question to consider, but does it reflect a student's ability to think critically about text?

One fall, Madeleine came up with the idea to exclude questions from the three-ways-of-thinking lesson altogether. That same year, when I was talking to my colleagues about test questions, we were discussing the idea of having students categorize the types of questions that often appear on the state tests. This reminded me of the three kinds of thinking—literal, inferential, and critical—and that's when it dawned on me. It now seems perfectly obvious that questions in response to text should break down into the same categories. The trick is to determine whether a question is literal, inferential, or critical based on the type of response the answer would be.

Questions like "What is the name of Isaac's village?" would yield a literal response if answered. So it can be considered a literal question. An inferential question requires the reader to make an inference to answer it. So the question "Why does the bridge keeper laugh at Isaac?" would be inferential, because the answer is only implied in the story.

> I love teaching this distinction to students: "The author *implies*, so that the reader *infers*."

Finally, critical questions require critical thinking to answer. "What is the significance of Isaac's not realizing the treasure is in his house all along?" asks us to think metaphorically. The answer is not stated in the text, and it would be difficult to point to the part of the text that implies the answer. Instead, we have to construct an argument to answer the question.

I teach this by telling another folktale or reading a short piece of text, perhaps a vignette from *The House on Mango Street* by Sandra Cisneros or . . . *And the Earth Did Not Devour Him* by Tomas Rivera. I ask the students to brainstorm questions about the text, and I write them down on the board or type and project them. Then I explain to students my historical difficulty with figuring out how to categorize questions using the three ways of thinking. I ask them to discuss in groups for five or ten minutes how we should categorize questions. Often they come to the same conclusion I did that day: that questions can be literal, inferential, or critical, and this depends on whether the answer to the question is literally in the text, implied by the text, or an opinion of the reader. We share ideas and then see if they work by categorizing the questions we asked before. Invariably the questions fall into the three categories, and we have a system.

COMBINING THREE WAYS OF THINKING: POWER STICKY NOTES

Three years ago, I introduced the three-kinds-of-thinking practice to my collaborative team teacher at Brooklyn Prospect at the time, Daniel Brink-Washington. He was enthusiastic about it and helped me tighten up many of the systems I had in place and push the thinking further. That's something I love about whole novels: there is always space to keep exploring. At some point Danny noticed that certain students were fleshing out their thoughts in their sticky notes, while others wrote brief comments that didn't probe beyond the surface. We also noticed that students who wrote lengthier notes had trouble categorizing them because they were moving naturally in and out of literal, inferential, and critical thinking. "In a way, we want them to be able to write a sticky note response that uses all three types of thinking," Danny said in a planning meeting.

"Hmm. I've never thought of that. Are you suggesting we have them try this now?" I asked. He was. I'm always wary of prescribing responses too much, but this seemed like a worthwhile experiment. It didn't mean we had to require it, and kids are usually up for a challenge. I also thought about the fact that later, when we introduced the literary essay, we'd help students discover how each of the three kinds of thinking plays a crucial role in the writing process. This seemed like a good stepping-stone on the way there.

So we brought the challenge of combining three types of thinking on a single note to the students.

"Who's having trouble categorizing their stickies because you've used more than one type of thinking in one note?" A handful of hands shot up. I ask Tamera to read one of the notes that she's identified with multiple types of thinking. She reads a note she wrote for *Make Lemonade* by Virginia Euwer Wolff: "'Why does Jolly ignore LaVaughn? She says it's because LaVaughn is part of her bad past. But that doesn't make sense, because LaVaughn's the one that got her into that better future!'"

"Wow," I say. "First of all, what do the rest of you think of her note? What's working about this note?"

A few hands go up.

"She really makes a point," Elvin says.

"And she, like, explains it," adds Mariah.

"I wanted to know what the bad past was," another student muses.

I was glad they gave the note some love, because that segued into the notion that pushing out ideas has value and that would provide a rationale for the power sticky note challenge. We analyze Tamera's note, identifying the literal and critical statements within it. One student thinks the question is inferential, because you might make an inference to answer it.

"I want to give you guys a challenge now. Mr. Brink-Washington and I were talking about the work you've been doing in your reading, and we wondered if you would be able to write a note that has all three kinds of thinking in it."

I gave them ten minutes to work through this, and most students were able to do it. We discovered a few ways that lead naturally to all three kinds of thinking. For example, by asking a critical question, attempting to answer the question, and offering evidence for their educated guess, students usually used all three kinds of thinking.

We named these "power stickies," and for a period of time, we asked that they try one each night, and the rest of their notes could be "open response," as we started calling it, which referred to free-form notes with any level of thinking that naturally came up. We had students practice identifying the literal, inferential, and critical statements in their own and each other's power stickies.

Consider this student's sticky note.

This statement, about Paulo Coelho's *The Alchemist*, that "the boy is really naive" is inferential because it's not stated directly in the text, but there is strong evidence for it. "He should have paid attention" is an

> LIC. The boy is really naive for trusting the man in the port town with all of his money. He should have paid attention to his friend's words: "Port towns are always full of thieves (37)" Also why does he trust EVERYONE he finds who can speak Spanish?

opinion, which puts it somewhere in critical territory, and the student provides some literal evidence for her conclusion in the form of a quote. The student finishes with a critical question. (I might encourage her to make a further inference or conjecture in response to her own question about why the boy might trust everyone who speaks Spanish.)

After a while we dropped the requirement of power stickies, but the practice seemed to have some sticking power. (Pun accidental!) Students started elaborating more in their responses, which helped them to recognize and strengthen their inference skills, which tend to be challenging to teach. Now, a year later in the spring of eighth grade, I haven't specifically required power stickies all year. This is because I don't like to attach too many requirements to the sticky notes. I do emphasize the importance of elaboration and a variety of kinds of thinking in notes. I think the power sticky exercise gave students a clear model and some explicit practice in this.

The invention of the power sticky and the success of its short-term use within a novel study gave way to the development of more exercises in specific formats for sticky notes.

HELPING STUDENTS EXPAND THEIR NOTE-TAKING SKILLS

As the year progresses, students become comfortable and pretty adept at writing literal, inferential, and critical responses on sticky notes as they read. My eighth graders have already been writing stickies for a year, and I'm observing several things that make me want to expand my students' practice of authentic note taking:

- I sense a need for additional challenge, or a shift in focus, in the practice of taking notes to keep it from becoming a repetitive assignment. The texts change and students learn more about literature, but the note-taking styles of students don't always reflect this growth. Struggling readers, I hypothesize, might benefit from a new angle to help them access a text more fully.
- I want students to apply official literary terms to their observations when relevant. For example, Allie comments on a conflict between two characters in the story using a combination of literal, inferential, and critical thinking. However, she does not use the word *conflict*, even though she's familiar with the term. If students aren't applying these terms independently, then they haven't fully acquired the concept, even if they understand what it is when they are prompted.
- I would like to see students pay closer attention to the language of the text as they read. There is a great deal to notice and comment on at this level, but since students are most compelled by the elements of character and plot, most do not take the time to make observations about language until we are rereading in discussions. I want to influence their process a little bit in this direction, without taking the general sense of freedom of response away.

Kelly Gallagher argues in *Readicide* (2009) that teachers need to find the "sweet spot" in teaching, where we are neither overteaching nor underteaching a novel, both of which can lead students to disengage from reading. While I'm certain that free-form response is an essential starting place, I've found that the sweet spot shifts a bit after students become adept at this skill. My colleagues and I have developed a variety of special formats for sticky notes, each of which encourages a new response habit, or simply the awareness of the new habit, to be used for short periods of time. The possibilities for creating new kinds of stickies are endless, and they can add a little excitement after students get used to the basic literal, inferential, and critical responses.

How to Avoid Getting Carried Away with Requirements

Helping my students respond authentically to their reading is essential to developing strong readers. Adding requirements to a process that is based on "no right or wrong responses" and "your real thoughts matter" can be counterproductive. Yet it's possible to find a balance between adding challenge to students' experience and letting them challenge themselves in their own time. Before I share the structured note types I've used in whole novel studies, here are some tips for avoiding the trap of too many requirements.

Use Small Doses

The key is to add some structure and challenge at strategic points so that students can access more during the reading experience, but not get carried away and take all of the freedom out of the response process or allow it to become too burdensome. I require some of the sticky notes each night—maybe one or two—to adhere to a special format. I create a code for each note type and ask that students label their notes accordingly.

Use Notes for Application of Familiar Concepts, Not Acquisition of New Concepts

Keep in mind that if students have to exert too much mental effort to accomplish a task attached to their reading experience, the "dream of fiction", as writer John Gardner put it, will be broken. The relaxed state of experience the mind has to enter in order to enjoy and comprehend the story is impossible if the student is overloaded cognitively. If students already have a working understanding of a literary element such as theme, then directing their attention to that element in their reading responses to an unfamiliar text can be a welcome cognitive challenge. However, if the concept is new and the text is new, the mental effort it takes to assimilate both new ideas will become disruptive to the reading process. The reading will stop being enjoyable for compliant students, and others will opt out of the response process or the reading process altogether.

Make sure the cognitive challenge is in bringing together a known concept and an unknown story. If you want students to apply a new concept to the whole novel, create occasions for this once they've completed the reading—in discussions, for example—so that the text is now familiar. Or if you want students to apply the concept along the way, allow this to happen in a group miniproject (described in Chapter 7) rather than connecting it to the individual reading process.

Limit Time Frames for Requirements

I never require the same type of special format for more than one whole novel study. I also never impose these formats on independent reading cycles. However, once a note type has been introduced, it is forever an option or tool, which students can then choose to use. Many do. Some turn to the formats consciously as a support. Others just naturally incorporate the terms or processes into their regular notes, which is what my real objective is anyway.

Ask Questions and Reflect

Since adding more requirements to responses is a delicate endeavor that can yield great or terrible results, I try to ask myself, "Why do I really want students to do X while they read? Am I attempting to control their experience? Can X be done equally well after students have completed the reading?" It's also important to listen to students about the effect this process has on their reading. In whole class check-ins during novel studies, I often ask them for feedback, and sometimes I make adjustments to the requirements in response.

Formats for Structured Reading Notes

The following sections describe the types of notes I've developed and their codes. The codes help me track students' use of the formats as I read through their notes. They also seem to help students remember the literary terms.

Open Response (OR)

Open response (OR) notes are basic free-form literal, inferential, and critical response notes, which I've described throughout this chapter. We needed a name to distinguish them from the special formats. In the beginning-of-the-year independent reading cycle and generally in the first whole novel study, I focus exclusively on open response notes. Since my eighth graders used sticky notes similarly in their seventh-grade class, I feel free to introduce two new note types in the first novel study, partly to differentiate "this year" from "last year," which can be important to students.

Worksheet 3.1 Sticky Notes Guide to *When You Reach Me*

Topics for Notes	Suggestions
Main characters	Investigate the characters in the story, especially Miranda and her family members. When you meet a new character: • What do you know about this character? His or her personality? • How does he or she act? • How does he or she connect to others? • How does Miranda seem to feel toward this character? Why?
Interesting/curious moments we need to discuss! (use blue stickies)	Take special notes on any parts in the book or thoughts you have while reading that would be good for bringing up in discussions. Use blue stickies and let them stick out of the book for easy access later.
Characters who change	When a character seems to be changing, write an observation or question about it.
Author's craft	What do you notice about the way the author writes? Interesting word choices? The narrator? What does the author do well? Not so well? Do you notice anything about the author's point of view? Biases?

Worksheet 3.1 provides an example of guidelines I included in the second seventh-grade novel study we were reading: *When You Reach Me*, by Rebecca Stead. There were no required formats, but I offered some suggestions that students could choose to use in their Open Responses or not.

Blue Notes (No Code Necessary)

I often add what I refer to as blue notes (the color choice is arbitrary; it refers to the color sticky note assigned to this) to the second novel study once students have experienced discussions once. I provide students with actual blue-colored sticky notes, and ask students to record comments and scenes from the story they specifically want to bring up in discussion. I rarely require a specific number of these notes; rather, I encourage students during class informally to collect interesting thoughts on these notes. This helps students to connect their thinking as they read with the opportunity to share in discussions later.

Language Notes (Lang.)

The language in *The House on Mango Street* is especially rich—laden with description and figurative language—and close examination of the language is crucial to comprehending and interpreting the story. Danny and I wanted to encourage students to record and explore interesting language as they read. We created a format for this called the language note (Lang.). This type of note seemed to click with certain students, and I was glad to have pointed them to explore strong language. Exhibit 3.4 gives our directions for these notes.

Theme Notes (TH)

In our planning discussions before launching *The House on Mango Street*, Danny and I agreed that in addition to setting, theme was probably the most potent literary

---

EXHIBIT 3.4 Directions for Language Notes

- Notice when a sentence or phrase really stands out to you as strong, interesting, or evocative (emotional)—or reread to look for one.
- Copy that sentence on a sticky note. Put the quotation in quotation marks, and add the page number in parentheses at the end.
- Explain why you chose this sentence. What is your response or connection to it?
- What do you notice about how the author has written this sentence? What makes it strong or interesting?

"Until then I am a red balloon, a balloon tied to an anchor" (p. 9). I found this sentence different from all the sentences. No one can actually be tied to an anchor. She's just saying how she's feeling. This is a metaphor. It's not an actual balloon. It's kind of saying that she's tied on. She can't do anything on her own, because her little sister puts boundaries on what she can do.

EXHIBIT 3.5 Directions for Theme Notes for *House on Mango Street*

After you finish reading a vignette:

1. Make a list on your sticky note of all the themes or ideas you think the author is bringing up in this vignette. Some examples of themes are hope, neighborhood, identity, oppression, and friendship.
2. After you make the list, circle the one you think is most important to this vignette.

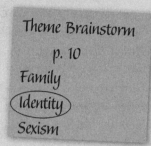

Theme Brainstorm
p. 10
Family
Identity
Sexism

---

element in this novel. In order to make meaning of the novel as a whole, which is composed entirely of short vignettes, the reader has to recognize the themes and patterns that run through the seemingly disjointed vignettes. We created the format for theme notes (TH) to help students trace themes. The directions are in Exhibit 3.5.

Students enjoy this format because it requires critical thinking, but unlike the other formats, it can be accomplished with few words. In subsequent novel studies, when this type of note was no longer required, most students continued to use or adapt it in their open responses. The part of me that questions the addition of specific structures to the notes feels satisfied when students voluntarily use a tool I've taught. Many students internalize the exercise and begin simply writing about a theme they notice. This is exactly the kind of shift I want to see: an assimilation of the literary language and concepts into their natural reading process.

Conflict Notes (CON)

In teaching seventh grade, I have students identify conflicts and teach them to distinguish between internal and external conflicts. In my eighth-grade curriculum, we look at the four classic types of conflict:

Students have sometimes asked, "What if the conflict is between two groups of people—as in a war? Is there society versus society?" I think this is a valid challenge. My answer is that we usually are talking about the conflict that the story's protagonist faces. If the protagonist lives in a society that is at war with another society, that protagonist is likely in a character-versus-society conflict with the "other" society, or his or her own, as the case may be. But in the world, we certainly have society-versus-society conflicts.

- Character versus character
- Character versus self
- Character versus society
- Character versus nature

When we read Sherman Alexie's novel, *The Absolutely True Diary of a Part-Time Indian*, we look at the layers of conflict and how they influence one another. In order to set students up for this novel, we first watch the film *Smoke Signals*, which Alexie also wrote. This provides an opportunity for students to get familiar with the setting and some of the cultural elements and themes of his work. In the film study, I introduce students to the four types of conflict and give them some practice identifying them in the film through a group miniproject (described in Chapter 7). This practice and familiarity with the types of conflict create conditions ripe for students to apply the concept to their reading of the novel without requiring too much mental effort. The directions for the conflict notes (CON) are in Exhibit 3.6.

EXHIBIT 3.6 Directions for Conflict Notes for *The Absolutely True Diary of a Part-Time Indian*

When you notice a conflict in the story, make a note:

1. Which type of conflict best matches this situation?
2. What does the character want?
3. Who or what is getting in the way?

Example:

CON Page 33

The conflict in this scene is character versus character. So Junior threw a book at his teacher. I guess he was just really angry that he gets the leftovers. He saw his mom's name on his hand-me-down textbook. His teacher, Mr. P, is only angry because everybody on the reservation has given up. He likes Junior and forgives him about the book because he hasn't given up on his life.

Mood Notes (Mood)

Students are usually able to pick up on the mood a passage of text creates for them, but they often don't remember that someone did work to create that mood, and using nothing but words. I ask students to pay attention to word choices that authors use to create mood in literature in mood notes. This also gives them practice generating a variety of words to describe different moods. I have students identify a section in their reading that has a strong mood and follow the process in Exhibit 3.7 for mood notes (Mood).

> **EXHIBIT 3.7 Directions for Mood Notes**
>
> For mood notes:
>
> 1. Pick a paragraph (or two) of text that has a noticeable mood (gives you a feeling).
> 2. Write down 5 words or phrases that the author uses to convey this mood.
> 3. At the bottom, name the mood.
> 4. Optional: Write more about it.
>
> Examples of moods in literature: uneasy, joyful, suspenseful, chaotic, peaceful, angry, cold, cheerful, dark, disappointment, hopeful, intense, jubilant, mellow, mischievous, melancholy, refreshed.

Vocabulary-in-Context Notes (V/C)

A colleague of mine, Craig Cetrulo, created a useful format for helping students to decipher the meaning of an unfamiliar word in their reading using context clues. I borrowed this format and applied it to sticky notes that we call "vocabulary-in-context notes" (V/C). The directions are in Exhibit 3.8.

> **EXHIBIT 3.8 Directions for Vocabulary-in-Context Notes**
>
> 1. Copy the sentence or phrase that includes the unfamiliar word onto the sticky.
> 2. Box the unfamiliar word.
> 3. Underline clues in the sentence (the context) or the word itself (e.g., root, prefix).
> 4. Write down your prediction of the meaning of the word.
> 5. Look up the word and check your prediction against the actual definition.
>
> Example:
>
> V/C Pg. 15
> Her high cheekbones and soft golden complexion are clear and beautiful, I think.
> Prediction: how someone looks
> Dictionary: the natural color, texture, and appearance of a person's skin, esp. of the face

I've had seventh-grade students practice this method in their responses to their independent reading books or in a book that has a lot of challenging vocabulary. Since we also study Latin roots, prefixes, and suffixes, students do enjoy using clues to decipher new words. If a book does not have at least one challenging word for the student per night, this can feel pointless for them. It is also an indication that the book may be too easy for the student. I don't believe that automatically means the book is not worth the student's time as long as the student also has opportunities to read more challenging texts.

Vocabulary Problem-Solving Notes (V/P)

Yusuf Ali, who cotaught eighth-grade English with me, wanted to help students apply multiple strategies to figure out the meaning of unknown words. By eighth grade, our students have experience using context clues and studying Latin roots and affixes. We asked them to generate a list of things they do when they encounter an unfamiliar word. They came up with around ten strategies.

We typed up these strategies and posted them on the wall in the room. Then we created a vocabulary problem-solving notes (V/P) format that asks them to share their process as they problem-solve an unfamiliar word in their reading (Exhibit 3.9).

This note-taking process is fairly labor intensive. Going through it just a few times makes a powerful impact on students, but the requirement of writing it down can become burdensome quickly. We used this as an in-class exercise in conjunction with a nonfiction book study and have not made it a daily requirement for students.

EXHIBIT 3.9 Directions for Vocabulary Problem-Solving Notes

1. Write the unfamiliar word at the top of the note.
2. Pick a strategy to use to infer the meaning of the word.
3. Write down the strategy and what you discovered when you tried it.
4. Write down another strategy and what you discovered when trying it.
5. Guess the meaning of the word using the information you have so far. Explain how you came up with it.
6. Look up the word and check your prediction against the actual definition.

Say, "What?" Notes (SW)

Yusuf and I also developed Say, "What?" notes to help students use a variety of strategies when they encounter a challenging section of the text and become conscious of their own processes. We began by having an open discussion with students about what they do when they come to a complicated or confusing part in their reading. We wrote down what they said:

> **Common Core Connection**
>
> Vocabulary problem-solving and Say, "What?" notes give students strategies to get at the first part of CCRA.R.1: "Read closely to determine what the text says explicitly and to make logical inferences from it; cite specific textual evidence when writing or speaking to support conclusions drawn from the text." This is important as students move into increasingly complex texts, which is emphasized throughout the Common Core standards.

Strategies for When You Say, "What?"

- Read the section over.
- Take a pause and think deeply about what it means.
- Look at context clues.
- Identify the few words that are confusing me most.
- Problem-solve the meaning of unfamiliar words.
- Make a sticky note writing out what's confusing.
- Ask someone else to help.
- Read the section out loud.
- Use a dictionary for unfamiliar words.
- Search the Internet for unfamiliar references.
- Reread the paragraph(s) before the section.
- Substitute words for unfamiliar words.
- Look for resources within the book, like the glossary.
- Envision what's happening.
- Use background information or own experience to connect with text.
- Write out what you understand and what you wonder.

Our directions for these notes are in Exhibit 3.10.

EXHIBIT 3.10 Directions for Say, "What?" Notes

1. Find a section that confused or surprised you. Write down your initial thought. (Code: SW)
2. Use one of your chosen strategies to reconsider the passage. Write the strategy you used if possible.
3. Write down any new thoughts and questions about this section of text.

 Visit https://vimeo.com /61677459 for video 3.1: Student Voices on Sticky Notes.

Balancing Structured and Open Responses

The structured formats for reading notes are tools to point students' attention to aspects of the text that might deepen their comprehension or experience. However, the experience of simply reading the story and responding subjectively is the most important thing. Students can't comprehend well if they cannot relax into the story. They cannot analyze well if they have no authentic experience and response on which to build. Without that requisite experience, the structured notes will not help students read more deeply. Structured notes cannot replace the habit of free, authentic response. They should be introduced as tools for students to incorporate into their general note-taking habits as they become ready for additional challenges.

Finding the right balance and following the shifting sweet spot is a challenge. I imagine teachers will find a variety of ways to accomplish this in their own classrooms. Table 3.2 provides some tips for keeping a student-centered approach while influencing the structure of students' reading notes.

COMING FULL CIRCLE: BACK TO OPEN RESPONSE

My objective by the end of the year is that students will have assimilated what they've learned about the literary elements as tools into their open response notes. In the spring, I drop the required structured notes and tell them, "All of your notes can be open response notes, but I'm looking for you to interact with the literary elements we've studied this year as you read. You all do this naturally when you comment on what you're reading, but I want you to use the language of the literary elements as you do this. For example, if you

Table 3.2 Tips for Structured Notes

Don't allow these to become the primary focus of the reading experience or responses of students.	**Do** ask students about their experience reading and responding. Listen and strike for a balance of enjoyment and challenge.
Don't use structured note types in the first whole novel study of the year or until the majority of the class has gotten the hang of open responses.	**Do** return to open response notes in the next novel study or independent reading cycle. If students are incorporating elements of the structured note into their open responses without any prompting, the exercise was successful.
Don't assign a structured note type for a literary element that is new to students. This will clog up the reading flow. **Avoid** assigning more than one structured note type per night, though this can be done with success.	**Do** admit when you've made a mistake. Once I got overzealous and asked students to respond to four different literary elements in one novel study. Students were lost, and many didn't follow my instructions at all. I realized I had gone too far, acknowledged it to the class, and adjusted the task.

comment on an idea in the book, make sure to call it a theme." I ask students to put a box around the literary element when they name it in their notes, so as to call my attention to it as I read through them.

In the whole novel studies of the final months of school, I provide all the previously introduced note types as optional guidelines for responding to each literary element. They serve as references, not requirements. Ideally, students find their own ways to note the author's development of literary elements and use of language in the narrative. As I assess these notes, I add to my criteria. I'm now looking to see that students explicitly comment on literary elements and the author's use of language, as well as showing literal, inferential, and critical thinking in their responses.

PARTS OF THE WHOLE

A View of Whole Novel Study from Start to Finish

When I describe the concept of a whole novel study and the discussions that are at the center of it, one of the most pressing questions I hear from teachers is, "What do you do in class while students are reading the book?" I describe the various layers of work that happen along the way in Part 2 of the book, but here is an overview of the progression of a whole novel study from start to finish. Each one is a little bit different, so this serves a general summary of the flow of a single novel study. This calendar in the table is for a novel of 210 pages. Students are assigned to read fifteen pages five days a week. The items on the calendar are explained briefly below.

Example of Daily Activities during a Whole Novel Study

	Monday	Tuesday	Wednesday	Thursday	Friday
Week 1	Prologue	Ritual launch and reading time	Minilesson on sticky notes and reading	Whole class check-in and reading	Introduce seeker books; Partner reading and peer feedback on notes
Week 2	Reading time and group miniproject	Reading time and group miniproject	Whole class check-in and partner or independent reading	Reading time and supplemental text/film	Reading time and supplemental text/film
Week 3	Reading time and discussion of supplemental text	Reading time and creative writing	Dramatizing scenes	Reading day	Books due! Discussions begin
Week 4	Discussions and creative writing	Discussions and creative writing	Discussions and creative writing	In-class literary essay writing	Creative writing share day

PROLOGUE

Sometimes before launching the novel, I open with an experience that provides some context for the whole novel study we're about to begin. For example, before reading Sandra Cisneros's *House on Mango Street*, a study in which we focus on the element of setting, I read the vividly descriptive beginning of Ray Bradbury's *Martian Chronicles* and have students write creative descriptions of real or imagined settings. Before Robert Cormier's *The Chocolate War*, we read and discuss an article about banned books to set students up to read the frequently banned novel and to connect to the themes of oppression and silencing in the story itself. I don't give away the connections between the prologue and the novel because I want to create opportunities for students to discover these connections.

RITUAL LAUNCH

Every whole novel study begins with a ritual launch, originally created by Noah Rubin, a former student of Madeleine Ray at Bank Street. The ritual consists of passing out to each student a gallon-size ziplock plastic bag containing everything the students will need on their reading journey and sending them off to begin. The baggie contains a copy of the book, a reading schedule, a letter I've written to students introducing the novel and expectations for the study, sticky notes, and a bookmark or other treat. I pass out the book baggie, and we read the letter together and look at the schedule and guidelines for the study. Then I send the students to begin reading. I describe the preparation and launch in detail in Chapter 6.

READING TIME

Once I've launched the study, I devote lots of time to reading during class. Sometimes students read independently. Other times I assign partners and a protocol for reading together. Sometimes we read portions of the novel aloud as a whole class or in small groups. I find I need to give students time to read at least three times per week to keep them going. If we will be working on something else for most of a class period, I have students read independently for about ten minutes when they enter the room. (More on reading time in Chapter 6.) During this time, I talk with individual students, observe their reading habits, and assess their sticky notes.

WHOLE GROUP RESPONSE PRACTICE

On the second day of reading, I like to have students choose a section from the previous night's reading to read aloud together and practice response. We do this as a whole class. Students or I read the section aloud, and students share their responses. I record them in a text box on my laptop that looks like a sticky note and project this for students to see. I generally do not ask questions or prescribe the content of their responses, but I use this process to model the general types of notes they should be writing. If we are working with a structured note type, I model the note format by asking students to "help me" follow the directions for writing, say, a language note. I do this at least two more times during the whole novel study at the beginning of class and then give students reading time.

WHOLE CLASS CHECK-INS

During a novel study, we spend about five to ten minutes several days per week checking in as a whole class about how the reading is going. Students share excitement, general responses, frustrations, and questions. Sometimes a common question from students leads us to reread a section of text together, or a strong response to a character leads to some impromptu discussion of an idea from the book. However, I limit the scope and time frame for these discussions; their purpose is for students to feel part of a venture, as they have their individual experience in reading the book.

MINIPROJECTS

Generally in the second week, we use two or three days of class to work on a group miniproject. I use my assessments of students' reading notes to diagnose the needs of the whole class or small groups of students and design collaborative projects that help address those needs. The projects are designed to aid students' comprehension and critical thinking as they read and also to help them explore the author's development of a specific literary element that is a focus for the study. During these days, I always give students some time to read independently at the beginning of class. I share more about miniprojects in Chapter 7.

MIDWAY READING CHECK

I spot-monitor students' progress in their reading and note taking informally on a daily basis and follow up with students and families after school when necessary. Midway through the study (or once a week if I can manage it), I do a quick check for completion either during class or by collecting books; I enter a grade in my grade book. I also use the opportunity to offer a comment or two to each student about his or her notes—what's working, an area to improve or find additional challenge, or a response to the content of a particular note.

SUPPLEMENTAL EXPERIENCES

I pepper the days during the reading portion of the study with additional text materials that connect to the theme, content, or structure of the novel. We might spend a day reading and discussing an article that helps students understand the novel's time period. We read and respond to a poem that connects to a theme in the novel. We watch a film with a similar story line, and I use the opportunity to teach the idea of a moral dilemma, which will come up later in the book (I don't tell them, though).

CREATIVE WRITING

We often write creatively during the reading portion of the study. This might include writing letters to characters, writing poems, or writing monologues in the voices of characters. The assignment could also focus on emulating the style or structural element of the author in the original work. I take these opportunities to teach lessons on some of the formal aspects of fiction writing, such as punctuating dialogue. Once students have finished the book, either during or after discussions, I often have them rewrite pieces of the novel for different purposes.

(See Chapter 5 for details.) Students usually share these with peers, giving and receiving feedback.

DISCUSSIONS

After students have finished reading the novel, we begin discussing the book. I describe the process for this in detail in the next chapter. For whole novel discussions, I allot at least three days. I prefer to run discussions for half of the class at a time, which means the other half of the class is working on a quiet independent activity—usually creative writing related to the novel. The homework during discussions is based on prompts generated by each discussion group.

WRITING PROJECT

The whole novel discussions lead to writing projects. These could be creative or essay writing projects. Essays are based on debates or questions that arise in discussions. These could be based on only the novel, or they could explore a connection students have drawn between the novel and the supplemental texts we've read. Sometimes I draw out the writing process: I provide minilessons on writing each piece of the essay and give students time to outline and get feedback from their peers on their ideas. These essays usually involve multiple drafts. Other times, I give students a timed in-class essay assignment (always based on their own ideas and questions about the book). Sometimes students write multiple drafts of these in-class writing pieces, and other times they serve as formative assessments, and we leave it there.

■ ■ ■

Creative projects are always based on elements of the book we've studied or discussed. For example, following their reading of *The House on Mango Street*, which is written in short vignettes, students wrote their own collection of vignettes. Following the study of various novels with the journey motif, students wrote original journey stories. After studying Louise Fitzhugh's *Nobody's Family Is Going to Change*, students experimented with rewriting scenes from different perspectives.

4

Whole Novel Discussions
Everyone Has a Voice

"You mean we can say anything we want?"

I think all teachers are familiar with that slight nervousness that enters our bodies and minds just before conducting a class for which we have spent a great deal of time preparing. *Will it work?* we silently wonder, because we have indeed experienced days when well-prepared lessons take frightening belly flops. Part of the reason the risk of a belly-flop lesson exists is that often we expect a specific response from students. Preparation is essential, but we may not recognize how much our lessons depend on the students' experiences of them and our responses to students in the moment. If students don't meet or even rebel against our expectation, we may feel we have lost the lesson we were counting on teaching.

We have to remember that teaching is not something we do to students; teaching is an interaction of the teacher, the members of the class, and the content. I'm certain that in order for us to help young adolescents develop critical-thinking skills, students must feel that their honesty is welcome into the conversation. Their honest response cannot just serve as an interesting sidebar; they must be an integral part of the lesson. When teachers always preconceive of the response they want or expect from students, then students learn to think, *What might my teacher want me to say right now?* This does not give them much opportunity to discover and develop the power of their own minds, which is what a strong student and a good citizen ultimately needs. The teacher has fallen into the familiar trap I call "the chief thinker."

With one person's mind always in control—the teacher's—the classroom eventually becomes predictable and dull. In an effort to gain power and fend off boredom, a student might begin to think, *What might happen if I say something the teacher especially does not want to hear?* In other words, the student begins to think of ways to throw the teacher's seemingly predictable lesson off its course, thereby fulfilling the developmental need to practice autonomous thinking and problem solving. At the same time, the teacher has found himself or herself in the throes of a belly-flop lesson. Hours of careful planning can fall by the wayside if the students opt for a different agenda. Aligning the agenda of the lesson with the agenda of the students is one of the greatest and most worthwhile challenges of teaching.

The whole novel discussion seminars that take place after students have completed reading a novel are the center of the program and consistently provide some of the most fulfilling moments of my teaching career. In these discussions, I've created a set of circumstances; the rest is now up to the students. I don't impose a list of questions or topics we must discuss, and I don't determine the ideas and interpretations we must end up with by the end of the period. I've learned not to be nervous about these discussions, because there are no belly-flop lessons to be had here. We take a ride on the boomerang and all roads essentially lead to home or someplace else equally important. When students realize they can say anything they want, amazing things start to happen. Time seems to stop, and we almost forget we are in school. The disappointment comes only when the bell rings and class ends.

OVERVIEW OF DISCUSSION SEMINARS

Once students have completed reading the entire novel and the due date on their schedules arrives, discussions begin. We discuss most often in half-groups and sit in a circle. Half of the class discusses with me, and the other half works on related independent work, silently. In cotaught inclusion classes, the learning specialist runs a second discussion simultaneously. In student-centered discussions, it takes time to explore the text and arrive at critical interpretations. Ideally each group meets three times, and the level of analysis deepens with each round.

In my first year of teaching, my students had great discussions on the first day, but on the second day, it seemed we had nothing more to say. Since then I have developed ways to keep the discussions going for multiple sessions. The purpose of sustaining a discussion over a number of days is to give students time to attain a deeper level of understanding of the novel, as well as develop the group process of literary discourse. I use these key techniques to facilitate a week's worth of student-centered discussions:

- Each night type the notes from the day's discussion and bring copies of them to the group to review the next day.
- Engage in rereadings of key chapters or passages in the novel that students have commented on in discussion.
- Assign student-generated homework or in-class writing prompts that help fuel further exploration of an aspect of the novel.
- Allow students to participate in the development of culminating projects or writing assignments that build on the content of the discussions.

Keeping records of the students' discussions assists the discussion process in several ways. The students find novelty in watching and reading their own words and ideas in written form. The notes also allow us to find avenues for further exploration the next day. After a day of discussions, I read over the notes and type them up. As I do this, I star or make a note next to comments that we could discuss in more detail the following day. When students express opinions but have not supported them with evidence from the text, or if two students have presented opposing opinions, I mark these places in the notes as possible areas of discussion for the next seminar. If, in the discussion, students have expressed confusion over a certain scene, character, or plot thread, I mark that as an area to which we should return. Finally, when students make discoveries about the novel, its elements, or the author's craft, I take these opportunities to introduce relevant literary terms such as *foreshadowing* or *character development*. Sometimes I don't recognize the opportunity until I read over the notes and mark the places later that day. Still later, the notes become a tool for assessment of students in their discussion skills and literary analysis.

Although I have my own ideas about topics we could discuss, I give the students the opportunity to direct the discussion each day. We convene for our session, and I hand out copies of the notes. I ask everyone to read over the notes and put a star or question mark next to anything they would like to comment on or question. Sometimes I hand out small-size sticky notes and ask them to write comments there. When everyone has read the notes, we begin with a round-robin, with each student making one comment. Other days we begin by sharing responses to the student-created homework questions aloud. Enthusiastic discussions can result from either of these techniques. Then the open discussion begins.

Over the years, I've noticed trends in the way the discussions tend to progress over several days (see Table 4.1). In the first session, students tend to air their gut reactions, opinions, and questions about the book as a whole and bring up controversial characters or scenes. There is always plenty to say. The second day becomes an excavation of the text. We find ways to look more deeply at the text than we did in our initial responses. It becomes essential for students to turn to the text to reread sections in question and find evidence for their ideas. However, it is the initial responses from the first day that have called attention to those ideas that merit closer study. By looking back at the notes, students often find topics they would like to continue discussing. If they do not, I point to something in the notes that raises questions.

By the third day, we generally have analyzed many of the book's most important elements: characters, conflicts, plot, and themes. I usually find that students are ready to take a step back and consider more closely the author's role, intentions, and strengths and weaknesses in writing the novel.

There are many exceptions to this neat progression of skills over three days depending on the students, the text, my facilitation, and other circumstantial factors. It is not necessary to force the discussion to adhere to this progression.

Table 4.1 Stages of Discussion

	Focus	Skills Practiced
Stage 1: Authentic, surface-level response	Students air their gut reactions to the book, strong opinions about characters, and exciting and controversial parts; critical questions and debates emerge from this mostly surface-level discussion.	Authentic response to literature; questioning; connecting; inference; voicing opinions; respecting differing opinions; turn taking
Stage 2: Evidence-based analysis	We delve deeper into questions that emerged from the first session by looking for evidence in the book, rereading sections together, discussing further, and asking new questions.	Rereading; supporting our ideas with evidence; challenging or revising ideas with evidence; close reading of text; analyzing language; application of literary vocabulary
Stage 3: Critical understanding	Students take a step back from the story and consider the role of the author in creating the novel; assess the strengths and limitations of the author's craft; and discuss the novel in the context of the world and other works of literature or film.	Drawing conclusions from evidence; analyzing the author's craft; inferring the author's purpose and intended audience; making connections across texts; connecting themes in the text to world issues; critical thinking

SETTING UP FOR DISCUSSIONS

"Good morning. Today we begin discussions of *The Jacob Ladder* by Gerald Hausman and Uton Hinds. Groups A and B are listed on the board, each with twelve students. Group A will discuss today with me in the Western hemisphere of the classroom, while group B works on the silent group assignments in the Eastern hemisphere," I begin. (My classroom is organized into table groups named after continents that seat four.) My teacher's assistant, a student who has applied for the

The Jacob Ladder, by Gerald Hausman and Uton Hinds, which takes place in rural Jamaica, begins when the main character's father is put under a spell by an obeah woman (one who does magic and casts voodoo spells) and leaves the family. Tall T has to help his family without his father's guidance. His father is a powerful figure in the town. He works on the banana boats and plays the "devil" character in the annual Jonkonnu dance. Tall T skips school and starts studying history under the tutelage of the local librarian. He also becomes the treasurer for the Jonkonnu dance, collecting and guarding the coins tossed by onlookers. In the end, he climbs the Jacob Ladder, a ladder made of vines that runs up a steep cliff from the beach. His ambivalence toward his father permeates the book, and it ends unresolved. An afterword explains that his father left the obeah woman but moved to the city and never returned to the family.

job and holds it for an entire marking period, hands out a copy of the silent group assignments to students in group B.

"Group A, you will need to push the North and South America and Antarctica tables together and bring your chairs around it in a circle. Make sure to bring your copy of the novel with your stickies inside to the discussion circle. Group B, if you have any questions, ask them now, because once we begin, you'll need to work independently."

I circulate around group B students as they get settled and answer their questions. They are familiar with the types of creative assignment choices that appear on the sheet for silent work. Killing off a character, adding a character, and writing the beginning of a sequel are all popular choices (see Chapter 5 for more on these writing assignments). Later in the week, after discussions are over, we'll have a gallery walk in which students read each other's writing pieces and leave warm feedback and suggestions for revisions. Students revise over the weekend.

The reading was due yesterday, but two students in group A and one in group B hadn't finished the book by the due date and took them home to continue working. I check in with these three to see if they finished. It is a rule that you must read the entire book in order to participate in discussions. Gerald shows me his book complete with stickies through the end.

"Yup, I finished," he says. "Can I go in the discussions?"

"Yes!" I say. "Go find a seat."

I walk over to Diana.

"I only have fifteen more pages," she says.

"Okay, you can keep reading at your table. Come join us if you finish during this period."

"I stayed up 'til 2 in the morning last night finishing this book!" Ty shouts from across the room.

"I'm glad you finished, Ty," I say walking over to him. "You're in group B, so you'll discuss tomorrow. Are your notes complete?" He looks down at his book. "No."

"So you know what you need to do tonight," I say. "For now, work on the silent work."

After a few minutes, both groups are settled. I sit down at the discussion table with my copy of the book and my laptop (or notebook and pen). I always take the seat closest to the wall, from where I can keep an eye on the entire room.

The Circle Is a Must

Any size group can engage in whole novel discussions, and the configuration of the group will vary with the space and size of the class. The key rule for the design of the physical space is that form must follow function. When a group's function is to discuss something together in a sustained, collaborative way, the best form is the circle. In a circle, all members of the group can see and hear each other, a big advantage for managing sustained, student-driven discussions. In rows or groups, it's easy for students to drift away from the focus of the group. In that case, the teacher becomes the focal point—the connector of the disparate pieces of the group—and this doesn't support the student-driven discussion process. I've seen the difference when a teacher struggles to lead a discussion in rows or clusters and then finally creates a circle. It's a relief to everyone, because it removes physical barriers to speaking and listening in a group.

There are a few ways to achieve a circle configuration. Sometimes I hold discussions in the meeting area of my classroom, with students sitting on the benches that form a semicircle at the front of the room. I've also had the discussion group sit in a circle on the rug on the floor in the meeting area. Whatever the space, I always want to make sure the group sits close together, knee-to-knee and shoulder-to-shoulder, so that we hear one another well and create some insulation from the rest of the room. One advantage of the meeting area is the ability to project the notes on students' comments onto the board so students can follow along and reference them.

In a room with no space for a meeting area, I recommend arranging half of the desks in a circle in one-half of the room and keeping the rest of the desks separate in groups or rows apart from the circle. Another option is to create enough space for half of the class to pull just chairs into a circle in one part of the room.

Finally, a whole class discussion is also possible. In fact, I conduct whole class discussions of shorter texts, such as the graphic novel *Anya's Ghost*, by Vera Brosgol, or the film *Smoke Signals*. I can seat my entire class in the meeting area for a whole class discussion. Without a meeting area, it's necessary to arrange the desks in a large circle or arrange chairs in a large circle around the perimeter of the room.

Scheduling Half-Group Discussions

The main benefit of discussing with half the class at a time is that everyone gets more airtime. The level of engagement and the quality of the learning experience for each individual student is greater this way. In half-groups, there is also a more intimate quality and a sense of togetherness in the group. Although I've had amazing discussions with entire classes, I notice a more fluid dynamic in the smaller groups. It seems that we are able to go into more depth and cover more when each person has more of a voice. The students also get a greater level of individual attention from me, and no one can hide in the whole group format. When students are more engaged, there are fewer management issues within the discussion.

The half-group discussions create two problems to solve: scheduling and management of the other half of the class. In my first school, I taught ninety-minute periods. I would have one group meet for about thirty minutes and then switch to the other group. We would follow this format for three days in a row. Now I have fifty-minute periods. I meet with half the class on one day and the other half the next day. In order to have multiple sessions of discussion for each group, I devote an entire week of class time to whole novel discussions. Groups A and B alternate days Monday through Thursday, and then Friday I meet for twenty minutes with each group to conclude.

It can also work to have two teachers each leading a discussion group simultaneously in the same room or in two separate locations. If possible, separate locations are preferable so that the voices from one discussion don't distract the other group. In my collaborative team teaching (CTT) classes, where I coteach with a special education teacher or if I have a student teacher working with me, each of us can lead a group. I have also begun seeking out other English teachers in my school who are available during classes I do not coteach. If they are interested and have time to read the book in advance, this can work really well. I see the transcription of the discussion, so I can keep tabs on students' progress.

I keep the other half of the class busy with what I call silent work. In my first years of teaching, creating the name "silent work" made a big difference in communicating the expectation to students. I tell them, "We need you to be silent so that we can hear each other well in discussion. Later it will be your turn, and we will do the same for you." Students seem to understand this; in fact, they often listen to the discussion. Some teachers may want to try a fishbowl method in which the silent group students observe members of the discussion and provide feedback.

I assign work that students can engage in with little or no help from me. I've had students revising written work based on my comments during this time—by hand or on laptops. I've also given them vocabulary workbook-type assignments. My favorite, though, has become short fiction writing assignments that connect to the novel (described in Chapter 5). Students are highly motivated to work independently on these assignments, and they create a unifying thread between the two groups.

I make sure that all students understand the assignment and I've answered basic questions. Then I leave the silent group to work while I facilitate discussion.

THE SEMINAR: STARTING WITH THE GO-AROUND

"As usual, we'll begin with a go-around, everyone speaking once," I tell the students. I do this so that everyone breaks the ice and contributes something to discussion right away. "You may say anything you want about the book. Something you liked, didn't like, a character you want to comment on, a favorite or least favorite part of the book, something that confused you, a comment you wrote on a sticky note, or any response to the book that comes to mind as others speak. After we've gone around once, the discussion is open and anyone may respond. Refer to the sentence starters if you like. Remember to respect community rules." I pass out a copy of the sentence starters for discussion (Exhibit 4.1).

 Visit https://vimeo.com /60986929 for video 4.1: The Go-Around.

EXHIBIT 4.1 Sentence Starters for Discussion

- I agree with what you said about . . .
- I disagree with what you said about . . .
- Could we talk about . . .
- I have a question about . . .
- The author does a good job of . . .
- The author doesn't do a good job of . . .
- I don't understand what you mean by . . .
- Can you think of an example of what you just said?
- I'd like to look at page . . .
- This reminds me of . . .

Community rules apply in our daily meetings as well as in discussion seminars:

1. Listen to teachers/classmates.
2. Raise your hand/take turns.
3. No private conversation.
4. Respect personal space.

During the discussion, I take notes on everything students say. I transcribe it like a script, putting students' names before their comments for future reference. (See Appendix A for an example of a full transcription of multiple rounds of discussion.) Students seem to like the sense of importance this gives to them and their words. It also helps them take turns, because I can type only one person's comment at a time. I use my own form of shorthand, which I clean up later to make the notes readable (Table 4.2). Sometimes I project the notes while students are discussing, mistakes and all, so they can see the transcript in real time. If I'm writing by hand, students know I'm writing down what they say, but can't really see it or follow my messy handwriting.

Oliver begins by saying, "Sometimes I got this part, but sometimes I didn't. Sometimes Mama Poon came out and yelled at Brother John while he was putting his pants on and I didn't get why. I don't know if that was supposed to be a big contributor to the storyline or just entertainment."

Table 4.2 Examples of Shorthand for Taking Notes

Word	Abbreviation
character	ch.
interesting	int.
Any name, including character, or students (e.g., Tall T)	After writing it once, use only the initial (e.g., T) or first two initials where necessary
because	bc
Author's name	Author's initials
confused	con
sometimes	s/t

Aliyah says, "I thought the book was very interesting because it's different from other books I read and I really liked how they struggled in their life. I liked how they started off with him not going to school but then he became interested in reading. He was poor, but when he got older, I don't know if he was rich, but he had more stuff than when he was younger."

"I thought the book was okay," Nellie says.

"Tell us a little more. Why just okay?" I interject. Students can say anything they want about the book, but their comment should be substantive, providing some possible area for further discussion.

"I thought books were supposed to have happy endings. But it seems like it came up to a sad ending with just a little happiness," she says.

"I wonder why the soup [callaloo] made Brother John stay with Mama Poon? Because maybe Mama Poon made a deal with him, like 'I will give you soup every day if . . . ' Why would Mama Poon want Brother John?" says Italia.

"I think that, and I'm just shooting at the stars right now. In my opinion, Tall T's spirit grew more mature as the book went on and on and on," says Rianne.

"I was sad for Tall T because he didn't have a father to support him. The end was *whack* [meaning "weak"] because his father doesn't come back and I was thinking he would," says Dominic.

"I wasn't really very convinced with the fact that Tall T climbed the ladder. He was always talking about the banana men being big and strong. Then at the end he just climbed it like it was so easy. I didn't really get the title. Why is it called *The Jacob Ladder*? Most of the book didn't have to do with it," says Simon.

The go-around continues, with each of the twelve students contributing one point about the book. They need not respond to one another's points unless they choose to. The initial comments become a bank of possible discussion points from which I can draw later if necessary. Each comment provides an area for the whole group to explore. If one student has been less vocal, I can always say, "Let's return to what _____ said in the beginning about . . . Can you elaborate on that point?"

During the go-around, several students put their hands up to respond to their classmates' comments, and I have to remind them to hold their comments until we've gone around the circle once. They may record their thoughts on sticky notes so as not to forget them. The go-around is so important because it sets a tone that everyone will be an active part of the discussions and breaks the ice right away for students reluctant to speak.

THE TEACHER'S ROLE: DRAWING OUT STUDENTS' NATURAL RESPONSES

"The discussion is now open for anyone to respond," I say after the last person has spoken. Six hands shoot up. I call on the first student, and the conversation evolves from there. (My primary role now is moderator and note taker. One teacher I know who works with whole novels has a student type the notes—a great idea I have simply never had the guts to try. Though students create most of the content of the discussion, the role of moderating takes some skill. The following sections outline some strategies I have developed to keep the ideas flowing and address some common situations that can arise during discussion.

 Visit https://vimeo.com /61675054 for video 4.2: Open Discussion.

Pushing beyond the Silence

Most often students enter into a natural discourse without my doing much more than calling on them to speak. But in rare cases there may be a silence after the round-robin. When this happens, I look at the notes I've recorded so far and pull out a student's comment that we could explore further or debate. I might ask, "What do you all think of Rianne's comment that Tall T's spirit grew more mature as the book went on? Or Nellie's comment that the end was not what she expected?" There is always enough in the initial responses to get a discussion going.

It is key that my questions or directions, when they are necessary at all in these discussions, build on ideas the students have expressed. This sends a message to students that their responses, ideas, and questions are essential to the discussion. Students who are silent at first are often fearful that their ideas are not good enough, or they do not trust that I will not use their comments to make my own points. It sometimes takes some time for the students to figure out they are really the ones controlling the direction of the discussion and that ultimately they do not really need a teacher to interpret literature or guide their understanding. The teacher is providing space and encouragement for students to explore their own responses and ideas.

When Students Say They Don't Like a Book

Some students test the validity of my assertion that they can say anything they want about the book by saying how much they disliked it. Sometimes this is less about the book and more about testing my response. Other times, the criticisms are genuine and deserve space in discussion, whether I agree with them personally or not.

 Visit https://vimeo.com /60122464 for video 4.3: Authentic Responses.

"Tell us more. What didn't you like?" I always ask in an even tone.

"Everything," the student might respond.

I then push: "Well, give us one part or one character that was especially bad." I allow a little silence while we wait for the student to offer an example. If my gut tells me the student needs more time, I'll say, "Go ahead and look for the part and we'll come back to you as soon as you find it. Don't forget you can read us one of your sticky notes if you choose." The goal is to get some material for discussion while showing the student that it's the clear articulation of an idea and the evidence for it that counts, not whether I agree with the idea.

Sometimes students who may not have liked the book end up loving the discussion because they get to tease apart their own complex responses to the work.

With the help of the community of peers, they figure out what the author was successful at doing and what was truly weak about the work. They also come away better able to articulate their personal reading preferences.

Still others leave discussions with a very different idea of the book than they came in with. Kara says on the first day of discussions of the 2009 Newbery Award–winning novel, *When You Reach Me*, by Rebecca Stead: "It was okay. The beginning was nice, but the end didn't make sense, and that made the book boring." The next day, she enters the discussion saying, "What I want to say was after we had discussion, I got a different view about the book. I liked it more, and I understood the ending. Now I think the beginning was more boring, like Marcus said. But I wrote in my homework that the book did deserve its award. Because of that discussion."

During the seminar on the first day, we had reread parts of the book together, specifically the end, clarifying many students' questions about what had happened. The homework question students generated that night had been, "Do you think the book deserves its award? Why or why not?" Sometimes their dislike of a text results from confusion and lack of comprehension, though not all students are self-aware enough to realize this. If I had frowned on Kara's initial opinion or if Kara hadn't felt comfortable enough to voice her opinion, we might have missed out on an effective learning experience.

When Students Talk Too Much—or Too Little

The other group dynamic to be prepared for is highly verbal, often long-winded students who sometimes want to say everything that comes to mind without thinking through their ideas and how they contribute to the discussion. It's possible to end up with an entire group of students with this tendency. Even more of a challenge is when half of the group is very talkative and the other half is reluctant to speak. I deal with this issue by stating that each student may make just one point when it's his or her turn to speak. I tell students they should decide what that one point is going to be before they begin speaking and keep it concise. (This is a good opportunity to teach that word.) About fifteen seconds should be enough to make one relevant point.

Encourage the group to follow a discussion thread for a while using sentence starters from the list instead of each student steering it in his or her own direction or jumping in with a laundry list of points about comments previously made. This makes everyone dizzy and keeps reluctant students from finding logical entry points.

If one student has been dominating, magic words I've seen Madeleine Ray use in college seminars are, "What do the rest of you think about this?" Sometimes if a particularly important and controversial issue comes up, I return to the round-robin: "Let's go around quickly and hear from everyone on this one," I'll say, or, "Let's continue with this idea, giving preference to those we haven't heard from yet." I ask students who have already spoken on this topic to lower their hands. I then wait the time it takes for someone who hasn't spoken on the topic yet to voluntarily enter the discussion. That awkward wait time makes an important statement to students: everyone's voice is essential here. Once the students become more practiced in the art of discussion, they begin to understand the value of having everyone's participation and begin to monitor themselves and make room for one another in the discussion, as we come to expect in college seminars or adult meetings.

Shaking Up the Pot

Sometimes the discussion has been moving toward an important discovery but not quite getting there, or going back and forth on one idea without gaining further insights. Often this happens when only a few students are participating. I find myself tempted to take a shortcut and just tell students the thing they're circling around or prompt them with pointed questions. A fruitful alternative, however, is to shake up the discussion pattern by asking students to talk to the person next to them for thirty seconds about the question at hand.

For example, in discussions of *The House on Mango Street*, we have reread the end of the book and students are grappling with the layers of suggestion Cisneros makes about the main character, Esperanza. Students are confused about what happens to Esperanza at the end of the book, since the author only gestures toward the outcome without stating anything directly. We've reread the ending, but students are still puzzled, with certain vocal students bringing up the same questions and others remaining shy and reserved. I ask them to talk to a partner for thirty seconds about what they think is happening. I listen in on their conversations as much as I can. Then I feel free to call on any of the students,

Visit https://vimeo.com /61676465 for video 4.4: Shake Up the Pot.

because all have had a chance to think out loud first. I often call on students who have been quiet during the discussion and find that the new voices push the conversation along, out of the "stuck place."

Throwing Students a Line

While my primary role is that of moderator, note taker, and encourager of scholarly habits, such as turning to the text for evidence (more on that soon), it would be dishonest to completely ignore the fact that I am also a reader with my own experience of the literature. I am reminded of one of my high school English teachers, who assigned us to read Shakespeare's *Macbeth*. I remember her style of quietly smiling through our discussion of the play, as though she were keeping a secret. She would say, "Oh, isn't that interesting," in response to anything we said. She was a new teacher, and she clearly wanted us to develop our own interpretations of the complex and provocative play, but I was extremely frustrated by her responses. The class floundered at a certain level of understanding, and for whatever reasons, she refused to throw us a line.

Drawing from this memory, I occasionally do offer some of my own insights or pose questions my students might not be mature or experienced enough as readers to voice. I make sure to do this seldom enough that students understand it clearly as the exception, not the rule. The teacher, though never an authority on anyone else's experience of literature, can be a resource to the students when appropriate.

THE TOOLS OF REREADING AND FINDING EVIDENCE

After many ideas are thrown in the pot during the round-robin, threads emerge. The most productive threads are often arguments, because they provide opportunities to dive back into the text and do close reading. This is what happened during our first round of discussing *The Jacob Ladder*, when Simon said, "I wasn't really very convinced with the fact that Tall T climbed the ladder. He was always talking about the banana men being big and strong. Then at the end he just climbed it like it was so easy. I didn't really get the title. Why is it called *The Jacob Ladder*? Most of the book didn't have to do with it."

Visit https://vimeo.com /61676370 for video 4.5: Close Reading.

Once the session was open, Julia picks up on his point: "About the title—I actually think it's good. *The Jacob Ladder* is an obstacle Tall T has to overcome. The whole book is about his obstacles."

Shakwon says, "I agree with Simon about the title. If the book was actually talking about the Jacob Ladder, it would have said so all along. Instead it kept on talking about Tall T and the family. During the book, I think Tall T was saying he was going to climb the Jacob Ladder, but when it happened, it was too late for it to be the main point of the book."

Paula adds, "The end of the book left me wondering about Tall T's future. He has this spiritual experience while climbing the Jacob Ladder. Is that going to last his whole life? Is that very important in the book?"

Maya says, "I really didn't like the part when he climbed the ladder. Was he dreaming? Was it real? Like Simon said, one minute he's all weak and can't climb, and the next he's climbing. I was hoping Brother John would come back at the end, not this."

Ana continues the thread: "I sort of agree with what Simon and Maya said about the Jacob Ladder thing. All of a sudden he's like, 'Oh, my gosh, it's so hard to climb, etc.' and then he just goes and climbs it. Sort of annoying, I guess, because he talks about how hard it is and you see all these big strong men climbing it, it makes it seem so easy."

Bianca says, "I have to agree with Julia. I don't think it was easy for him. Like in life, it's hard for him to do any big task like that."

Luca says, "But the banana men only climb the ladder at the end of the day—when they're really weak. So Tall T and the banana men are probably at about the same level of strength. It's not so unrealistic."

Dominic, who was reluctant about reading the book and can often be disengaged from academic activities, weighs in. "I disagree with Simon and whoever said about the Jacob Ladder, because at the end when they said he was climbing, they did say it was hard. He slipped. He said it was very tired when he got to the top. It didn't say it was easy."

Paula adds, "I sort of agree with both sides. It's kind of weird that he'd be able to get that much strength to climb, but if you're thinking about something and convince yourself you can't, you won't, but if you convince yourself you can, you will."

"I disagree with Dominic," Simon responds. "I don't think the author described it as being that hard. He slipped once, but that's just once; the slipping is not that big a deal."

Here I see a place ripe for textual analysis and ask: "Can someone find this part so we can look at it together?"

Ricardo changes the subject, "Wasn't that soup under a spell or something that made him stay forever, I mean it wasn't just soup?" Some students respond and have a short dialogue about whether the soup is real or symbolic and why Brother John really left.

Bianca says, "I have the page now. And I'm reading this and it sounds intense. On page 110 and 111 when he climbs the ladder."

"Everyone turn to page 110 and follow along," I direct the group. I wait to make sure everyone opens to the page.

Bianca begins reading from the text. "'It seems that I'm higher than I really want to be . . . ascending to heaven.'" She stops reading and says, "It's not really that it's about his strength. It's that he's Jacob, from the Jacob Ladder in the Bible. On the front," she says, pointing to the cover of the book, "he has bony arms. He doesn't really look like a strong kid. But he's a believer. That's how he climbs it."

Simon interjects, "Going back to the beginning of that section—'I dreamily hoist myself up . . . 10, 20, 30.' That doesn't make it sound like it's hard. 'I stop for a moment and catch my breath.' You could be catching your breath anywhere."

Dominic comes back, "It also says, 'I grab a strong vine. My cheek touches clay. My eyes are shut.' He's praying for his life. It is hard."

Bianca adds, "It says, 'I twist my head and open my eyes. Behind me the blue sea. Above me finally the blue sky.' It's like he's finally reached something."

Lucilla says, "I agree with Simon, but also think that Tall T's the one that wrote the book, so I feel like he could have put more into it. But at the same time, if I try to remember something that happened in the past, it's hard to get exactly how I was feeling—I think that was the best he could do."

"The Jacob Ladder could have been a symbolic ladder. It actually existed all of Tall T's life. He has to climb higher and higher and had to reach happiness," Paula says.

Maya adds, "I think Paula's point is true—the book was about facing obstacles. But it felt like it was rushed, like he was given a 120-page limit to the book or something."

"I agree," says Bianca.

Here I want to help everyone understand the unique circumstances under which the book was written, which are no doubt important to their experience of it. So I say, "Let's look at the two authors' names on the front cover. As people pointed out, Uton Hinds is Tall T. What about the other guy?"

"Maybe Tall T told him what happened and the other guy wrote it down," Julia says.

"I think Tall T wrote it, too," says Lucilla.

"In the end, I think you have to dig deeper into it to get the meaning, rereading it," concludes Maya.

In this excerpt of discussion among seventh graders (this is not the entire session), with minimal direction from me, several important things happened quite naturally. The argument revolved around what was intended to be the climax of the book, when the main character, Tall T, climbs the Jacob Ladder, a ladder of vines that leads up a cliff in his town in Jamaica. Simon's initial assertion in the round-robin that he was unconvinced by this passage opened up a question about the intended significance of the moment and whether the author had been successful at it. This argument, built on one reader's authentic response to the novel posed to the community, created an occasion for rereading a section of the book. The result was a close reading of the climax of the novel, propelled by student interest. (I introduced the term *climax* on the second day of the discussions.) During this close reading, students made claims and supported them with evidence from the text. They looked at the literary device of symbolism in the ladder. Finally, they began to construct an understanding of what the author was trying to say in creating this event at this point in the book and critiqued the author's skill in doing so.

We arrive at the same skills, concepts, and understandings of a traditional literature classroom, but the path we took to get there is different. The students take us there through their honest responses and by, as Maya puts it, "digging deeper into it to get the meaning."

It sometimes takes two or even three sessions to reach the level of analysis that this group reached in one session. The students seemed to progress through at least the first two stages of discussion rather quickly, once Simon astutely challenged the author's writing of the climax, and Dominic took him up on the challenge. Simon is quite a mature reader. His initial comment that he was "unconvinced" by the event of Tall T climbing the ladder demonstrates his awareness that somebody—the author—intended to convince him of something. That may or may not have swung the discussion, were it not for Dominic—a reluctant reader—who took him up on the challenge and rebutted his point with evidence. Others took interest and stuck with the thread long enough to pursue a close reading of the passage and the beginning of an analysis of the author's intentions and possible shortcomings. Although it is somewhat unusual for this to occur so quickly, remarkable things happen fairly regularly in this open discussion format. Rather than an exceptional example, I see it as a lesson not to underestimate students by prescribing the process and content of literature discussions.

In general, I allow day 1 of discussion to flow, simply facilitating student participation in a general way. By day 2, I emphasize turning to the text to find evidence for claims students are making. It's much more effective to bring this about by asking students, "Can anyone find a part that shows what Joey is talking about?" than it is to give general reminders to the group to "remember to find evidence for your claims." I also find it helpful to review the notes after day 1 and identify a few comments that are ripe for rereading.

Visit https://vimeo.com/ 61675784 for video 4.6: Using Evidence in Discussion.

STUDENT-GENERATED HOMEWORK QUESTIONS

"It's time for us to stop for today," I say, five minutes before the close of the period. It is really difficult to keep myself from allowing the group to use every last minute, but I know this causes everyone to madly rush around the room packing up and putting the desks back into their normal formation at the end of class. I hand out the homework sheets that have a space for the student to write in the homework assignment.

"What would make an interesting homework question to write on, based on our discussion?" I ask.

"I know," Shakwon says. "'Do you like the ending of the book? And why?'"

"That sounds good. Any other suggestions?" I respond. I like Shakwon's idea, because so many students were interested in this question and brought up plenty of rich evidence. The question would give those students who were actively participating and also those who did more observing a chance to process their thoughts in another form.

Rianne offers, "How about, 'How do you think Tall T changed by the end of the book?'" I appreciate Rianne's attempt to draw others back to her initial wondering about the book with this question. We didn't get back to it explicitly. I do think our discussion pointed toward some answers to this question, but students would need to examine the story again in order to answer it fully. Some students would be more interested in that than dwelling on today's argument.

"Both great questions. Choose the one that interests you more and record it on the space on your homework sheet. Remember the requirement is one paragraph, but you're free to write as much as you want."

"Can I type it?" Simon asks.

"Yes, you may type if you prefer."

"Can we e-mail them to you?" Maya asks.

"I'd like you to print a copy to bring to discussions tomorrow. If you don't have printing capabilities at home, you may e-mail it to me with a message to print," I respond.

The parameters for discussion homework are that students must write at least one paragraph of commentary, response, or a creative piece, depending on what the group decides. Homework can serve several purposes simultaneously. It allows students to continue the discussion after our time is up. Students who are less vocal during discussions can write their responses and then share the next day. Some benefit from the opportunity to process content from discussion in writing. These writing pieces can become longer pieces— essays even.

 Visit https://vimeo.com/ 61675328 for video 4.7: Student-Generated Homework Questions.

Sometimes the homework assignment can be useful for students to reread sections to clear up confusion. I remember a group one year that was both upset and confused by the end of *The Dream Bearer,* by Walter Dean Myers. It became apparent by the end of the session that a majority of the group had not understood what happened. When I brought up this possibility, several students admitted they had rushed through to finish on time. Others said they had read it but not understood it. Our homework assignment was to reread the end and write a paragraph explaining what happened. The next day the majority of the group now understood the event that took place at the end. Those who still had questions had much more specific questions. We reread sections and had a great discussion about the significance of the ending and their responses to it.

Sometimes on the second day of discussion, I'll use the homework question to push students toward an analysis of the author's intentions. For example, if students have been discussing their dislike of a particular character, a student will likely suggest a homework question, "Do you like character X? Why or why not?" even though we have already discussed that in depth. I might suggest an adjustment to the following question: "Why do you think the author created a character nobody liked?" Students are appreciative of the added challenge.

At the end of the day, I spend some time cleaning up my notes so they are readable for students the next day.

The Learning Cycle

When students make observations and discoveries about the novel and its formal elements, you can take these opportunities to introduce vocabulary to describe the things the student has brought to attention. The learning cycle, a theory of instruction designed by Lawson, Abraham, and Renner (1989) originally for teaching science concepts, posits a three-stage model for inquiry in a standards-based curriculum. The learning cycle begins in stage 1 with *exploration*, in which students explore and respond to new situations. These responses lead to discoveries—not the teacher's discoveries, but those of the students. In stage 2, *term introduction*, the teacher introduces terms that refer to the patterns discovered during exploration. Stage 3 is *concept application*, in which students apply the concept they learned to a new situation—in their own writing, for example, or in their reading of a new text.

OPPORTUNITIES FOR INTRODUCING LITERARY TERMS

I use discussions as a springboard for introducing students to literary terms that help name their discoveries. I don't predetermine which terms I will introduce in discussions, but find opportunities to work this learning authentically into our process. (Chapter 7 looks at miniprojects I use to teach literary elements to the whole class during the reading portion of the novel study.)

I review the notes for opportunities to introduce terms. I note *climax* as a concept students analyzed in today's discussion that I will name for students tomorrow. Later in the year, we'll study plot arch more formally with the whole class, and they'll get to discover it again across multiple texts. But this is a good opportunity for students to hear it in advance and also to see that their observations about the text have significance beyond this single text. Terms name patterns that exist in the world of literature, and they've just found one.

Discoveries made in discussions create a much more exciting context to teach literary terms than direct instruction. For example, in discussing *The House on Mango Street*, we often reread "The Three Sisters," one of the vignettes, because students find it confusing, and even out of place in the book. In this vignette, Esperanza meets three elderly sisters at a viewing of a dead child. The tone is shadowy. The three sisters read Esperanza's palms and speak as if they can tell the future.

Students remark on the strangeness of the sisters. Do they have magical powers? They seem like witches maybe. And then someone often says it: they're like the Fates! My students (and most others in New York State) studied Greek mythology in sixth grade, and many have a decent memory of these characters. Some other students have read Shakespeare's *Macbeth* and connect these three sisters to the Witches. You can see the light bulbs go on for students and hear a chorus of "Ohhhh yeaaaahhhh! The Fates! What was that again?" as they access whatever previous experience they have with this archetype. I ask someone to explain what the Fates do in Greek mythology.

"They weave, and they can cut the thread to decide if you live or die." Other students contribute more specifics. Often one student knows Greek mythology well and can provide more information. In fact, the popularity of Rick Riordan's Percy Jackson and the Olympians series, about half-breed children of Greek gods and goddesses and humans who have superpowers, has created a generation of Greek mythology fans. I also may allow a student to search the topic on the computer right then or suggest that interested students research it for homework.

Then someone notices the cover. The original cover of *The House on Mango Street* pictures three women holding thin scarf-like material, almost like weaving. "Is this them?!" a student cries. Another round of "Ooohhhs" ensues. We discuss the significance of the author's reference to the Fates at this moment of the book and the decision to include them on the cover, even though they are in only one scene in the whole book.

"What a great discovery you've made here!" I say. "There is actually an official name for what the author has done here. When a writer refers purposely to another story in literature, either directly or by suggestion like we see here, it's called *allusion.*" I write it on the board so they recognize the unique spelling. "The writer wants you to make a connection between these two stories, characters, or ideas, just like you have done with these three sisters and the Fates."

Students gain experiential understanding of various terms throughout the year in the discussions; I also plan in times to teach most literary elements to the whole class at key points in the year and often use shorter texts or films for this. For example, I know that another allusion will come up in *The Chocolate War*, by Robert Cormier, which we'll read later in the year, in which the main character has a poster in his locker that reads "Do I dare disturb the universe?" a line from "The Love Song of J. Alfred Prufrock" by T. S. Eliot. I plan to give students an opportunity to look up the poem during the reading process to access the allusion and use it to better understand the author's purpose.

Common Core Connection

CCRA.R.4—"Interpret words and phrases as they are used in a text, including determining technical, connotative, and figurative meanings, and analyze how specific word choices shape meaning or tone"—specifies that in eighth grade, students can interpret allusion. Knowing where important allusions in whole novels exist in advance and setting up conditions for students to discover them is a way to teach this concept authentically.

CONNECTING REAL AND FICTIONAL WORLDS IN DISCUSSION

Throughout this chapter, I've emphasized students' use of the text in rereading to answer their own questions, examining language, and finding evidence for their claims. However, the study of literature does not just place us in a conversation with a single text or confine us to the world of literature. When we discuss novels together in the classroom, we are responding to characters and situations that have relevance in the real world and our own lives. We share a lot of our selves and our views through our responses to stories. Literature generally creates a safe place to explore challenging issues.

There are times in whole novel discussions when students begin to depart from the text and discuss the real world. Sometimes this is off-topic in a way that may be unproductive. In such cases, and they don't happen often, I redirect the group back to the novel. But there are times when students' discussion of the novel leads to a discussion of a real-world issue, which can be just as much of a learning experience as discussion of the book. Since time is limited, it can be a tough decision whether to let it continue, but I've learned to take notice when it comes up and go with my gut on whether to cut it off or let it go on.

For example, one year the boys in my class had read *The Dream Bearer*, by Walter Dean Myers. The main character's older brother, Ty, seems to be involved in drugs or in dealing drugs. He's not a well-developed character so we have only a few clues as to what's really going on, but the boys seemed to dwell on him a lot. Here is how their discussion went:

KHALED: I don't like that Ty was acting like he was a gangster, like a punk. If I was David, I would have slapped him, too.

MS. SACKS: Why do you think Ty's acting that way?

SAM: Look at where he lives—look at the environment.

QUINCY: He probably sold drugs because he wanted to make extra money.

KHALED: It's not always about your environment. Maybe he did it because he didn't have a father figure around.

MS. SACKS: He doesn't have a father?

KHALED: He does, but Reuben's not acting like a father.

QUINCY: They probably pressured Ty, the people around him, where he hangs out.

KHALED: Maybe he felt like it's a family, the gang he gets into

MASON: Adding onto what we were talking about before, I think Ty should have looked for a real job, but he is trying to support his family.

The boys continued discussing what Ty's involvement in drug dealing and what his reasons for it might be. I was tempted to ask them to find evidence for their claims in the text, but when Quincy said, "They probably pressured Ty, the people around him," I realized this discussion wasn't about Ty anymore. Ty's character had opened up a safe space for them to discuss something they were witnessing and trying to understand in their own neighborhood. I thought that letting them continue the discussion they were having would be worthwhile. Soon enough we got back around to the novel discussion and came to some insightful conclusions about the book's central theme. When it was time to go, one of the boys said, "That was, like, the best discussion *ever!*"

Now and then a thoughtful digression from the text can fuel a discussion. It lets students know that their life experiences can be valuable and relevant to the discussion. It also makes a valid statement about the intersection of the real world we live in and the virtual worlds that writers create. It wasn't by accident that the Myers book provoked a group of thirteen-year-old boys to discuss the reasons a teenager might join a gang or start selling drugs, and the relationship between this choice and the dynamics within his family. In fact, this may have been one of Myers's intentions.

Literature asks questions and makes statements about the real world. Daniel Brink-Washington, one of my coteachers (who now works in science), put it this way:

> One thing I really enjoyed working with you on was thinking about what opportunities and challenges lie in each novel in terms of content—not just skills, but themes that would be an opportunity to either tap into what I know a kid is already interested in, or to expose a student to something that might be new to him or her. Those things can present challenges as well. Oftentimes those challenges—and overcoming them—is where a lot of the learning happens. I think of all the challenges that you address with those eighth-grade novel choices: challenges of diversity, power, and conflict in all of its forms. When kids read about it, it causes them to have to confront a lot of the conflicts in their lives. It becomes a huge learning opportunity for them.

When we read fiction, we gain experience and exposure to ideas that we must work to assimilate into our previous experiences and understanding of the world. The novel community provides space and occasions to confront and process these experiences, both in and out of the book.

INCREASING STUDENT AUTONOMY IN DISCUSSIONS

Ultimately I want students to become skilled in the process of directing their own discussions. In the winter, I begin ceding control over who speaks by experimenting with ways to have students call on each other or take turns without raising their hands. I pose this to students as a discussion. I ask, "What are the benefits of raising hands and having me call on students? What are the drawbacks?" Students recognize that it's more orderly when I call on them to speak. It's easier to ensure one speaker at a time. However, I also control who speaks. They note that this often leads students to look at me while they speak instead of at their classmates.

"How could we do this differently?" I ask. I take suggestions from students. We experiment with students taking turns instead of raising hands for limited amounts of time. Eventually students talk over one another, and we have to stop. We solved the problem by having one student speak and then call on the next student. We discuss how to ensure that we have a good balance of students speaking. Students try calling on members of the group who do not have their hand raised. "What do you think, Angie?" a student tries, when Angie hasn't spoken. For adolescents especially, this is a way to build community and independence in the second half of the year once norms are in place for discussions.

Students also expressed frustration with raising hands in discussion, because sometimes by the time they get called on, the conversation has changed and the point is no longer relevant. We want to be able to follow threads of discussion. My students last year came up with a solution of hand signals. Instead of just raising a hand, students put up one, two, or three fingers. One finger signals that the student has a very quick point (about five seconds) that is in direct response to what has just been said. When "ones" are called on, the discussion can go back and forth among a few speakers quickly without anyone changing the subject. Two fingers signal a comment that is on the topic but takes a little longer to explain. There is no time limit for a "two." Three fingers mean the student will change the focus or bring up a new idea (though still about the book or general activity at hand). Sometimes a "three" is a welcome change when a discussion is going around in circles.

STUDENT-LED DISCUSSIONS

In the final novel study of the year, students lead their own discussions. Students choose from five novels that all follow the journey structure and form smaller novel groups of about four to eight students. Each group then conducts its own discussion.

 Visit https://vimeo.com /61680450 for video 4.8: Student-Led Discussions.

One student is the facilitator (taking on the role I usually play), one student takes notes on the laptop, and another tracks participation. Participation trackers create a Harkness circle, a diagram that follows the flow of discussion (the name comes from the Harkness method of discussion developed at Phillips Exeter Academy). In the Harkness circle, we write each student's name on the circle. The tracker simply draws a line from the first speaker to the next, and so forth, following the chain of conversation. The resulting diagram shows who speaks a lot and who speaks little.

All students are accustomed to the format, beginning with the go-around, taking turns, turning to the text for evidence, and rereading sections for greater meaning. They are poised to do this on their own without me, but leadership does matter. Each group nominates a member to facilitate discussions, and then I share some of my facilitator tricks with the chosen leaders. I share, especially, phrases I use to keep a good balance of speakers and move the discussion to deeper levels:

- "What do the rest of you think of that?"
- "Can someone find evidence for this?"
- "We haven't heard from _____ in a while. What do you think?"
- "Let's try rereading that part."
- "Let's go around again and hear from everyone on this."
- "Do you think the author did that on purpose?"
- "Why would the author do that?"

After the first round, I read the transcript of each group's discussion notes and make a few comments. I note a few great moments, as well as places where students can explore further by rereading. Before the second session, I have students reflect on how the first round went and set goals for that day.

On the whole, I've been impressed with how much the students internalize the processes and are able to lead their own meaningful text-based discussions. With some groups, I've felt the need to sit in for portions of the discussion to help them stay on track. Although some groups encounter challenges in leading their own discussions, I think the experience is valuable, no matter what. This is an area I hope to develop further by giving students more chances to practice with shorter texts, and sooner than the end of the year. I also would like to give more students the opportunity to facilitate discussions.

Some readers might wonder why student-led discussions are not a part of the whole novels method throughout the year given the student-centered focus of the pedagogy. My answer is that leading a discussion of literature and participating in one are different skills. I offer my students lots of opportunities to take on leadership in the classroom because leadership is an important skill for young people to develop. But students need to develop their own skills and maturity in analyzing literature in a group before they are ready to lead their peers effectively in discussions.

PARTS OF THE WHOLE

Lessons from Beginning Teachers on Whole Novels

Beginning to teach is an enormous learning experience, the scope of which few who have not done it understand. I know that experience made a lot of things about teaching clearer for me, but I also found a great deal of excitement using this method as a new teacher. What are the particular benefits and challenges of implementing whole novels as an inexperienced teacher? I spoke with two teachers at the beginning of their careers who have been working with whole novels.

■ ■ ■

Liliana Richter teaches seventh-grade English in a high-need school in Staten Island. Her classes are heterogeneously grouped, and many of her students read below grade level. She began teaching whole novels as a first-year teacher, and she reflects here on the lessons she took into her second year.

ME: What obstacles did you run into trying to lead a whole novel study as a first-year teacher?

LILIANA: I didn't know what to watch out for in terms of students not challenging themselves in their notes. I also failed to properly model the three kinds of thinking responses enough, or to look out for students mixing up literal, inferential, and critical thinking.

Working with a behaviorally challenging population made class discussions difficult as well. I did not hold students to a high enough standard in their speech. It would have been a great opportunity to reinforce formal speaking and careful word choice, but I was too permissive in the way students expressed their thoughts, which were often quite complex, but their use of language didn't allow them to express themselves clearly.

ME: What lessons could you pass on to new teachers trying this method?

LILIANA: It's an excellent way to give students a sense of responsibility for their learning.

Trust your students to bring up the questions you would have asked them, and more! I was at first hesitant and thought I would have to feed my students certain questions to ensure we touched on themes and Common Core standards, but these topics and methods resulted naturally from their own inherent curiosity and interests. Of course, not all students will ask questions key to understanding a text or push their thinking and understanding to a rigorous, challenging level, but their classmates did, and they benefited from that more than if I had done it.

A great way to improve students' sentence complexity in speech and in writing would be to provide sentence starters. For instance, one could ask students to begin an inferential note with *although*.

Be sure your students are speaking to one another in the circle and not to the teacher. Simple reminders are helpful, but at times I even left the circle to observe the students talking to one another.

ME: What areas do you think beginning teachers might need support in to implement this model while also working all of the basics of classroom teaching?

LILIANA: Students may need more modeling than you'd expect (my students did). Also, collecting and giving feedback and/or grades on notes more frequently would have avoided many problems with students. Informing parents about the process in the beginning of the year also helps.

ME: Are there any pieces or moments you could point to that were particularly successful or intriguing about this method, despite challenges?

LILIANA: The students' critical notes were impressive and very revealing at times. The students enjoyed the discussion and listened relatively well to one another. Knowing a discussion is coming at the end of the book shapes their entire reading.

Their questions and comments often address other readers in the class rather than simply the teacher. They ask about the opinions other students had. Their questioning of one another was one of my greatest triumphs brought on by this method, since my first year I had trouble getting away from a teacher-centered room while still maintaining a sense of order.

■ ■ ■

Meredith Byers, a second-year teacher, began leading whole novel studies with her ninth graders at my school in Brooklyn. She teaches a racially and economically diverse group of students in an academically tracked class, with abilities ranging from mid- to high performing and gifted.

ME: What obstacles did you run into trying to lead a whole novel study as a first-year teacher?

MEREDITH: The challenge for me has always been figuring out what to do during three weeks the students are reading the novel. The whole novel approach is wonderful in that it gives teachers tremendous freedom to explore, but it can feel overwhelming to know what to focus on. Our conversations about teaching *Catcher in the Rye* stand out to me. I remember feeling lost about where to even start. There's so much to say about that book, and I want to make sure I am saying as little as possible so the students are able to experience the text for themselves! Still, you helped me find a balance of what we could do in class. We talked about complex characters, the rise of the American "teenager" and teen culture, we close-read the Robert Burns poem "Comin thro the Rye." Those few weeks felt a bit daunting in that I had to figure out what we could cover without "giving it away." I want the students to experience as much of the book as they can on their own.

ME: What lessons could you pass on to new teachers trying this method?

MEREDITH: I had a setback, where I wanted to see what would happen if I didn't check stickies for a week. When the book was due, only four students had completed the stickies! All of them had read the book, and that was clear to me when we started to discuss, but almost no one had done the stickies! We had a conversation about this, and the students admitted that even though writing stickies helped them gain deeper understanding of the book, they lost motivation to do it when I wasn't regularly checking. We decided there would be more frequent checks during the next book. I appreciated the students being honest with me, and we are off to a strong start on our current book!

ME: With your higher-performing students, do you think the sticky notes take away from their experience of reading? Do the notes have value for them?

MEREDITH: I think the notes help kids keep track of what they are thinking. My ten-year-old sister was afraid of the whole novel idea because she "wouldn't remember the important parts." The notes mitigate that fear and give kids a chance to reflect on what is happening in the text. It also helps with tracking themes, and the kids are so quick to find passages in discussion. They can find a passage before I can!

ME: What areas do you think beginning teachers might need support in to implement this model while also working all of the basics of classroom teaching?

MEREDITH: I found that students with challenging behavior really chill out when they are genuinely engaged in exploring something that they are interested in. If kids are reading books that are appropriately challenging and engaging, they respond well to whole novel studies. Kids are so intuitive that they recognize the trust placed in them by the teacher. Taking that risk is something that new teachers need encouragement and support to do.

ME: Are there any pieces or moments you could point to that were particularly successful or intriguing about this method, despite challenges?

MEREDITH: The moment that consistently amazes me is the discussion. The students so anxiously anticipate the discussion, and it's thrilling to see them so excited to discuss a book. The students go above and beyond my expectations and surprise me with details that stand out to them. I truly learn new things from them each time we discuss a text. I don't mean to sound trite, but their ability to find meaning within the novel stuns and amazes me every time we discuss.

I have one group of students reading *A Yellow Raft in Blue Water*, by Michael Dorris. The novel is told from three different points of view. Today during our reading time at the beginning of class, one of the students blurted out to me, "Oh my gosh! The next part of the book is from the mother's point of view! That is amazing." He was really that excited to find out that the novel would change narrators throughout the book. I loved seeing him figure that out on his own and have the experience of processing what this meant for the book. He didn't need a lecture from me on narrative structure to find this meaningful. Instead, he has figured this out on his own, and he will reflect on it throughout the rest of the book. When he's finished, I await his thoughts on why the novel is structured this way and what it means and why it matters. But for now, I know he is experiencing the book on his own and having small epiphanies like this along the way. That's the beauty of teaching this way.

I have truly loved applying the approach to ninth grade. I often worry that the classic high school texts might feel too dated and may not resonate with my students. The whole novel approach allows me to pair traditional texts with contemporary texts that I know the students will love. I also love selecting increasingly challenging and complex texts.

5

Making the Writing Connection

Harnessing Students' Drive to Say Something

"Try it out at the dinner table."

I once had the opportunity to hear Susan Orleans, author of *The Orchid Thief* and other works of journalistic nonfiction, speak about writing. She said something that really stuck in my memory. It went something like this:

> To write, you first have to have a story. You have to have something to say.
> I always test out whether my idea will be interesting to others by telling it to
> friends, like over dinner. If it holds up at the dinner table, it's worth writing.
> At first, use a voice similar to the one you'd use if you were telling it to friends.
> Later you can craft it, cut things out, work on pacing and language.

Students are often asked to write on a question we've created, and they spend time looking for what they perceive as a predetermined right answer. In other words, they're not beginning with something they want to say. Instead, they're insecure about what they're saying because they don't know if it meets the teacher's expectations. This stunts their writing process. Many adults suffer from this same stunting because they never discovered their writer's voice. Whole novel studies take away this pressure by giving kids space and encouragement to speak their minds about books and translate their thoughts into writing. The thinking they share in discussions is their own, and they're willing to take risks. The discussion sessions are a place where students test out ideas, push them to their limits, and work together to determine their validity—at the dinner table of the classroom, if you will.

Students generate great content for writing in whole novel discussions. I shelter the transition from speaking to writing by beginning with student-created homework questions (described in the previous chapter). These allow students to continue the conversation we've been having outside the classroom with pen and paper and determine the direction this conversation will take. In these responses, I ask for a minimum of one paragraph, but I allow them to transfer their thinking freely in an open response format, rather than a formally structured paragraph. (Students come to me having learned many formulas for paragraph writing. While these can be helpful, I want students to get away from the formulas here and simply explore their thinking on a particular topic or question on the page.)

Common Core Standard Connection

By exploring both short, informal and long, formal structures for writing about a topic, students develop skills in CCRA.W.10: "Write routinely over extended time frames (time for research, reflection, and revision) and shorter time frames (a single sitting or a day or two) for a range of tasks, purposes, and audiences."

Sometimes these homework exercises are rooted in personal response in questions like "Who's your favorite character?" After the second or third session and as the year progresses, students ask more analytical questions:

- "What is this character's role in the book?"
- "How does this character change throughout the book?"
- "Why do you think the author wrote this book?"
- "Why did the author end the book this way?"

What start as personal responses, such as "I didn't like the end," are interrogated in discussion. Students work together to solve the problem of why they didn't like the end. They make connections between different scenes and elements of the story and cull the text to take a closer look at the sources of their responses. This process leads students to reframe their personal reactions on a more analytical level to consider the author's role and possible motivations. The chance to do this thought work out loud with peers lifts a heavy burden for students when it comes time to write responses to literature. They come to writing with increasingly sophisticated things they want to say.

DEVELOPING CLAIMS IN OPEN DISCUSSION

A strong curriculum should have a balance of opportunities for students to develop divergent and convergent thinking processes. The discussion seminars and the homework questions invite students to practice divergent thinking—open, creative, uncensored kind of thinking—in their interpretations of the literature. A strong literary essay begins by making an interesting argument, often the result of creative, divergent thinking. In my experience, the freedom that allows students to practice divergent thinking in response to literature (and risk being wrong or ridiculous) leads to much stronger motivation for students to shift toward the convergent thinking task of crafting a focused argument.

I can often trace the direct connection between students' development of ideas in discussions and their choices to explore them further in writing. I encourage this transition by building in opportunities for students to write in between discussion sessions. In a discussion of *The Absolutely True Diary of a Part-Time Indian*, by

Figure 5.1 Students Sharing Writing in Discussions

Sherman Alexie, Jelissa shared a comment about a line on page 189 in which the narrator, Junior, says "So many ghosts . . ." The discussion went like this (see Figure 5.1):

JELISSA: About how the author writes the story . . . After the sister writes the letter, he never really writes the thoughts about the letter. I think Alexie is trying to get you to think how he would be feeling. Like on page 188 towards the bottom, he writes "So many ghosts." He doesn't explain what he means by saying it. You have to think, *What does he mean?*

AMELIA: I think that line stands out to me as well. I think that all those ghosts are metaphorically ghosts and literal . . . not that you see it standing in the room but his family. Three family members are dead. That would symbolize the literal ghosts. Metaphorically . . .

MS. S: How could it be metaphorical?

AMELIA: It could stand for his tribe?

SAMUEL: On the last page it says, "I hope that they would forgive me for leaving the rez." I think the ghosts would stand for his tribe. Kind of in connection to

144

Mango Street. Esperanza was gonna leave Mango Street, because the people there weren't going to do anything with their lives. This kind of related because he's saying how once he went to Reardon, he discovered a whole new world. And like three of his family members are dead. The rez is becoming a sad, lonely place. Not good. He probably wants to get out of there. He'll miss Rowdy. He belonged to all these tribes, but didn't want to leave this one because of Rowdy. That's why he says, "I hope you'll forgive me."

JOSUE: I thought maybe it wasn't metaphorical, but just literal about the deaths— Eugene, sister, grandfather. Three deaths of people really close to you is devastating. Ghosts symbolize death.

Later in this discussion, I asked students to come up with questions for a five-minute writing activity. We had a double block that day, so there was no opportunity for homework between sessions 1 and 2. Amelia suggests the question "What does the author mean by the line 'So many ghosts?'" There are about four other questions, and I ask students to choose one to write about independently for five minutes.

Amelia chooses her own question. After students write for five minutes, I ask them to tell me which question they wrote about. I direct students to meet with the others who wrote about the same question. "Question 1, meet at table 1," I begin. They are to share their written responses, and then see if they can keep the discussion going for a few minutes. I give them about five minutes, spending some time with each group. Amelia and Jelissa are the only two who choose this question, and they meet and talk through their ideas.

After three rounds of discussions and a few open writing opportunities like this, I plan for students to spend a period doing in-class essay writing. An ideal time for students to write literary essays is following whole novel discussion sessions. I make this transition by pulling out the major topics or debates from the discussion notes and framing them as essay questions. Sometimes I have students participate in this process by creating a list of good essay questions with me. They then choose the one they are most interested in, or they may propose their own. In these essays, students really have *something to say*. They are writing to communicate and using a form that is often difficult to get students to authentically engage with. My assignment sheet is in Exhibit 5.1.

EXHIBIT 5.1 In-Class Literary Essay Assignment Sheet

In-class Writing 11/29: *The Absolutely True Diary of a Part-Time Indian* Essay

1. Choose ONE question below for your essay.
2. Take out your copy of your group's discussion notes.
3. Write your essay following the format provided.
4. Use loose-leaf paper.

ESSAY QUESTIONS

Students raised the following questions about *The Absolutely True Diary of a Part-Time Indian* in discussion. Choose ONE to answer in an essay.

Essay choice 1	How does Junior and Rowdy's *friendship change* over the course of the book? What message does this piece of the story send? Use evidence from the novel to support your answer.
Essay choice 2	How did *alcoholism* affect Junior's life? Use evidence from the novel to support your answer.
Essay choice 3	Did Sherman Alexie write a compelling (strong) *ending* to *The Absolutely True Diary of a Part-Time Indian*? Why or why not? Use evidence from the novel to support your answer.
Essay choice 4	By the end of the story, is Junior a *part-time Indian* or a *full-time Indian*? Use evidence from the novel to support your answer.
Essay choice 5	Pick a minor character (Gordy, Ted, Mary, Penelope, or another). Why do you think Sherman Alexie put this character in the book? How would the story be different without him or her? Use examples from the novel to support your answer.
Essay choice 6	Were there stereotypes in this book? What message does Sherman Alexie send about stereotypes of Indians, white people, or others?
Essay choice 7	Pick one important line in the book. What does this line mean? How does it connect to the characters? What is its significant to the book overall? For example, Junior says, "So many ghosts" (p. 188). Write an essay about this line. Or Rowdy says, "You're an old-time nomad" (p. 229). Write an essay about that line. Or pick your own.

ESSAY OUTLINE

Aim for 5 paragraphs. If you run out of time, skip paragraph 4 and move to the conclusion.

Paragraph #1: Introduce the topic. Answer the essay question in a complete sentence. Briefly state your reasons for your answer but do NOT go into detail.

Paragraph #2: Explain one piece of evidence for your answer—an example from the book. Use a quote to show what you mean.

Paragraph #3: Explain a second piece of evidence for your answer—an example from the book. Use a quote to show what you mean.

Paragraph #4: Explain a third piece of evidence for your answer—an example from the book. Use a quote to show what you mean.

Paragraph #5: Conclude your essay. Begin, "In conclusion . . . " Restate the main idea of your essay (your answer to the question). Then offer a final thought or two. How does this connect to our lives or the world of literature and stories?

Amelia chooses to write about the line "So many ghosts," which she explored previously during the discussions:

On page 188 of The Absolutely True Diary of a Part-time Indian, when Junior says, "So many ghosts," I think that he is referring to the literal ghosts and the metaphorical ghosts.

The literal ghosts Junior is thinking about are his grandmother and Eugene, a role model, (his sister hadn't died yet). He mentions right before the ghosts line on page 188, "Yeah, that Eugene, he was a positive dude even as an alcoholic who ended up getting shot in the face and killed." At this moment, Junior is thinking about Eugene and how he died, and him being a literal ghost.

I think Junior might also be referring to the people of the reservation for the metaphorical ghosts. The people on the reservation are alive, but they don't really feel alive. By being on the rez, their hope is gone, because they don't think they can have a good future. That's why they turn to alcoholism, to, as we said in discussion, "numb

(continued)

(continued)

their pain." On page 192, Junior says, "Or maybe I was raising my mother's or father's hope for me." This shows that Junior is giving his parents hope, which they have lost forever since they stayed on the reservation and turned to alcohol. This makes them kind of like ghosts.

In conclusion, Junior means by saying the line, "So many ghosts," there are both metaphoric and literal ghosts in his life and others lives.

She runs out of time before concluding her argument, and some of her evidence needs clarifying, but it's clear she's seized the opportunity to organize her thinking about this line into the format of a traditional essay and begun to connect the single line and its levels of meaning to the big ideas of the book.

Common Core Connections

When students choose to write about a particular passage of the book, they engage in close reading, which they often start in discussions and practice. CCRA.R.4: "Interpret words and phrases as they are used in a text, including determining technical, connotative, and figurative meanings, and analyze how specific word choices shape meaning or tone."

Students put their thinking into essay form and practice CCRA.W.4: "Produce clear and coherent writing in which the development, organization, and style are appropriate to task, purpose, and audience."

The in-class essay is an example of an opportunity for teachers to work on the short-form aspect of Common Core Writing Standard 10: "Write routinely over extended time frames (time for research, reflection, and revision) and shorter time frames (a single sitting or a day or two) for a range of tasks, purposes, and audiences."

LITERARY ESSAYS WITH A PURPOSE

English teachers often work to give students authentic audiences for their writing. Students can write letters to senators about local or national issues; they can write short stories and read them to younger kids or senior citizens. But literary critics, the experts in our discipline, who've made a career of literary studies, write for an audience of their peers—a literary community inclusive of both fiction writers and other critics of literary art. The whole novel community, especially the discussion seminars, creates a community of adolescent literary critics. The students are motivated to engage with the diversity of opinions and perspectives within the community, sharpen their own thinking, critique the authors they read, and become persuasive with their arguments.

Common Core Connections

In essay writing, students sometimes struggle to imagine an authentic audience and may feel stunted by the pressure of writing for a teacher. Discussions provide students with a real and engaging audience for their ideas allowing them to work toward CCRA.W.4: "Produce clear and coherent writing in which the development, organization, and style are appropriate to task, purpose, and audience."

Once students have something they want to say, teachers have an occasion to help them develop the technical skills of presenting evidence, embedding, and analyzing quotes. Often these skills are taught first in isolation, and later students are expected to apply them to a new context. The problem is that students have no real motivation to learn these skills without an authentic need for them. ("This is a state standard" or "This will be on the test" won't mean much to many of our students.) When students finally get to apply the skills in more authentic contexts, their writing style is mechanical and dry. This is an example of an approach that gives students *a place to stop* rather than places to go. ("Places to go" is the phrase I use when I think about differentiating instruction for the individuals in my class. It's my job to help every student find new places to go and ways to get there. I discuss this idea more in Chapter 8.)

By contrast, Cecile turns in the following essay, which came out of a discussion session that revolved a lot around the relationship between two characters in *Like Sisters on the Homefront*, by Rita Williams-Garcia. Cecile is a student who tends to perform in the middle and sometimes lower third of the class and struggles to elaborate on her ideas in writing.

Gayle and Cookie both learned a great deal from each other. Being around 2 totally different life views made them alter theirs. Cookie was more of the goody two shoes church girl. While Gayle was the wild child that didn't care what anyone else had to say. As these to girls learned to come together Cookie became just a little more lose and Gayle thought things over just a little more.

You can tell that Gayle learned from cookie because of many instances in the book. Some big things are that Gayle actually started to respect Great which in the beginning she really didn't.

Another place that shows Gayle learned from cookie is throughout the whole book Cookie has been telling Gayle "Let me save you" and by the end of the book Gayle actually told cookie that she wants to save her which to me seems like a big step forward.

You can tell they changed because they didn't just act randomly different. They started acted like each other. Not completely but enough to tell. If you read the book closely you would know. At least be hinted by the end.

This is how I see these two girls started acting alike. They even cared for each others well being. Which is a big step for both of them.

At this point, she has drawn a conclusion about the relationship between Gayle and Cookie and has done some work toward finding evidence to support it and structuring her ideas.

Common Core Standard Connection

When students feel genuinely motivated to argue a point, they are ready to learn and apply techniques to analysis and incorporate evidence into their writing. The whole novels writing process presents the opportunity to focus on CCRA.W.1: "Write arguments to support claims in an analysis of substantive topics or texts, using valid reasoning and relevant and sufficient evidence."

As I look at Cecile's essay, I can think of many places for her to go with it and her expository writing in general. Cecile's first draft provides an opportunity to help her build or practice the following skills:

- Finding quotes to support ideas
- Structuring paragraphs
- Connecting the change in the characters to a theme of the book or author's purpose for an effective conclusion
- Writing an effective introduction

In the following unedited example, Sophia, a high-performing student, argues a similar point with more evidence and technique, coming out of the same discussion group:

In the novel *Like Sisters on the Homefront* written by Rita Williams-Garcia, two of the main characters, Gayle and Cookie, change very dramatically by the end of the book. Coming from very different environments, they both have a strong effect on each other and that's one of the big contributing factors to the way they change. Cookie is a modest goody-two shoes from a large plantation in Georgia and Gayle is a rebellious teen mom from South Side Jamaica in Queens. Throughout the book, they change each other's views on sex and how that affects your life.

Cookie is a demure 16 year-old who relies very much on her parents. She hasn't had her first kiss yet. A completely different situation from her cousin Gayle, a fourteen-year old mother who has done things Cookie would never even think about doing. In a conversation at the beginning of the book between them Gayle finds out how modest Cookie is.

"Girlfriend, your problem is you need to think more about that.' Gayle said 'What's the most you ever done?"
"Nothing"

(continued)

(*continued*)

"Not even a kiss? Come on, Cookie. You nice looking. Sort of. You must be turning someone on.'

"Cousin, don't talk so loud!" Cookie said.

Here Gayle is trying to wrap her mind around the fact that Cookie doesn't do anything with boys. It's sort of difficult for her to understand because where she comes from everyone has had their first kiss at an early age. Cookie, later in the conversation, reveals that a boy she once dated did kiss her but she thought it was disgusting and pulled away. Gayle had never been exposed to someone like that, so of course her reaction was surprised at her response to his kiss.

At the end of the book they both have a very different conversation. Cookie decides to go to her current boyfriend's, Stacey Alexander, house. She wanted to have sex him. Gayle suddenly realizes that what she's doing is a bad idea and decides to stop her.

"Wait," Gayle said as Cookie went out the back door.

"Go back, Cousin," Cookie said, heading straight for the car.

Gayle followed. "Thought you was saved Cookie."

"Leave me alone, Cousin." Cookie told her.

"And what if I don't?" Gayle asked.

"I'll make you," Cookie told her.

"Go through me you, so bad," Gayle dared.

Gayle realizes all the mistakes she's made, some of them the result of sex. Gayle made these mistakes because she had no one to tell her not to, but Cookie does. And she just doesn't want Cookie to mess up like she did. She sees how lucky Cookie is, she has a house and a loving family and a place where she feels happy and safe. She has a home, something Gayle never really did. Gayle doesn't want Cookie ripping her home apart.

In conclusion, at the end of the book Cookie got more daring than she was before because Gayle exposed her to new things, and Gayle got more mature because Cookie showed her that being grown up doesn't necessarily mean doing things that are "not meant" for kids. She finally saw she had no idea what she was doing and decided to stop being oblivious and selfish. She had Cookie to thank for this because she saw what not being crazy and confused can do. It can give you a home. A home is where people help you and don't support you in doing something that they know is wrong. A home is where your family is. Where your roots are. Where you are meant to be. A home is something Gayle realized she wanted more than anything by the end. Gayle did have a house in New York but it definitely wasn't a home. This idea of house vs. home is something that reoccurs in literature and in real life. We may live some place but then later in life find somewhere we just belong.

Sophia has written a strong first draft. I want to point her to find out how to properly embed quotes within a paragraph, cite page numbers, and reflect on how she can make the focus of each paragraph in relation to her thesis clearer to readers.

What's interesting is that the main idea that both students are communicating through the essay was developed in discussions, giving both of them a chance to work on their essay writing skills, while feeling confident in their purpose.

> **Common Core Connection**
>
> Discovering new tools during the writing process prompts students to work on CCRA.W.5: "Develop and strengthen writing as needed by planning, revising, editing, rewriting, or trying a new approach."

ESSAY STRUCTURE AND THOSE ANNOYING FIVE PARAGRAPHS

I'm not crazy about the classic five-paragraph essay format; professional writers don't really use it, and many high school graduates spend their first years of college unlearning this format that has been ingrained in them for too long. I think a lot of the problem with the five-paragraph essay comes when students focus on the format without a clear purpose for writing, teachers overprescribe structure at the sentence level, and students never get to think critically about how to structure expository writing or study other formats of essays and falsely assume everything should be a "five-paragraph essay."

Nevertheless, a five-paragraph structure can provide a decent way of organizing an argument, and there's some convenience to it, because students come to me familiar with it. I do use a five-paragraph essay structure with students, but I make sure to give them experience with other forms of expository writing throughout the year. For example, at the beginning of the year, I introduce the narrative essay (a personal story that leads to an idea) and the argument essay (the five-paragraph essay based on a claim). Later, students study the format of a feature article.

In teaching the argument essay, I strip the classic format of sentence-by-sentence requirements some students have learned and emphasize just the most important parts of it:

- An introduction that includes a thesis or claim and possibly a hook.
- Several paragraphs (two to four) of evidence-based argument to support the claim. Each paragraph has its own focus and should include analysis of relevant quotes.
- A conclusion that summarizes the argument and connects it to the greater world of literature and our lives.

I often have students with little prior experience with essay writing begin by working together on a miniproject to outline an argument on a big piece of chart paper. They develop a thesis statement about the novel or film, which they write in a large rectangular box at the top. I teach them to name the full title and author of the book. Then the group must find three pieces of evidence to support their argument, which they list in bullet points below the thesis. They must select one or two quotes for each piece of evidence and explain how each piece of evidence supports the overall argument.

The collaborative work outlining the ideas provides lots of opportunities for students to give and get feedback on each other's thinking. I also circulate, asking questions. When I find groups listing evidence that doesn't clearly support the claim, I don't tell them this directly. Instead, I ask, "Why did you choose this piece of evidence? What does it show? How does it help you make this argument?" The assignment itself leads students through this same line of questioning, so my role is to point students to reconsider choices. Sometimes I ask the same questions when the evidence is well chosen, to encourage students to clarify and defend their thinking.

At various points in the year, I explicitly teach writing skills to the whole class: writing a claim (the thesis statement), outlining, quoting from a text, and analyzing evidence, for example. Literary essays that come out of whole novel studies can be used to teach, reinforce, assess, and provide feedback to students on any essay writing skills, though generally not all of them at once. The length of time we spend on these essays varies from a single period of in-class writing to a week of fine-tuning each component of the essay. The number of drafts also varies. Sometimes students write a single draft, and other times we go through two or three drafts. Students may receive feedback from me or from peers, and I may provide guidelines for students to assess their own writing. With 105 students, it's impossible for me to give substantive feedback every time we write without writing rather infrequently. I've had to become comfortable with having students write and not providing feedback on it every time.

STUDENTS AS CRITICS OF AUTHOR'S CRAFT

Another way discussions benefit the writing process is that students can develop much more sophisticated ideas in discussions than they do if we just give them a writing assignment we've developed in response to a text. The discussions often bring out students' critiques of the author's writing choices, which the Common Core Standards require and many teachers are struggling to find ways to accomplish. It's difficult and unnatural for most kids to critique author's craft decisions as they are reading the book for the first time because they are focusing on getting and enjoying the story. However, this type of analysis becomes quite natural after they have read the entire book and discussed it with peers.

When students develop ideas about the author's craft in discussions, they can write more confidently about them in essays, something that is often difficult for them to do authentically. Teachers sometimes resort to feeding ideas to the students, so that they can then teach them the writing skills to communicate those ideas. This distorts students' understanding of what writing is about—the purpose essayists and critics have when they put pen to paper—by creating an illusion that the purpose of writing is to adhere to a structure rather than to communicate content.

In his first draft of the literary essay that follows, Raafi, a student who comes from a non-English-dominant household and struggles with both reading and writing, offers a detailed critique of Walter Dean Myers's novel, *The Dream Bearer*. This followed a heated discussion among the boys' group as to whether the book was "good" or not. There were a lot of differences in opinion among the group. As always in discussions, I remind students that the book doesn't just exist; it was written by an author. When we have reactions, positive or negative, we have to look at what the author had done to make this impact on us. Raafi does just that in this essay, teasing apart the two sides of the argument that ensued in discussions. This is the most I had ever seen him write.

Walter Dean Myers wrote a compelling book for young readers but the begging of the book was shaky but throughout it went well and it was an excellent book. Well what I mean by this is that in the begging he could have created an event or conflict that would have made young readers interested. Cause if you look at a 13 year old he or she will need something that will make them be interested and to pay attention.

For example in the beginning it just rushes in with all these characters like sessi, Loren and David. Then it begins with this scene on the roof. this makes it confusing for me and readers because their first thought will be like " what is this?" My thoughts will be to explain the setting a little bit and also describe the characters. Cause Walter Dean Myers just start to talk about a roof that sessi was building and unlike all the other books their will always be an introduction with many description, he always just brings an event that is irrelevant in the stories that i had read from him. I thought Walter Dean Myers could do better.

When Walter Dean Myers brings the character named Mr.moses the book enlightened for me. He was my favorite character in the book because his emotion throughout the story was calm. The thing that Walter Dean Myers did was bring an important event and make it the number #1 thing throughout the story. It made me pay more attention because when he said he was a dream bearer it was surprising and cool cause that was an important gift from whoever he had gotten it from. At first when he got introduced i thought he was a homeless man or a scout cause he would come to the park and watch David and Loren play basketball every time they came.

Through going towards the end of the story it was very interesting cause there was problem after problem with Tyrone dealing with drugs and him betting and Reuben being kind of mysterious. What i mean by this was that like he kept a occupied living style and he was bad. I thought he was using drugs cause he was hanging out on the streets and stuff. But I sill wonder why he was abusing Davids mom well i think it was because of the alcohol cause alcohol makes you act a different way.

In conclusion well I think that Walter Dean Myer's wrote a compelling book for young readers a little bit cause of the little mistakes in the beginning cause of the way he introduced it with this random setting and also just him rushing all these characters. So this way how he organized it wasn't well but he did a great job going towards the end. Many people do this mistake in my opinion and get better and better in the end.

Despite some obvious places to go for Raafi in his next draft of this essay, he's taken on the position of the critic or editor.

In a letter to his students, Kurt Vonnegut assigned them to read fifteen short stories and respond in a term paper, published in *Kurt Vonnegut: Letters* (Wakefield, 2012). He asks them to give each short story a grade of A through F based on their own satisfaction with it. He warns them not to think too academically but to offer feedback to the writers of the stories "as a sensitive person who has a few practical hunches about how stories can succeed or fail" (119). By critiquing Myers's writing in his own voice in this essay, Raafi has done exactly what Kurt Vonnegut asked of his college students.

Here's an example of a more meandering seventh-grade essay draft that attempts to critique the author's choices in *The Jacob Ladder*:

After reading the book *The Jacob Ladder*, by Uton Hinds, I find that the story being told only in first person refreshing. I say this for two reasons. One it's original and refreshing, and two, it really gives you a sense of what Tall T is thinking and what Jamaica is like in the 1960s.

For number one, I say it is refreshing let me tell you why. I am a big book reader. A lot of the time the books I read are in third person. So when the class first started reading The Jacob Ladder, I was very excited. It also makes the story read a lot better. For instance. When Uton is climbing the Jacob Ladder in Oracabessa, instead of the author giving an "outside" description, he put it through Uton's eyes and made it a lot

(continued)

(continued)

clearer and exciting. This is why I think That The Jacob Ladder being written in first person is refreshing.

For number two I think that first person helps give you a sense of what Tall T is thinking and what Jamaica is like in the 1960s. I say this for a few reasons. One when Tall T is thinking instead of the narrator giving a proper description, you hear how Tall T would actually think. With the 'iff' 'dems' an' 'botsuh' included. For my second point, when Tall T is describing Oracabessa, he gives it how he sees it. He sees a community of characters, opportunities, fun and people who he loves, loathes and fear. It feels sincere and truthful, more than anything. So I really like that.

In conclusion I like the first person narration of The Jacob ladder for two reasons. One it's refreshing. And two it really gives you a sense of what Tall T is really thinking and what Oracabessa is like in the 1960s.

LITERARY ESSAYS USING MULTIPLE SOURCES

Later in the year, we begin to draw from several texts to explore ideas authors put forth in fiction and how they do it. *The Chocolate War*, one of our whole novel studies, takes place in a Catholic boys' prep school in the 1970s. The novel brings up the theme of power dynamics and the structures that influence them and the roles of oppressor, victim, bystander, resister, and martyr. We watch the film *Swing Kids*, which takes place in Nazi Germany and brings up similar themes. Finally, we read "The Lottery," a short story by Shirley Jackson, which brings up the idea of tradition in relation to power structures. Seekers have the opportunity to read *The Book Thief*, by Markus Zusak, and *Lord of the Flies*, by William Golding, which also contribute to a discussion of power structures. In discussions, we focus on *The Chocolate War*, but students make comparisons to the other texts and the film. They readily compare characters, messages of the stories, and themes that come up in multiple texts.

Following discussions of *The Chocolate War* and related texts, I frame essay questions that build on the connections students are already making, and I ask them to use more than one text to answer the question.

At this point in the year, my students are nearing the date of the New York State English Language Arts test, given annually in grades 3 to 8, so I am a bit more specific in the prompts to give them a chance to work on the skill of understanding an essay question. Nevertheless, all of these questions came directly out of discussions students had on these topics:

Common Core Connections

Each whole novel study includes supplemental texts and other materials that relate thematically to the core novel. This provides rich opportunities to practice these Common Core state reading standards:

CCRA.R.7: "Integrate and evaluate content presented in diverse formats and media, including visually and quantitatively, as well as in words."

CCRA.R.9: "Analyze how two or more texts address similar themes or topics in order to build knowledge or to compare the approaches the authors take."

CHOICE 1: Compare the message Robert Cormier sends in *The Chocolate War* about resisting oppression with the message Shirley Jackson sends in "The Lottery" or the writer of *Swing Kids*, Jonathan Marc Feldman, sends about resisting oppression. Use evidence from the text to support your answer.

CHOICE 2: Choose a *character* from *The Chocolate War* and a character from either "The Lottery" or *Swing Kids*. In an essay, discuss the similarities or differences, or both, between these two characters' *roles* (e.g., oppressor, victim, bystander, resister, and/or martyr). Include evidence from the text to support your answer.

CHOICE 3: Choose a *theme* that is present in both *The Chocolate War* and *Swing Kids* or "The Lottery." *Compare* the *message* the author sends about this theme in each text.

The student essay that follows was written by Patricia, who likes to read but often struggles to structure her ideas clearly in writing. Here, she decided to work on choice 2, but she wanted to make a complex comparison between two characters and the shifting roles they play in the stories. The depth of the experience of this whole novel study and the increasing complexity of the texts we read across the year set Patricia up to be able to make this argument confidently. Her confidence about her idea allows me to focus my support on helping her think through her organization. What should she communicate in each paragraph, and how would that connect with her thesis? She does a solid job of finding a logical way to structure her rather complex argument in this first draft. Note that she realized her argument required more than five paragraphs to adequately make her point.

Arvin from the "Swing Kids" and Jerry from "The Chocolate War" both started as resistors but ended extremely differently. The "Swing Kids" is a 1993 film that shows a little bit more what people in Germany had to give up, specifically music in this film because of the big power of the Nazi. The Chocolate War is a book written by Robert Cormier. This book takes place in a high school called Trinity. In this school the group of people with all the power are called "The Vigils". This book shows that resistance against power might be impossible.

Arvin from the swing kids was a resistor and followed his belief. In this movie the Nazi did not agree with Swing music, and if they heard you or saw you dancing to swing music they would have put you down. Arvin refused to give up his swing music. For example, one day he was walking up a block holding a record of a swing artist while singing the artists song. The Nazi youth then broke his new record and put Arvin down for singing the swing song. Arvin still resisted, prayed, and listened to his favorite music, A second example of how Arvin resisted was that he knew the Nazi youth hated swing music, he knew what could have happened to him if they saw him but he still played his guitar in swing clubs because he loved it. This is what made Arvin a resistor.

Although Arvin at first was a resistor, his role changed through out the end to a higher level. Arvin was playing his guitar in a swing club when a German man asked him to play a German song. Arvin got upset, and he denied and denied and told the man "i will never play a German song in my life." He then left the club dramatically. One of his friends which was also part of the Nazi youth started it argue with Arvin. His friend told him that night "Watch yourself Arvin because we are coming for you next." Arvin that same night went home packed his favorite swing stuff and killed himself in his bathroom. That's when his role changed from a resistor to a martyr. He was willing to die for his religion and his beliefs, and also for what he loved.

Jerry from "The Chocolate War" also started with the role of a resistor. In trinity, the group with the power is The Vigils. The Vigils give out special order and assignments to specific kids. In the school, every single student must sell at least

50 boxes of chocolates. The Vigils gave Jerry an assignment to deny for 10 days to deny his teacher, Brother Leon, about selling the chocolates. So Jerry did exactly that. For example, on page 118 it is a conversation between Brother Leon and Jerry as Brother Leon is checking how many boxes of chocolates the students have sold. On page 118 it says 'Renault' he said again his voice like a whip. Jerry Renault replies 'No, I am not going to sell the chocolates' The vigils then got very upset and the "leader" Archie called a vigils meeting and invited Jerry. On page 172 you can see Archie gives Jerry an assignment that Jerry needs to accept the chocolate the next day. But on page 177 Jerry said to himself "My name is Jerry Renault and i will not sell the chocolates."

Although Jerry started with the role of a resistor, at the end his role changed and went down. He became a victim of violence. For example, on page 213 Jerry got attacked by Janza, a vigils member and few of his friends and it says "they were swarming all over him, hitting him to the ground as if he was some kind of helpless Gulliver." Then he got into a fight with Janza one on one but the whole trinity was against Jerry. Archie knocked him out, interfering in the fight, almost killing Jerry. On page 259 it says "the doctor said that Renault may have sustained a fracture of the jaw and there may be internal injuries." Jerry totally regretted his resistance against the great power the vigils after his experience of being a victim.

Arvin and Jerry both started with the roles of resistors but ended with different roles. Jerry ended up resistance against the vigils after he practically almost got killed. Arvin didn't regret resistance and showed he was willing to die for what he believed in. The authors are trying to say to not resist on a power that is way bigger than you without a plan, without a team. Think before you do or accept the consequences.

Some students chose to identify a theme and compare the messages the authors send on this theme in two or three different texts. For example, one student wrote about the theme of tradition in *The Chocolate War* and "The Lottery" and what the authors were trying to say about the relationship between tradition and oppression. At this point it's spring, and students have built up some facility analyzing a single work of literature. This strength allows them to focus on the new challenge of applying their analysis to two texts at the same time and creating an argument that considers the precise connection between them.

CREATIVE WRITING IN THE WHOLE NOVELS PROGRAM

Creative writing is always one of my students' favorite parts of my class, and it's true for me as well. Young people have active imaginations and need space and encouragement to channel their creativity into writing. The immersive experience of reading a novel and the admiration and criticism for the author students articulate in discussion provide a springboard for students' own writing.

Every year when I survey students about my class, they ask for more creative writing. And every year when I send them off to high school, they return to me saying they don't get to write creatively at all anymore and that mine was the class in which they wrote the most creatively. I'm saddened by the lack of creative writing in students' high school education. I'm convinced that fiction, poetry writing, and narratives of any kind are the key to developing voice and style in writing. Creative writing also seems to give students a feeling of control that is often missing in their lives, where so much is out of their control. The imaginative writing has a therapeutic effect. This draws students into their school experience in a positive way that can extend past the singular experience of writing fiction.

During writing time, I often let students find a space in the room, where they can imagine being by themselves. I introduce Virginia Woolf's *A Room of One's Own* and the concept that a writer needs space to think and write. I give them thirty seconds to find a space in the room—or they can stay at their desks (Figure 5.2). This is something I adopted from Madeleine Ray and Nancy Toes Tangel, and students love it. Some teachers may be thinking this sounds chaotic, but students appreciate the novelty and rise to the challenge.

Nearly all of the creative writing in my class connects to our whole novel studies. Following are examples of the types of creative writing my students do in conjunction with the books they read. I generally make decisions about which assignments to use based on the literary focus of the study.

Figure 5.2 Students Writing in a Room of Their Own

Connecting to Characters Through Writing

Three of the creative assignments I might use during a novel study focus on character.

Character Pen Pals

When students are new to whole novel studies, I love to assign them to write a letter to a character in the novel. We do this at the beginning or in the middle of the novel study. They must pretend the character is a real person and just talk to the character about what's happening in his or her life. I encourage students to comment on

Common Core Connection

The pen-pal exercise encourages readers to think about the novel creatively as well as analytically and develops CCRA.W.3: "Write narratives to develop real or imagined experiences or events using effective technique, well-chosen details, and well-structured event sequences."

specific things the character says or does and end with a few questions for the character. When students have finished reading the novel, they pretend to be the character and write a reply letter to themselves.

The character pen-pal exercise gets students engaging subjectively with the world of the novel toward the beginning of the novel study. I hang these letters around the room and keep them there throughout the study. The assignment also provides an opportunity to teach or refresh students on the proper formatting for a friendly letter. And the final letter serves as an assessment of the students' understanding of the character and plot of the book.

A variation or extension of the assignment is to have students pretend to be a character in the book and write a letter to another character in the same novel. Their replies at the end of the novel study can be revealing of students' understanding of the development of that relationship. In another variation, students write an epistolary exchange between two characters from different novels.

Voices

Voices is another creative writing exercise that gets students interacting with the world of the novel during the reading process. In this exercise, they pick a character from the book and write a poem from the character's perspective. I don't focus on poetic devices or anything technical about poetry in this activity. Instead, I ask, "How would this character speak in a poem?" It's interesting to see which characters different students pick and how they take on that character's voice. The responses are lovely and sometimes humorous, and I've had success getting a wide range of readers to write at least a few lines. It need not be long—four lines can be sufficient.

After writing time, we come to the meeting area. I tell students, "When I point to you, begin reading your poem. Give no introduction to your writing; just begin. When I bring my hands together [I bring my hands together in a single clap], pause.

I will point to someone else to read. If I come back to you later, begin reading where you left off the first time." What we get in this activity is a poetic mash-up of different voices of characters from the novel, as interpreted by the students. Hearing the characters' voices juxtaposed with one another can be revealing. Sometimes disparate characters seem to be communicating the same thing. Other times the differences in tone of the characters' thoughts become pronounced.

Moral Dilemma Monologues

Characters in novels often face difficult situations where there are two actions that both seem right on some level but the character can choose only one. I introduce the concept of moral dilemma to students and then ask them to identify a character who experiences one.

I have used this in relation to the film *Swing Kids*, in which all three of the main characters face moral dilemmas around whether to join the Hitler Youth, and each one makes a different choice. Students write a monologue in the voice of the character exploring these two choices. Students have to make clear why the characters feel compelled in two different directions and why each direction seems right on some level. The students can invent minor details to help build out the monologue, but they can't change anything about the story and should make use of the details the author writes into the story. The monologue needs to lead to the choice the character makes. This activity is a good opportunity to teach the concept of a moral dilemma, and it forces students to closely examine a character's internal conflict.

In a variation of this exercise, students can decide for their character, either in keeping with the plot of the novel or departing from it. If the student changes the character's decision, this can lead to an interesting question: What else in the story would have to change if the character makes this decision? Advanced middle school students can even consider ways to foreshadow the revised decision.

Rewriting the World of the Novel

Through whole novel studies, and especially the discussions, students learn that authors have to make many choices in creating a story. Each choice has an impact on the story and also on the reader's experience of that story. The author has an incredible amount of control, and crafting a convincing and compelling story is also an incredibly difficult thing to do well. Middle school students can have a hard time grasping this concept because of the egocentrism of their thinking at their developmental stage. However, adolescents are developing critical thinking, which helps them balance their egocentric thinking and eventually evolve out of it. One of the most effective ways for students to understand that author's craft exists is to try their hand at fiction writing.

I have students begin by using the world the professional author has created in the novel but experimenting with pieces of it in scene-writing exercises. Madeleine Ray calls it "permutating the story."

I want students to play with elements of the story, but it's important that they have read the entire novel before doing this. They need to understand what they're playing with before they do it. For starters, Madeleine always suggests picking a character from the book that you really didn't care for and "kill 'em off!" In other words, write the death of this character into the story! Kids absolutely love this idea. I have never seen every student so thrilled to write. Later, an important analysis question is, "How else would the story have to change if this scene takes place? Would those changes, in the end, make for a better or worse story?"

I suggest exercises that derive from students' responses to the book. For example, if students find the beginning of the book boring, as they sometimes do, I'll give them the option to rewrite the opening scene. If they notice, as they do reading *The Chocolate War*, that there are no female characters in the entire story, have them create a female character. She could be a sister for the main character, Jerry, or a crossing guard, for example. I ask them to play around with writing a scene in which this character enters the story and how this character's arrival might change the rest of the story.

Often students are frustrated because they want to know what happens to the characters after the story. "There should be a sequel to this book!" I hear them say. This is a great chance for students to write the opening scene of the sequel. Then they can think about what else might happen in a sequel. What would the central conflict be?

In these exercises, students can practice their own fiction writing craft while learning about the decisions authors make in story creation. Skills like writing dialogue, describing setting, describing characters' actions, and writing interior monologue can be taught in minilessons during these sessions.

In addition, this assignment can be paired with dramatic improvisation. Through improvisation, we can make the learning three-dimensional for students, get them really playing, and generate ideas for scene writing. For example, if a student is working on adding a character, that student can play his or her character and have a classmate play another character as they improvise a scene. The class can offer feedback or suggestions for what could happen next.

This form of writing, especially when paired with dramatic improvisation, gives students a sense of the immense control they have as writers of fiction. I have found this to have a powerful effect on adolescents. Madeleine has pointed out that one of the reasons kids like video games so much is the feeling of control it gives them. In the virtual world of the video game, they get to drive, whereas in real life, so much is out of their control. Writing fiction seems to give kids, especially boys in my observations, that same sense of their own power.

In some novel studies, we have time to spend several days or a week working on this writing. Other times I don't feel that I can devote that time, but I want students to have the chance to write fiction. A practical short-cut is to have students work on their scenes while half of the class is discussing with me. When I am the only teacher in the classroom, I need a highly engaging but silent activity to keep the other half of the class busy while I run discussion. Writing these scenes has been one of the most successful of these silent group assignments because of the accessibility of the assignment and the high motivation kids feel to write. The drawbacks are that they work without teacher support and that the assignments don't connect as clearly to the criticisms that students raise in discussions of the author's craft. (A sample assignment is in Exhibit 5.2.)

Chris chose to give a scene from *Nobody's Family Is Going to Change*, by Louise Fitzhugh, a makeover. Many students felt that the long section of the novel that revolved around a group called the Children's Army was boring. Chris tends to be a quiet student, but like many of my other students, he shows another side in his creative writing. On page 168 is Chris's twist on the "Children's Army" section of the book.

EXHIBIT 5.2 Scene Writing Assignments *Silent Work!*

Shh . . . your classmates are discussing the novel.

Your Task: Write a fictional scene based on the novel *When You Reach Me*. You will write two scenes over two days.

Length: Each scene should be *at least* one page, but I encourage you to write more.

Your Choices

#1: *Give a Scene a Makeover!* Pick a scene from your novel that you felt was boring. Rewrite it in a more compelling (interesting) way. Give it a title, and explain at the top of the page which scene you're rewriting.

#2: *Kill off a Character!* Pick a character from the book. Write a scene in which that character dies. Make sure to use dialogue, description, and detail.

#3: *Add a Character!* Make up a new character for the novel. Write a scene in which your character enters the novel. Make sure your reader can really picture your character. What does he or she say to the other characters? How do they meet? What kind of personality does he or she have?

#4: *Change the Point of View!* Pick a character from the novel who is NOT the main character. Rewrite a scene from that character's point of view. This could be done in either first person or third person.

#5: *Change the Setting!* What would happen if your novel took place in a different place or time? Rewrite a scene from the novel in a completely different setting. You may change other things in the scene, too. Remember to use dialogue, description of setting, and detail.

Student Gives a Scene a Makeover

As i walked in to the meeting of the childrens army everything was different. There was no longer brigades and people talking, i just saw everyone standing in big cluster, the ones who were talking seemed to intimidate the ones who were not.

I then saw Harrison Carter sitting at a giant chair almost a throne, with the three officers conversing with him. I expected Harrison to address the rally held on thursday. The rally was relatively small and did not draw much public attention. Unfortunately it got out of hand and a riot was started. Not many of us were hurt but severaL police officers were hurt.

Slowly Harrison Carter got up and started to address the crowd here is what he said "Hello Childrens Army i am proud to announce that the rally on thursday was a big success" (Success?,But police officers were assaulted, by us?!) "Unfortunately this has brought some a small amount of public attention, luckily though we posed as the "Young Persons Against War" " This did help us realize that we cannot hold protest in NYC for it is too big of a city." "We have decided to move all of the Childrens Army to a very small and isolated town in Long Island". (Long Island?! Was he mad.

Oddly though no one seemed to protest it, everyone seemed to go along with the plan. Perhaps Harrison had scared them into joining. Why is he suddenly acting like this?" We shall set up a mass camp in the woods surrounding the town posing as boy scout & girl scout troops. If the town tries to kick us out or call the police we will take the town . . . by force if necessary." Thank you and like always Children First!!"

Everyone else gave the salute, but i was too horrified to. A officer gave me a dirty look as i just stood there while everyone else was saluting. After that everyone broke up and i tried to make my way to Harrison, Maybe i could try to talk some sense into him. Two officers tried to stop me but Harrison protested "Let her through" he said. "Sheridan right, how are you".

"What are you talking about moving the Childrens Army, we can't possibly due that, the childrens parents will report us a missing and they will find all of us."

"We've taken care of that" Harrison said a smug look. "We told lies about school retreats and other stuff like that so parents don't grow concerned."

"Still" I said "What are we going to do just sit there forever and have more committees" "Well no will take the town" He replied "But the childrens army does not use violence" I said "Wake up, Sheridan did you really think that "Riot" was an accident?" His face became suddenly serious as i looked at him in horror "We need to send a message and if the only way is with force we will result to that" "How do you even expect to fight a whole town" I said " Our numbers have grown exceptionally and we greatly out number them. " Well am not going and i will stop you"

Harrison slowly stood up and said "You will come with us to our new location, or you . . . will . . . die."

Chris uses strong vocabulary and syntax, and his narrative leads his characters quite naturally into decisions that don't actually take place in the novel, which reflect Chris's active imagination. In addition to these strengths, Chris's work demonstrates a clear need to review some of the rules of punctuation and practice proofreading his own work. When I spoke to him about it, he said, "Yeah, I didn't really know how to do the dialogue, and I usually forget about punctuation even though I know how to do it." I had him edit the parts he knew how to do first, and then I paired him with a classmate who knows well the rules for writing dialogue. I find it's effective to have students work on aspects of writing mechanics in the context of a high-interest assignment like this one.

Emulating Author's Craft

Love them or hate them, all of the authors we read have some aspects of their writing worthy of emulation. In fact, at the close of each novel study, after discussions and writing projects, I ask students to write down some aspects of the author's craft they want to remember for their own writing. We set these up in a chart form with a column for "author," "title," and "craft elements to remember." They add to the chart throughout the year in the back of their notebooks. Many of these strong elements become the basis for creative writing assignments, in which students borrow ideas and make them their own.

Emulating Style

The House on Mango Street, by Sandra Cisneros, has a distinct and inviting style: descriptive language and surprising similes and metaphors to describe places and feelings that are familiar to so many students. It seems to beg for students to try writing about their own lives in this expressive style. In reading this novel, we focus on identifying themes in each vignette and looking at how common themes connect the otherwise disjointed chapters.

To get their feet wet, I often have students write their own version of a single vignette in the book. For example, "My Name" is a powerful piece in which the narrator, Esperanza, illustrates her feelings about her name using figurative language. I read this chapter aloud with students in the meeting area and have them talk about what they notice in the writing. Then I assign them to write an original piece, using similar techniques, about their own names. The writing students produce is full of expression. Sometimes I use "Hairs" instead. It's similar and uses a series of surprising similes about the different kinds of hair of Esperanza's family members. Students enjoy writing their own versions of this one, too.

When students have finished or nearly finished the novel, I assign a creative writing project called variations on a theme (an assignment sheet is in appendix G). In this project, students apply aspects of Cisneros's writing style as well as the structural format of *The House on Mango Street*. Students select a theme that we've identified from the novel (there are many, so this is not a limitation) and write a collection of vignettes, each exploring different people, places, or feelings but connect around this theme. Students choose themes such as home, family, neighborhood, and belonging.

Students write in the first person about topics connected to their own lives but fictionalized by changing details and names. They practice the skills of using descriptive and figurative language and developing a personal voice in their writing. It has consistently been some of the most interesting and powerful writing students do. Some students are able to embed a subtle plot line, as Cisneros does, that develops over the three vignettes. However, it's important in this assignment that students don't write a linear narrative. The objective is for them to connect the pieces thematically, not chronologically. Here is one of Naima's vignettes:

90s BABY

"We all come from the 90s," my older brother, Gavin says. "That's where baggy pants, overalls, huge sweaters, and Lauryn Hill were the deal." I laugh a little. The thought of "baggy pants" being in style seemed a little corny.

I was born in 1999, and my older sister, Abbie was born in 1998. My other older brother, Cedrick says that we're not "real" 90s babies because we have no memories of that decade. I disagree with that claim. But I just love that period of time. All I listen to is Boys 2 Men and Lauryn Hill. All I wear is huge sweaters and big boots. I don't know why the 90s is "my thing", but a lot of people differ from what I think. Maybe it's because of the way church used to be. Or the way "shout music' used to make people jump. Or maybe Lauryn Hill and the Fugees are just too good to be compared to the stuff they play today.

(continued)

(*continued*)

In the 90s, my mom would play the bass or the organ or even the drums in every church service. In the 90s, the heart of man wasn't so desperately wicked with nothing but evil filled inside. In the 90s, our economy wasn't struggling as bad as it is today. The makes me sad; the thought of the way things used to be, and not knowing why they changed.

Sometimes I wish that I could go back in time, so that I could look at things that makes me happy, and just observe and observe and observe. "But you can't," says reality, and I know that reality is right. I try to look on the bright side, eventhough the bright side seems to be getting very dim. It's getting dim because it seems as if nobody cares anymore, and they're just too depressed to think anything matters. The world is suffering from a serious case of depression. Things can still change. I know that they can. The 90s is "my thing" because it brings me back to happier times. I'm an artificial 90s baby to my brothers. So what? I am what I am to myself. And according to me, I *am* a 90s baby.

Here is an example of a student who channels a different aspect of Cisneros's writing: creating rhythm by playing with sentence structure.

DRUNK

The bum hit the car. One car. Two cars. Three cars. That idiot caused the crash. Friday night. That crazy drank to much. He didn't care about us. About our streets. If he did he would have not harmed it. He took off. Speeding down the street. My street. Our street. "licenses plate number 113ky5. Remember that. will ya?" He left. The police. They found the car abandoned, but thats it. Don't even know if they found the bum that hit those cars. Doesn't matter. The fact that this one bum brought the neighborhood together is amazing. the fact that someone called the police is amazing. A neighborhood looking out for each other. I don't know what anyone would do without a community like this. Is it even possible? That bum hit the car. One car. Two cars. Three cars. That idiot caused the crash. Friday night. On the brownstone on 8th street. he broke those cars, but he didn't break our community.

There are other authors whose styles students can learn from and emulate. *Bronx Masquerade*, by Nikki Grimes, for example, is written as a series of monologues from the perspective of different characters, all students in an English class studying poetry. Grimes also includes poems written by each of the characters. When my students in East Harlem read this book, I had each of them create a fictional character in a fictional English class. We collaboratively made up some details about the class for students to reference in their pieces. They wrote a monologue and a poem in the voice of their characters, and then we put them together into a book—our own "East Harlem Masquerade." It was gratifying to see how students wove together elements of their own lives and their imagined characters' lives. They loved reading each other's pieces. It was June, and I made a copy for each student to take with them.

Borrowing Plot Structure

As a child, I wrote stories. They were short at first, and then I started having ideas for longer pieces. I'd write detailed opening scenes that suggested a novel-length story would follow. But I never kept at them. I would quickly lose direction and quit. I didn't know how to make the story live up to my grand vision. In retrospect, what I didn't have any idea how to do was plot a story. Over the years, many of my most avid student writers have come to me for help because they have the same problem. I tell them what Madeleine Ray taught me in graduate school (I didn't even learn much about plotting in college), that all the great plots have already been invented. They are in the folktales. All modern literature is some permutation of these basic archetypal stories.

In the final whole novel study of my eighth-grade class, students study the structure and elements of a classic plot, the journey. After examining multiple journey stories in their reading, they listen to Joseph Campbell's theory on the hero's journey structure through his interviews with Bill Moyers in *The Power of Myth* (2001). Then students synthesize the information by plotting out the general pattern that journey stories take. (See appendix H for a worksheet for this activity.) Students use this knowledge, along with the skills and techniques in fiction writing they've developed over the course of the year, to write original stories with the elements of a classic journey story. (A sample assignment is in Exhibit 5.3.)

EXHIBIT 5.3 Journey Story Writing Project Assignment

Assignment: Write an original fictional story that follows the basic plot structure of the hero's journey. Use descriptive detail and dialogue throughout.
Length: 5 scenes. Each scene should be approximately 2 pages, handwritten.
Due dates: See schedule below. Complete first draft is due Tuesday, May 29. Complete second draft is due Thursday, June 7 (typed).

Scene 1: At Home	Scene 2: Journey Begins	Scene 3: Adventure/ Challenge(s)	Scene 4: Confronting the Challenge	Scene 5: Return Home
Exposition	**Conflict**	**Rising Action**	**Climax**	**Resolution**
Introduce main character and his or her home life. *Describe setting. Use dialogue between characters. There may be hints of conflict.*	A conflict occurs; main character leaves home. (He or she may not know it will be a journey yet.) *Balance dialogue, setting description, with action.*	While away from home, character encounters a new challenge in a new setting. *Describe new setting, probably new characters. What new conflicts could arise here?*	Character confronts final challenge; rising intensity leads to climax of story. *Character may do something heroic. Remember to include dialogue and interior monologue.*	Character returns home, changed as a result of the journey experience. *Use description! What does home look like now? How do characters feel and act toward one another?*
Due Tuesday 5/22	Due Wednesday 5/23	Due Thursday 5/24	Due Friday 5/25	Due Tuesday 5/29

You may choose to add scenes at any point; these are a minimum requirement.

Remember there are four types of conflicts you may use throughout your story:

- Character versus character
- Character versus society
- Character versus self
- Character versus nature

Your story may be a *realistic* journey or it may include elements of fantasy/sci-fi. It may be set in a familiar setting or in a foreign country, time period, or world.

Students are ready at this point to write a story of length, and using a known plot structure is a relief and a catalyst for their writing. I have the class divide their stories into five chapters and require approximately two pages per chapter. A ten-page story sounds like a lot to many students, but they've built up some ability in narrative craft, and even my most struggling writers are successful. Breaking the story into parts that students fully understand through varied reading experiences helps them effectively write longer stories that are well paced. They enjoy crafting multiple settings and creating reasons for the character to move from one place to the next. They have enough practice with scene writing to write dialogue and interior monologue to develop the characters.

In writing fiction, I see my students process the details of their own lives while creating new identities for themselves. They work through emotions and confront conflicts in creative ways in the safe place that the virtual world of fiction provides. Through the whole novels method, students also become immersed in the language of the author, and it influences the quality of their own use of language.

Most important, I want to help my students develop their writing voices and use their voices to say what's on their minds—creatively or critically. The immersive experience of reading many novels throughout the year and the repeated opportunities to construct their own interpretations of these novels in discussions are huge benefits to students as they find their voices as writers.

 Visit https://vimeo.com /61680457 for video 5.1: Connecting to Writing.

PART 2

Making Whole Novels Work in Real-World Contexts

6

Setting Expectations,
Building Accountability
The Launch and Beyond

"Everyone wants to be close to the sun."

When you throw a boomerang, there are several key factors to pay attention to if you want it to return to you in a manner that allows you to catch it. The location, the weather, and the finish of the boomerang are all important, but the most critical factor is the way you release it into the air. The boomerang that is thrown with no technique won't return—or, worse, it can return and hit you right on the head!

In the whole novels program, we send students off into a literary world. We want them to return to us armed with rich experience and increased skill, ready to work together to make meaning of their journey. The organization, expectations,

179

and launch of the study make all the difference in influencing the shape and outcomes of the students' journeys.

LAUNCH A NOVEL WITH A RITUAL

It's 6:45 a.m. and I arrive at school with five boxes of gallon-size clear ziplock bags—one for each student. I'm not an early bird, but today is an exception: I'm preparing the ritual launch of a first whole novel study.

I open a large package of sticky notes and lay them next to the stack of reading schedules with guidelines for sticky notes on the back and the stack of letters to the class. I also pull out bookmarks I've printed on card stock from a template the art teacher created. I pull all of the copies of Sandra Cisneros's *The House on Mango Street* out of the storage space inside one of the three giant meeting area benches and lay them on the table. I check to make sure that all of the books are numbered. I begin stuffing each bag with a copy of the book, the schedule, the letter, a bookmark, and a stack of sticky notes. Often I get help with this from my coteacher or students. However, this is one of those rote teacher tasks that I actually get a little excited about doing. It's meditative as long as I allow enough time. I put the stuffed bags inside several large plastic shopping bags and set them aside until class starts.

After my first class finishes their entry routine, I ring the bell, calling them to the meeting area. Students see "New Novels" on the agenda that is posted daily on the front board.

"What book are we reading?" a student asks excitedly.

"You'll find out in a moment," I say. I like to keep the titles a secret to build up some excitement and suspense. Students are now seated in the meeting area.

"The meeting is now in session," says the class griot, a student with an official classroom job. (The term *griot* comes from West Africa, referring to a historian or storyteller known for vocal expertise.) Another student taps a mallet on the wall two times (imitating a gavel) to signal that meeting area rules are in effect.

"As many of you know, today we begin our first whole novel study of the year. I'm going to give each of you a bag with a copy of the book and everything else you should need for the study inside. When you get your bag, you may take a look through it. Then find the letter. We'll read that together once everyone has a bag." I walk around the meeting area, personally passing each student a ziplock bag with the book inside it.

The ziplock bag method serves a practical purpose of helping students keep their belongings organized and in good condition. It also helps create a metaphor for the reading process. When we send students to read a novel, we are sending them off on a journey of sorts. Like a parent who packs a bag full of the necessities for a safe journey, such as snacks, water, rope, and a pocketknife, I like to think that I am sending my students away to the world of novels with necessary materials for their successful return.

Although I normally let students pass out materials, I keep this task for myself, allowing it to be part of the ritual. By personally handing out a book bag to each student, I send a message that I believe each of them can do this and that I'm interested and invested in each one of their journeys.

 Visit https://vimeo.com /61678473 for video 6.1: Ritual Launch.

Once everyone has received the package, I instruct students to take out the letter.

"Dear eighth graders," I begin. "Kali, please read," I say, and he begins reading. After one paragraph, I call another student's name, and she begins reading, and so it continues (Figure 6.1).

The letter frames the novel study, so its content varies depending on the novel, the particulars of the study, and how it connects to the rest of the curriculum.

Here is a list of what I generally include in the letter introducing a novel study (see Exhibit 6.1 for a sample letter):

- *Introduction to the novel:* A very brief introduction to the novel, author, main character, and something else about the story that I think might catch the students' interest. I might mention an unusual setting, an intriguing conflict, or a theme that doesn't give the story away, or a noteworthy structure. This is my marketing piece.
- *Connection:* A few words about how this book connects to the rest of our curriculum—as long as this doesn't give away the concepts that are ripe for student discovery. I might mention that the novel builds on some of the ideas we came up with in a previous novel study or the history they are learning about in their social studies class.

Figure 6.1 Reading the Letter Aloud

- *Contents:* A list of the items that should be in the bag. Sometimes I omit this later in the year if it's becoming repetitive and I want space on the letter for other information. I always keep the letter to a single page.
- *Expectations:* A description of the expectations for students' reading and notes. Often this is the basic requirement of keeping up with the schedule and writing sticky notes. Sometimes we devote a lot of class time to partner reading; other times, we may have comparatively less reading time in class. Sometimes the format for notes varies.
- *Literary focus:* A suggestion of a literary element or device to pay special attention to, as we'll be focusing on this in class. In the case of *The House on Mango Street*, I note that the plot of the story is not especially clear, so I suggest that students focus on the language, imagery, setting, and themes. Depending on the novel and time of year, I may ask students to keep track of conflicts or characters' changing.
- *Other:* Any other point specific to the novel study. For example, if the book has some explicit content or language, I make a statement about it—perhaps,

"The author put this in the novel because he wanted it to be part of the world of the story, but this does not make it appropriate for our classroom or community." Students and I often share these letters with parents, so it's important to keep them in mind as an audience of the work as well.

- *Encouragement:* I always end by expressing my own excitement about the study, especially about hearing their reactions to the novel in discussions. I sometimes remind students that any reaction to the book is valid—they just need to read it and be able to share their response with the group. If the book is longer or denser than students may be accustomed to, I often add a line about accepting challenge and perseverance.

Exhibit 6.1 is addressed to a group of seventh-grade students who were new to the whole novels program. Exhibit 6.2 is addressed to that same group of students the following year, as eighth graders. Though it was our first novel study of the year, the process was familiar to them. The guidelines for stickies referred to in the eighth-grade letter include two types new to these students: theme notes and language notes.

EXHIBIT 6.1 Letter Introducing the Seventh-Grade Novel Study

Dear seventh graders,

We are beginning our second novel study of the year. For this study, we will all read *When You Reach Me*, by Rebecca Stead. This book was the 2009 winner of the Newbery Medal, the highest award for literature written for kids. It is part realistic fiction, part mystery, with a little science fiction mixed in. I guess you've got to read for yourself to understand! We will focus especially on the characters, exploring the ways in which the events in the book affect them and cause change.

This packet contains the following contents:

- A hard-cover copy of the novel
- A schedule and reading guide
- A bookmark (*Thanks to Ms. Walsh!*)
- Sticky notes (including blue ones)

We will read in class some days and also for homework. You are always responsible for keeping up with the schedule and writing at least four sticky notes for each night of reading. (This applies even if you are absent or if we miss a day of class.) Keep the books in the bag provided. Keep them in good condition, and *bring them to class every day!*

When you finish the entire book, we will begin true discussions (like we did for *The Jacob Ladder*). Bring your honest reactions, questions, and ideas about this book and its story. I look forward to very interesting conversations! This is an unusual and remarkable book—-you've just got to stick with it.

Enjoy!

Ms. Sacks

EXHIBIT 6.2 Letter Introducing the Eighth-Grade Novel Study

Dear eighth graders,

Today we begin our first whole novel study of the year. We will read *The House on Mango Street* by Sandra Cisneros. Organized in short vignettes, it is a novella about a girl named Esperanza who was born in Mexico and lives in a neighborhood in Chicago. In its twenty-seventh year of publication, it has become a modern classic.

In this packet you should find the following:

- A copy of *The House on Mango Street*
- A letter and reading schedule
- Directions for sticky notes
- Sticky notes to get started

We will read portions of the novella aloud in class; however, you are responsible for reading according to the schedule and writing four sticky notes each night. Follow the directions on the Guidelines for Sticky Notes sheet provided [see Exhibit 6.3]. Bring your book to class every day, and keep it in the bag when you are not reading it.

Keep in mind that this book is a little different from others you may have read. It is full of poetic language and imagery, and it is not always clear what is happening or why the author includes each part. It's okay to feel a little confused. Your sticky note guidelines are designed to help you respond with literal, inferential, and critical thinking as usual—but also to keep track of themes in the vignettes and take note of interesting language and its impact on you as you read. Pay special attention to the language of setting in this novel. I hope you are up for trying something different. Let the writer transport you with language!

Looking forward to your honest responses in discussions,

Ms. Sacks, Mr. Brink-Washington, & Ms. Stiman-Lavian

After we read the letter, I ask several simple questions and cold-call on students to answer them. I then ask students to take out the schedule (Exhibit 6.4) and ask, "When are the novels due?" I wait while they locate the due date. "On what day should you be up to page 130?" This easily gets everyone involved and makes sure they are clear about how to read the schedule. I take time to answer questions students may have.

"Can we read ahead?" someone asks.

"As always, the schedule is just a minimum requirement. You may read ahead, and finish the entire book if you like! We just need to make sure everyone has completed the reading in time to participate in discussions."

"Phew!" a few students usually sigh, relieved not to be held back in their reading.

"For those who finish early, we have several seeker opportunities, which we'll talk about later this week." (Read about these opportunities in Chapter 8.)

"If there are no more questions, you may now return to your tables and begin reading. Take a look through the guidelines for sticky notes if you want, but we'll be looking at that together tomorrow."

I send students to their tables to begin reading. It takes a minute or two for students to get settled into the reading, and I allow them some processing time. After all, it's the beginning of a journey. Some want to read through all of the materials in the baggy before starting to read. Others like to place a few blank stickies on the pages to remind them to record their thoughts.

 Visit https://vimeo.com /61680451 for video 6.2: Reading Time.

EXHIBIT 6.3 Guidelines for Sticky Notes

DAILY REQUIREMENT

For each night of reading, you must write at least:

2 open response notes
1 theme brainstorm note
1 language note

DIRECTIONS FOR OPEN RESPONSE NOTES

Open response notes are your basic responses to your reading:

1. You should have a variety of literal, inferential, and critical thoughts in these notes.
2. This is the place to ask questions, voice opinions, record things you notice, summarize, and make connections, for example.

DIRECTIONS FOR THEME BRAINSTORM NOTES

In theme brainstorm notes, after you finish reading a vignette:

1. Make a list on your sticky note of all the themes or ideas you think the author is bringing up in this vignette. Some examples of themes are hope, neighborhood, identity, oppression, and friendship.
2. After you make the list, circle the one you think is most important to this vignette.

DIRECTIONS FOR LANGUAGE NOTES

In language notes, after you have finished reading a vignette:

1. Find a sentence that really stands out to you as strong, interesting, or evocative (bringing out emotions).
2. Copy that sentence in quotation marks onto the sticky note. Put the page number in parentheses at the end.
3. Explain why you chose this sentence. What is your response or connection to it?
4. Explain what you notice about how the author has written this sentence. What makes it strong or interesting?

EXHIBIT 6.4 Whole Novel Reading Schedule for
***The House on Mango Street*, October**

Monday	Tuesday	Wednesday	Thursday	Friday
10/3 Read the opening of Bradbury's *Martian Chronicles*; setting writing exercise	10/4 Read pp. 3–20	10/5 Read pp. 21–38	10/6 Read pp. 39–78	10/7 Read! No school
10/10 Read! No school	10/11 Read pp. 79–102	10/12 Read pp. 102–110	10/13 Books due!	10/14 Discussions/ writing begins
10/17 Discussions/ writing	10/18 Discussions/ writing	10/19 Discussions/ writing	10/20 Writing celebration	10/21

I send the class librarian around with each student's library page from the sign-out binder that sits on a shelf. Students must record the title, book number, and date on their sheet. I also send my teacher's assistant around with a marker for each table and instructions for students to write their names on the outside of the ziplock bag to make them easy to identify. Some students take time to write their name in special lettering or surround their names with hearts. I allow this as well (to a point).

With some books and groups of students, I'll read the first page or few pages aloud. Sometimes this is a tool to help students get located in a challenging beginning of a book. Other times the purpose is to hook students' interests with an engaging reading and give a sense of the tone of the opening.

 Visit https://vimeo.com /61681631 for video 6.3: First Page Read Aloud.

Figure 6.2 Reading Time

Within a few minutes, everyone has usually begun reading. Occasionally I feel the need to make a quick announcement to let all students know it's time to start: "I see that almost everyone has begun reading. We'll now have quiet reading time for the next fifteen minutes" (Figure 6.2).

The study is launched.

Students look forward to the ritual launch of a whole novel study. They are curious about the world they'll be entering, excited about the autonomy they'll have over the reading process, and anticipate the stimulating discussions they'll engage in together once they emerge from the literary world. A definitive initiation of the study helps to reinforce and capitalize on this excitement.

HOW TO MAKE SURE THE BOOMERANG RETURNS

When I went through the steps of the ritual launch of my first novel study, my students were excited when I passed out the books. They liked seeing the schedule, which created some known future points in an otherwise nebulous, though positive, class run by a first-year teacher. They seemed happy to start reading in class on that first day.

For the next three weeks, however, I have no recollection of how we used the class time. I may have occasionally given students a portion of a period to read, though not much. There were some hopeful signs. Two girls skipped into class after a few days saying, "Miss, this book is soooo good! Do you have more like this?" But I had very little notion of how the majority of my students were doing.

When the books were due, I set up discussions—and it was quickly clear that many students had not read past the first few pages.

Madeleine Ray was visiting my classroom that day, and she saw the confusion on my face. "May I make a suggestion?" she said from the side of the room. I nodded. "Why don't you make a small group for the people who finished the book. The rest of the class can sit at their tables and work on the reading."

We did just that. I didn't treat the students who hadn't read punitively. This was one of those situations where I, the teacher, had missed something important. I didn't want to start blaming kids when I didn't understand what happened. We made a circle of desks and seven students sat with me for discussions. The others read quietly.

Those discussions went well. Madeleine sat with the discussion group, observing. In a little while, there was another surprise.

"I finished!" a boy called from the next table over. He had been reading steadily since he'd been given the chance.

"Great! Join us!" I said. He did, and his comments demonstrated that he'd indeed completed the book. By the end of the period, several other students had finished the book and joined the discussion.

That day provided a powerful demonstration of two things. First, as Madeleine put it, "Everyone wants to be close to the sun. And you, the teacher, are the sun." The discussion circle was a powerful motivator for my students, and it wasn't about the grade they would get. It was about attention, belonging, and the chance to express ideas. The students wanted to do this and might have done the reading if they had understood what would follow. Second, if I wanted everyone to read the whole book, I had a lot to learn: some of my students later told me they'd never before read an entire novel on their own.

The first thing I learned is that though children want to succeed, their paths are often not predictable. A boomerang, if crafted perfectly and thrown well in ideal weather, will return, and all we have to do is stand there while it makes its journey. But kids come in all shapes and sizes, and the weather changes. We can't just stand there. At the same time, we can't do the work for students or overstructure the experience to the point that they can't enjoy the story.

In this section, I describe the structures I use to support the whole class during the reading period of the whole novel study, so that they have a successful journey and return. (In Chapter 8, I'll turn to the supports I offer individual students.)

Give Students Reading Time

One thing I knew for sure was that I needed to get students to read at home. For many, this did not appear likely at first. Some were not accustomed to reading much at all, and especially not at home, where there could be all kinds of other distractions. I talked to each of them about finding a quiet place at home or at the library to read, but this wasn't nearly enough. I needed to create a new habit of reading for my students. How do you form new habits? Practice.

I came to the conclusion that I wouldn't be able to influence my students to read at home if we weren't also reading in class. That's one of the golden rules of teaching: you have to spend time on the things that you think matter. Saying it isn't enough. You have to *show* students what matters. If organization matters, you don't just tell kids to be organized; you have to devote class time to it. If vocabulary matters, you have to pause regularly to notice new words or carve out time for formal word study. If the way students treat one another in class matters, you have to spend time talking about how we should interact and working on it when conflicts arise. If I wanted my students to read at home, we would begin by developing the habit of reading at school.

How obvious this seems today. However, in my own middle school, teachers did not give me time to read in school. It was against some unwritten principle that if the teacher wasn't talking in front of the room, it wasn't really teaching. And so that's how we studied literature: with the teacher talking in front of the room and me reading a different book or writing notes to my friends under my desk.

I started giving students regular class time to read—independently, in partners, and sometimes as a whole group. Although reading time every day is ideal, it's not always possible with all of the curricular demands of English language arts. I've found that three days a week works well, and students can make up the difference outside class. With fewer than three days, students seem to disconnect from the practice and their books.

During a novel study, reading is not always the focus of our class activities. Sometimes we work on writing, a miniproject related to the novel, watching a film, or reading a supplemental text. To balance this out, I usually give students the first ten minutes of class to read independently. This is a relaxing way to start class, and students are happy to have the time to read.

> **The Silence of Everyone Reading**
> The silence of everyone
> reading
> at once
> is not a fearful silence,
> but one more like flying . . .
> breathing air of the same
> room/
> different worlds;
> the language is more
> influential
> even than our eyes.
> Who does not belong here?
> Only maybe me—
> standing at the runways
> directing lift-offs and landings
> and staying out of the way
> of the silence of
> everyone reading
> —*Ariel Sacks*

During quiet reading time, I often spot-check notes or confer with students about their reading. But I also like to sit and watch my students read or read silently along with them.

Some teachers may feel this isn't teaching anything and therefore isn't a good use of class time. I think it sends a message to students that the most important thing we can do right now is read. (In Chapter 8, I outline the ways I support individual students during reading time.)

Expect Students to Meet the Deadline

The first and most important expectation is that students read the novel and complete it by the due date. When I talk to teachers about the whole novels program, the most frequent concern I hear is, "What if they don't read it?"

This is a reasonable question. However, one important aspect of these conditions is the teacher's expectation of the students. In fact, research shows teachers' expectations of student success increase students' chances of success substantially.

With appropriate book selection, positive relationships with students, structure, and support, we can realistically expect all of our students to read a novel. It's worth taking a moment to make a cognitive shift toward this idea. Otherwise we're simply avoiding what we really want students to be able to do for fear they might not do it. The whole novels program requires that we purposely aim high and then take on the challenge of helping all students succeed in getting there. The trajectory will look different for different students, but it starts with our expectation that they take on the challenge and our belief that they can do it.

Resolve the Homework Conundrum: Expect Students to Read at Home

With the schedule, I set out the minimum requirements for reading each day. I make it clear to students that whatever they don't read in school, they must read for homework. Students seem to like the idea that they can manage the time however works best for them. This policy also helped me solve the tricky question of homework.

As a beginning teacher, I often didn't know what to assign for homework. Some assignments made a lot of sense, because they were things that needed to be done outside school, such as interviewing a parent about something. Other times I just felt pressure to assign something because of expectations from my school and even my students; there was a sense that "serious classes" assigned a lot of homework. I found myself making up questions at the last minute and then forgetting to collect the homework.

Research shows that there is little academic or developmental benefit to homework for homework's sake. Alfie Kohn writes extensively about this in his book, *The Homework Myth: Why Our Kids Get Too Much of a Bad Thing* (2007). But research, such as the 2007 National Endowment for the Arts report, "To Read or Not to Read: A Question of National Consequence," also shows that regular reading for pleasure is one of the greatest predictors of academic success, as well as financial and employment success. Veda Jairrels, author of *African Americans and Standardized Tests: The Real Reason for Low Test Scores* (2009), argues that reading time and, especially for older students, reading for pleasure, is the single action that would make the most difference for African American students' academic success.

In my second year of teaching, I solved the homework issue with a simple and meaningful assignment: the homework is always reading. This assignment is consistent whether we are in a whole novel study or an independent reading cycle. Either way, the requirement is roughly fifteen pages per day (or night). When I taught transitional English Language Learners (ELLs), the requirement was ten pages, but I have increased it to fifteen for a general education classroom. Toward the end of the year, I often increase the pace to about twenty pages per day for novel studies if I am confident my students can handle it.

Sometimes this homework assignment is confusing for students. A few days into a novel study in one year, I was surprised to discover that a student who was otherwise quite motivated had not read a lick of his book outside class. When I asked him what was going on, he first said, "I don't know."

"Well," I started, "you haven't been doing your homework . . . "

"Oh no," he said. "I do all my regular homework. I just don't do my reading outside school." This was an eye-opener for me! We also had a Latin roots vocabulary workbook that students were working on in and out of school. In his mind, the workbook was "the regular homework," because it looked like regular homework. This served as a reminder that my reading expectations also required a cognitive shift on the part of many of my students.

I occasionally add other homework activities, such as vocabulary workbooks (which students love finding ways to get done during the school day). Reading is the homework staple for my class because it is a worthwhile habit and because we really cannot read a lot of literature if students don't put in some time out of school. I've known a few teachers who read novels aloud to their middle school students. This can be a great experience for kids, but I'm always struck by the amount of time it takes to get through a novel, especially if it's not a daily immersive experience. One teacher read *To Kill a Mockingbird* aloud to his students for three months. Neither teachers nor students really want to be stuck in one book for so long. In order to avoid this, we must help our students develop the practice of reading both in and outside school.

Set Clear Expectations for Reading Notes

In Chapter 3, I described the habits of response I teach my students to develop as they read. Essentially students record the literal, inferential, and critical thoughts they have as they read on sticky notes. By the end of that first novel study nine years ago, some students had written lots of sticky notes, fully embracing the practice; others had written just a few when it had been part of an in-class assignment. Though the reasons for their incomplete work were varied, one reason seemed to be a lack of understanding of what—or how much—exactly they were expected to do. On the one hand, I didn't want to designate an arbitrary number of sticky notes they needed to write each night. I wanted students to respond when they had a reaction. On the other hand, I wanted to rule out confusion or avoidance as an obstacle. Also, when I read an interesting book, I felt capable of making a comment on just about every page, as some of my students were already doing, because there are so many layers to comment on.

As I was deliberating over how to set a clear expectation for sticky notes that I could hold students accountable for, I wandered into a colleague's classroom. She was also an English teacher who used sticky notes with her students. When I explained my problem, she told me that she had her students write a minimum of three sticky notes per night in their independent reading books. During reading time, she would walk around and read her students' notes, getting a peek into each student's experience of his or her book and using the notes as a starting place for her reading conferences. She would also note a homework grade for each student on her clipboard as she made her rounds. Apparently this system was working quite well, and I liked the clarity it provided students. I thought, *If that's what it will take to ensure that everyone reads and respond daily, then that's what I'll do.*

I began requiring a minimum three sticky notes per day, along with the reading. That was with transitional ELLs. I now require fifteen to twenty pages of reading and at least four notes. Exhibit 6.5 shows what my daily homework board during a novel study most often looks like.

Check In with the Whole Class

The success of the whole novels program, and reading in general, depends on the students' experiences. I meet with and assess the work of individual students, but I also want to keep my finger on the pulse of the class in general so that I can build on successes and make adjustments as needed. One way I take the temperature of the whole class is through an informal conversation in the meeting area. In the days following the launch of a novel study, I call a class meeting and simply ask students, "How's the reading going?" I listen to what they have to say and respond to questions and concerns.

When the book has a difficult or slow beginning, I remind students that the author is introducing elements of the story (the literary term for this being *exposition*) and urge them to stick with it because something will definitely happen soon! I encourage them to note their reactions, both positive and negative, to the story and author's ability to tell it well. Other times

> ### EXHIBIT 6.5 Reading Homework Board
>
> An example of an assignment for a whole novel study:
>
> **Tonight's Homework**
>
> - Read pgs. 121–137+
> - Write 4+ sticky notes
>
> An example of an assignment for an independent reading cycle:
>
> **Tonight's Homework**
>
> - Read 15+ pgs. in your book
> - Write 4+ sticky notes

 Visit https://vimeo.com /61680452 for video 6.4: Whole Class Check-In.

students are shocked by a provocative event in the story and feel the need to comment and process a little bit with the group. I have a check-in at least once a week, sometimes more frequently during novel studies, but I don't let them go on too long. Five minutes is usually about right. When an interesting conversation about the book emerges, I say, "Wow, this is so interesting! Let's remember this topic for our discussions next week." This builds up excitement for the seminar discussions.

When important issues come up in these brief conversations, I often get ideas for additional activities that can help support students along the way (see Chapter 7 for examples of these activities). At other times, these conversations just help students feel heard—which is important and motivating for adolescents. Finally, although students are reading the books mostly independently, these check-ins help strengthen the group process within the novel study.

I also have students write biweekly reflections in which they share thoughts and responses to various threads of our class. This provides an additional outlet for students to share their thoughts and offer feedback on the curriculum. Anna, a student who is often quiet during meetings, wrote this in her weekly reflection about a book we had just started: "At first I couldn't understand a lot of the words in the book, but then I saw that there was a type of 'dictionary' at the beginning that defined most of the slang words that were in the book. The dictionary helped a lot." After reading that, I asked her to share her discovery with the whole class the next day, which she happily did. The lesson is to always be listening and find ways to use student feedback to propel the study forward.

Give Feedback in Real Time

It's impossible for me to "check reading homework" every night, because students would have to give me their books, which would leave them unable to read that night. Instead, I spot-check informally during reading time. I spend time sitting with students and reading their notes. At the beginning of the year, I make an effort to get around to every student several times per week. I read their notes and assign a homework grade on a scale of 1 to 4. If the student has read the required pages, written the required notes, and the notes show evidence of literal comprehension, inferential thinking, and critical thinking about the story, I give the student a 4. This is really a placeholder grade. I write it on a clipboard and tell the student what grade I've given and why, but it doesn't go into my grade book. The purpose of this grade is to show students that the sticky notes do "count," to keep tabs on who is keeping up with the work, and to give some initial feedback about the quality of the notes.

I tend to go easy on them in this beginning stage, while they are still learning the three kinds of thinking, and give out lots of 4s when students have done the work reasonably well. If a student is only summarizing, for example, I'll give him or her a 3 and say, "I notice that you're doing a great job writing down what is happening in the book. For tonight, work on adding some of your own thoughts, opinions, and questions as you read." I have students do a lot of self and peer assessment of their notes, so these quick conversations are more of a reminder to students that I will hold them accountable for completing the work and for the quality of their responses. I always catch some students in the beginning who do the reading but don't write sticky notes, thinking it won't matter. The spot checks generally prompt students like this to complete the assignment that night—and beg me to check their work again the next day.

This is another reason it's crucial that I know my students as readers before beginning the first novel study. I need to know the difference between a student who is avoiding the work because he or she has not yet built a solid habit of reading and a student who is avoiding it because he or she is unable to read the text. Obviously these students require totally different approaches. Knowing my students' reading levels before beginning a novel study allows me to plan ahead to make the texts accessible to students who read far below grade level, so that I'm not discovering major skills deficits once the study has begun or embarrassing struggling readers by misunderstanding the reasons for their behavior.

In addition, I collect students' books and assess their work in more detail. It is quite time-consuming at first, because I need to get the book back to the students the following day, but it is worth the investment. These formative assessments help students understand the expectations for their annotations, identify areas that need improvement, work to improve them, and see the results fairly quickly.

The rubric I start with is in worksheet 6.1. In novel studies that use structured note types, I add a field to the rubric that corresponds to the skills students practice in the notes—for example, "Analyzes conflict" or "Engages with language."

At the beginning of the year, I invest the time to give students feedback using the rubric in the first independent reading cycle and the first whole novel study. I collect and grade once per week, or try to check everyone formally during class throughout a week. Assessing notes during class is ideal for conserving time, but it's not always possible. When I collect all 105 of my students' books, though, it takes me about seven hours to get through all of them. This is not fun and not sustainable! Nevertheless, it is an investment to set my students' habits. I sometimes do this in one marathon evening and the following morning. Other times, I break it up and collect work from a class each day, putting in one or two hours every afternoon and just have a heavy week of grading. In my current position, I've been able to get help with this grading from my coteachers; scheduling the "grading party" in advance makes this more enjoyable, and with more people, it goes much faster.

As students internalize the habits and process, I'm able to formally assess less frequently. I move quickly to a combination of informal spot-checking and quick conferences with students during class, a midway official homework check, that

Worksheet 6.1 Rubric for Sticky Notes

Name_____ Date_____

Book Title(s) _____

_____

		4	3	2	1
Reading habits total: _____	Reading in class				
	Completed required pages				
	Completed required sticky notes for the night				

		4	3	2	1
Reading process/quality response total: _____	Evidence of literal comprehension				
	Evidence of inferential (thoughtful) response to text				
	Evidence of critical thinking (asking important questions, forming opinions, making meaningful connections)				

Grade: _____

Comments: _____

_____

goes in the grade book, and the real, summative assessment at the end of the study when the books are due completed.

When I collect books midway through a study, I don't spend long on each one. I look for completion and then read through some of the notes to get a sense of the style and quality of the students' work. I leave a homework grade and brief comment. This can be done in one or two minutes per book, or about three hours for all my students.

After the first or second novel study, depending on how well students demonstrate their understanding of the annotation process and the expectations for the quality of their responses, I stop using the rubric officially. I don't stop assessing the same things, so the rubric is still in effect, but I move more quickly through the process, giving a more general grade that reflects a combination of the factors on the rubric. I write comments and a percentage grade on a sticky note and attach it to the front of each student's book to return to them. My comments include strengths, an area to improve or stretch their thinking, and sometimes a response to their ideas about the book. I find this method much more personal and don't think much meaning is lost by dropping the rubric as a feedback form.

> How long is your class period? When I taught ninety-minute blocks every day, I gave about thirty minutes of reading time every day. I checked and graded students' sticky notes during class almost every day. There was no need to collect books, and students always got immediate feedback. Now I have only fifty minutes per class, so I give ten to thirty minutes of reading time two or three times a week. During that time I spot-check, but usually can't get around to everyone. That's why I need to collect the books once a week.

Communicate through Grades

Philosophically I'm not a fan of grading. I'd rather help students set goals for themselves and learn to monitor their own progress while giving them feedback along the way. I worry that grades create and reinforce a system of external reward that does not motivate students to take risks and think critically and creatively. However, I work in a school system that requires grading in the traditional sense, and it's likely that I always will. (There are many other sweeping changes I can see taking place in the educational landscape before grading goes away.)

Since I must assign grades, and ultimately everything gets distilled into one number for an entire marking period of work, it's important that the grades are reflective of what's most meaningful in my curriculum. Little is more important than students reading in my class, whether in whole novel studies or independent reading cycles. A student who doesn't read has not really experienced the curriculum, and his or her contributions to the classroom community are limited. I've experimented with different categories in the grade book and assigned different weights for these categories. What doesn't change is the requirement of reading. I always look at my categories and think, *Would it be possible for a student not to read and pass the class?*

Here are all of the things that relate to the reading and are represented somewhere in my grade book:

- Sticky notes
- In-class reading
- Participation in novel discussions
- Writing projects related to the novels
- Contributions to group miniprojects related to novels

The single number grade is pretty vague, but I make sure that my categories are weighted so that it would not be possible for a student to somehow skip reading and still pass English class. Like many other teachers, my school uses an online grade book that allows me to create weighted categories. Instead of separating homework and class work, I have a category for reading notes and whole novel discussions. This category counts for 30 percent of a students' overall grade. Another category, writing projects, counts for 25 percent of the overall grade. In a progress report, the category averages provide a picture of where a student might be falling short. If reading completion is the main issue, it becomes clear with these category weights.

Grades are an established way of communicating with students about what works and what doesn't in the classroom and in their learning. And yet they get a lot of mixed messages through grades. I think of Leon, for example. At the beginning of the year, he told me he didn't much like reading and that he never really read books for his classes in the past. He was a student who had no significant deficits in his ability to decode and comprehend texts; he just felt that there wasn't anything in it for him and he'd rather not bother with it. That marking period, Leon did all of his other work for English class. He participated in lessons and activities related to the novel study and read a little bit during class. When it was time to turn in his book to be graded, there were no notes in it, and he received no credit. He did not participate in discussions because he had not completed the reading. He ended up with a 60 percent overall grade on his first progress report.

Leon seemed embarrassed about this outcome, as if the grade didn't match his perception of himself as a student. I, too, was surprised at how completely he had missed the mark given his ability. I met with him and his parents, and we talked about the reasons for his low grade and what he needed to do differently. In the next novel study, I noticed that he wrote a few notes during class but still wasn't completing his work outside class and quickly fell far behind.

A few days before the book was due, I asked him to stay after class. I called his mother and asked him to explain to her what was going on with his reading. In that same embarrassed tone, Leon told his mother that he hadn't kept up with the reading schedule and that the book was due in two days and he needed to catch up. He returned the phone to me. His mother thanked me, and she assured me that Leon would have the time and space to catch up. Leon's embarrassment seemed to dissolve. He smiled and nodded and said, "I'm gonna finish by Thursday. Don't worry." I must have looked a little uncertain that this could be done, because he added, "Just watch, Ms. Sacks."

On Thursday, Leon came bounding into English class with his book in hand. He practically slammed it down on the table in front of me enthusiastically.

"What does this mean?" I asked him, my curiosity piqued.

"I told you I'd finish," he said smiling. I thumbed through the book, scanning the sticky notes. I was worried about the possibility that he'd written a bunch of notes without actually reading the book. That happens once in a while, and it's always a big disappointment for both the student and me when I discover it. The notes looked pretty good, but I wasn't completely convinced. I'd need to read them in more detail. But first we would have discussions.

When Leon participated in discussion that day, all my doubts faded. Not only was he insightful with his comments, he became a leader of the group. He had an incredible memory for detail (perhaps because the entire book was so fresh in his mind) and easily offered specific passages as evidence for points he and his classmates made. He even built on classmates' ideas about symbolism in the novel. I was impressed.

Leon received 100 percent on his notes and participation in discussion and brought his grade into the 80s by the end of the marking period. More important, from then on, he seemed to understand the expectation of the whole novels work and put effort into meeting it. He did have a tendency to procrastinate a bit, but he always followed through and did well.

I believe that in his case, the grade was an important factor in his turnaround. It painted a blunt picture of him as a student that he and his family didn't like. He knew he could change that picture, and he received the support and push he needed to do it. Though I'd love to believe this would have happened without the grade, sometimes the blunt communication of a single number grade is the quickest way to get the point across.

Collaborate with Families

Leon's story underscores how important it is to be able to collaborate with families about their child's work in the whole novels program. Parents in all three schools where I've worked have been a huge support for me over the years, and I try to reach out to them in several ways throughout the year. Parents are usually looking for ways to help their child do well in school and keep up with assignments. Middle school students, however, are looking for increased autonomy from their parental figures and don't always communicate easily with adults about their academic responsibilities.

I try to help parents keep up with their students' work in English class by keeping the homework assignment simple and consistent: reading about fifteen pages and responding on sticky notes each night. I send a letter home for students and parents explaining the homework policy (worksheet 6.2).

I also talk to parents on curriculum night, on the phone, and in parent conferences about how they can help their child with this work. The common complaint I hear from parents is, "I ask my child if he's done his homework, and he always tells me it's done! Then I find out later that wasn't true. I don't know what else to do, though." I have two pieces of advice for parents about this issue.

Worksheet 6.2 Eighth-Grade English Reading Policy

Reading is essential to the study of English language arts and the advancement of students' literacy skills. For this reason, students are required to become active readers and build a practice of reading both in and out of school.

On most days this year, the *required homework* for English class each night will be the following:

1. Read a minimum of *fifteen pages each day/night* in your current book.

2. Record your understanding of and responses to the reading on *4 sticky notes*, which you place on the exact pages in the book to which they refer. Students are encouraged to respond honestly to the books and are entitled to their own opinions and experiences of all texts.

3. *During independent reading units*, students may choose an appropriate level book from the classroom library. *During whole novel studies*, students will be assigned a book to read with the whole class.

4. Students are required to *bring their current book to class every day* in the plastic bag provided. (This protects the condition of the book.)

5. Typically during reading units, we will devote some class time to read on *Mondays, Wednesdays, and Fridays*. However, reading is required every day (and one day of the weekend), totaling seventy-five pages of reading per week.

6. Students' *reading grade* will count as 30 percent of the overall English language arts grade and be based on the following:
   a. completing the required reading and notes on time,
   b. the quality of the responses and thoughts on the notes,
   c. reading in class and conferences with the teacher, and
   d. participation in literature discussions and related activities.

I have read and understand the reading policy. I will share my questions or concerns with Ms. Sacks should they arise.

Student signature _____ Date_____

Parent signature _____ Date_____

First, when parents want to check their child's homework, which many middle school parents are interested in doing, they can begin by asking to see their child's book and reading schedule. I provide students a reading schedule for whole novel studies, and they fill out their own schedules for independent reading cycles. Caregivers can read their child's sticky notes, or just check to see that they are on schedule with their reading and annotations. This is far more helpful than asking the student for a yes or no response to whether the homework is done.

Second, I want to move parents away from the yes-or-no question of "Did you do it?" toward more qualitative questions that can start a conversation between parents and students about reading. Middle school students often resist parental supervision of their homework; however, they usually do want attention from parents and may respond better to engagement about the content of the reading. I often suggest that parents ask, "What's happening in your book?" and follow up. Often this leads to topics of conversation students will rarely bring up on their own with parents but that are interesting and important. This type of conversation can take place in English or another language. Non-English-speaking parents often feel lost as to how to engage with their children about schoolwork. I encourage them to start a conversation with their child about their reading in their home language.

I created the handout in Exhibit 6.6 about this for English teachers at my school to distribute to parents at our conferences. See appendix B for a version in Spanish.

In addition to relaying these tips to caregivers, I send out e-mail newsletters to families when we begin a new novel study, which includes the reading schedule and guidelines for sticky notes. I hand a printed copy to students whose families do not have access to e-mail. Parents respond, expressing appreciation for the updates and sometimes with specific questions about their child's work. The e-mail creates an opportunity for another layer of parent support for the work.

EXHIBIT 6.6 Letter to Parents about Reading

TALK TO YOUR CHILD ABOUT THE READING

Your student has assigned reading every night. Get involved in their homework and academic progress by talking to your child about their daily reading!

PROVIDE A QUIET TIME AND SPACE FOR READING

Make sure there is a time and place each night where your child can focus on reading. Turn off television, video games, and the Internet for reading time.

ENGAGE IN CONVERSATION ABOUT READING

Ask your child to tell you about his or her book:

- Avoid the question, "Did you do your reading homework?"
- Replace it with, "What happened in your book today?"
- Show interest by asking follow-up questions about the story, its characters, and conflicts.
- Ask your child what he or she thinks of the characters in the book, or the book in general.

This is a wonderful, neutral way to have conversations with adolescents about a wide variety of issues, as they become more independent. (Book discussions can be done in any language!)

DEVELOP A RELATIONSHIP AROUND BOOKS

The following activities can help build rich relationships with your child around reading that will increase his or her motivation to read:

- Find out what kind of books your child enjoys. Take a trip to a bookstore or library to select exciting new books to read.
- Read together. Have your child read aloud to you, or read aloud to him or her from the chosen book.
- Share a book you are reading or have read with your child.
- Read silently at the same time. When your child reads his or her book, take out your book and read in a quiet place together. Then have a conversation about what you are reading.

■ ■ ■

The whole novels program gives students immeasurable opportunities to grow as readers and members of a learning community, but they will thrive only if certain conditions are in place. Clear framing of expectations for student participation, structures for accountability, and layers of support for students, including collaboration with families, are all essential elements of a student's successful journey through a whole novel.

In the next chapter, I share the collaborative activities I design to support and challenge small groups of students during the reading process. In Chapter 8, I address the ways in which I work with individual students who need support or additional challenge to grow in the whole novels program.

PARTS OF THE WHOLE

My Classroom Setup

Throughout this book, I refer to aspects of my classroom configuration that are unusual for upper-grade teachers and support the activities in my program. The physical layout of a learning environment is an important factor

 Visit https://vimeo.com /61990643, video P6.1: Classroom Tour.

in teaching, and often overlooked. Here I explain how and why I set up my room this way and offer some alternatives for teachers who may not have these space capabilities.

AREAS OF THE ROOM

Meeting Area

At the front of my room, I create a space for the whole class to meet with three large benches in a U-shape around the front board (Figure P6.1). There is a carpet in the middle of the benches. Each seats five to six students. Ideally we would all fit in one meeting circle, but my classes have about twenty-five students; to accommodate everyone, I allow a few students to sit on chairs in the circle between the benches, and others sit on the rug in front of the benches. I sit in a chair in front of the board, where I can project from a laptop or write on the board. The meeting area creates a space for whole-class activities, lessons, and discussions, where the acoustics make it easy for everyone to be heard and (almost) everyone can see each other without turning around.

My benches were built by a carpenter for fellow Bank Street alumna and teacher of whole novels, Nancy Toes Tangel. (She gave them to me when she left classroom teaching to consult.) They have storage space inside, and I use them to house class sets of novels throughout the year when we are not using them. In the past, I used three benches I bought from IKEA. The Norden benches cost seventy dollars each and lasted me six years. Cushions are cheap and add a lot to the environment.

Table Groups

In the rest of the room, I arrange the individual student desks in clusters of four (Figure P6.2). The meeting area takes up quite a bit of real estate in the classroom,

Figure P6.1 Meeting Area

but the clusters help maximize the rest of the space and create easy pathways for people to move around the room. The table groups are also important because they allow frequent collaboration, both formal and informal, between students in their table groups. I've used tables before, and I like the simple, unified quality they have; the benefit of individual desks is that each student's personal area is clearly marked, and we can occasionally pull the desks apart and create rows for occasions such as tests.

Classroom Library

Along one wall, three bookshelves form a classroom library space. On the bookshelves are bins that hold the books, labeled by genre, author, or any other category that might spark students' curiosity. The bins make it easy for students to browse. I allow students to check out and return books from the library at the beginning of class or during any reading time. I have also been in a classroom without the

Figure P6.2 Table Groups

bookshelves I needed to create this type of library. Then I lined the windowsills with bins and created a library that way. The only problem was we had to make sure to close the windows when it rained!

INDISPENSIBLE ACCESSORIES

Laptop Wheelie Desk

I have a small desk on wheels made for a laptop that I keep in the front of the room. I use it in the meeting area to hold my laptop, speakers, pencils, markers, and other paraphernalia. Without some kind of surface, I can't effectively use projection in the meeting area, but I can't use anything large like a regular teacher desk because it would take up too much space in the meeting area. I have a normal teacher desk at the back of the room. I almost never use it during class time. Laptop desks run about forty dollars.

Carpet Remnant

A carpet is a great classroom accessory for any age group. Many students love the opportunity to read on a rug, and it makes the room softer, physically and acoustically. I have been able to get several free carpet remnants donated from a local carpet store when I explain my purpose.

Carpet Sweeper

My carpet gets very dirty with more than one hundred students walking over it all day every day. But I teach in a secondary school, where most teachers do not have carpet and therefore custodians don't have regular vacuum duties. I have a manual carpet sweeper that easily cleans dirt and lint off the carpet. It makes no noise, and students love to clean the carpet. Carpet sweepers run about forty dollars as well.

Four Crates—and a Few Heavy Cloth Bags

Most teachers have at least some crates, which come in handy for all kinds of things. Mine are specifically for collecting students' books to assess their sticky notes. I have four classes, and I need to keep the books separated by class. I also need a place for these for the days when I have the books, or else they will pile up somewhere and make the room feel chaotic. Four crates, color-coded by class, solve the problem. Crates are about eight dollars each, but sometimes can be gotten for free from delicatessens or other stores. I also have a collection of heavy cloth material bags for times when I take home a bunch of books to grade.

HOW WE USE THE SPACE THROUGHOUT A PERIOD

The following sections outline the general routine my classes follow during one period. There are many days where we depart from the routine—whole novel discussions, being one example—but most days follow this structure.

Entering Class

When students enter the room, they sit at their assigned desks, which are arranged in groups of four. They get settled, copy their homework assignment for that night from the board, and take out their homework and other materials for class. There are directions on the tables for the opening activity. Most often this activity is reading.

Meeting

After the allotted time, which ranges from five to fifteen minutes, depending on the opening activity, I ring a Tibetan meditation bell. This signals to students to come to the meeting area. If I ring the bell twice, it means to bring their book or notebook (depending on what the opening activity was).

Students have regular spots in the meeting area that correspond to their table group and switch throughout the year when I change the assigned seats at the tables. At the beginning of the year, I call students to the meeting area table by table, and we spend time working on the transition. At this point, I ring the bell, and students know where to sit and do so efficiently.

The meeting is for minilessons, whole-class discussions, student presentations, checking in with the class on how their work is going, and discussing classroom issues in a democratic fashion. I have strict but simple community rules, which I borrowed from fellow Bank Street alum and teacher of whole novels, Nancy Toes Tangel. Her students created these rules:

1. Listen to classmates and teachers.
2. Raise your hand to speak/take turns.
3. No private conversation.
4. Respect personal space.

We have a clear process for responding to "errors" made by students with respect to these rules, which involves leaving the meeting for that day and following up with a quick conversation with me. (For more on this, go to arielsacks.com.) I encourage students to invent new processes, such as passing a "talking ball" to call on the next speaker (Figure P6.3).

I try to keep the meeting short, no more than fifteen minutes, though sometimes this is not possible.

Work Time

When the meeting is over, students go to their tables to work independently or in small groups. For certain activities, like partner reading or individual creative

Figure P6.3 Talking Ball

writing, I allow students to find their own space in the room. They may stay at their desks or go anywhere else in the room, but they may not sit at anyone else's desk. During independent work time, my coteachers and I sometimes call individual students or small groups to the meeting area to meet with me.

Exit Routine

When class is over, I give students a signal to pack up and straighten up their tables. I have a student with the official classroom job of "director of maintenance" dismiss tables as they are ready and watch that they push in their chairs on the way out.

ALTERNATIVE SUGGESTIONS FOR ROOM SETUP

I have used a meeting area since my first year teaching. Although meeting or rug areas are standard in elementary school classrooms, they are unusual for an upper-grade classroom. The meeting area was a suggestion of Madeleine that I took up and never looked back. It's a structure that continues to develop new functions within my teaching. At this point, I would not consider teaching without it. That said, it is an investment, it takes up space, it takes some time to figure out how to use, and it may not be possible in every classroom.

In a classroom without a meeting area, I have two suggestions for supporting whole novels work with the physical setup of the room.

Circle of Desks

Assuming you have desks, arrange them in a large circle around the perimeter of the classroom with a space in the front of the room for the board, where you write or project teaching materials. Put a rug in the center with some cushions to create a reading area or space for small groups to meet. You can even put short bookshelves in the center to shelter the reading area and make books accessible. For whole novel discussions, half the class can sit inside the circle on the rug, while the other half stays at the desks and works independently. Or you can run whole class discussions in the large circle.

The drawback to this setup is that your desks are not set up for group work. You would need a procedure for forming groups for certain activities. Perhaps every four students along the circle can push their desks together to form groups and return them to the circle at the end of the period. Or two students out of every four bring their chairs in front of the desks of their two neighbors to form a group of four around just two desks. This would work if the activity required minimal materials.

Table Groups and Circle of Chairs

Table groups make it easy to build in short bursts of group work—"share at your tables for two minutes"—in addition to longer group projects. You could arrange your desks in groups of four or six, which maximizes space in a crowded classroom. For whole class discussions, create a procedure with your students in which they bring their chairs to the perimeter of the classroom to form a large circle. You probably need to keep table groups away from walls in order to accommodate this.

Practice the procedure with students and allow them to come up with solutions to challenges that arise. Use a stopwatch and work on how quickly they can make the transition. For half-group discussions, push half of the table groups together to form a circle or square on one side of the room. Have students bring their chairs around the large cluster of desks.

7

Developing Students' Critical Reading and Comprehension
Activities We Do along the Way

"And at the side of the road . . ."

When I talk to teachers about whole novels, here are the questions they ask me most frequently:

1. What are students doing in class while they are reading the novel?
2. How do you make sure kids learn the literary concepts?
3. How do you help students who are struggling with the reading?

In this chapter, I focus primarily on answering questions 1 and 2 and go into more depth about question 3 in Chapter 8. The answers to all three questions are intertwined in the intentional offerings I make to students as they take reading journeys.

When I was little, I adored *Mouse Tales* by Arnold Lobel. One of the stories in it features a mouse that goes on a long journey. It is an arduous one, and during it, he needs many things. Fortunately, at each breaking point, there is a man at the side of the road selling exactly what he needs—water, socks, shoes. And finally, when his feet are so worn out they can't walk anymore, he needs new feet. I got a huge thrill every time I heard the line, "Fortunately, at the side of the road, there was a man selling feet!" How humorous, exciting, and comforting it was to find that the mouse's journey was not doomed. He would get what he needed and be able to keep going.

When I send students off on a literary journey in the whole novels program, I want to encourage and protect each individual's experience of the literary work, but I also need to make sure students are supported and growing in their reading and thinking. To these ends, I provide students tools and supplemental experiences throughout the process to help them make their way toward completing the reading and growing as critical readers of literature. What I won't do is walk the route for them. The students must take the journey themselves. The line between providing helpful tools "at the side of the road" and doing the work for students can be a subtle one. When students appear to be struggling or there is pressure to cover certain content, it can be tempting to do some of the work for the students, or overly prescribe the route, taking much of the experience away from students.

In this chapter, I share examples of the activities and experiences I provide to help propel students forward in their reading and thinking: group miniprojects around a literary element build skills and understandings, and the use of film and picture books builds background knowledge and experience with analogous texts. All of the activities create opportunities for collaboration and mentorship, which build community around the otherwise solo endeavor of reading a book.

 Visit https://vimeo.com /61676638 for video 7.1: Miniproject.

HELPING STUDENTS AS THEY GET INTO THE NOVEL

In, "What Happens When We Read (2)," psychologist and literary critic D. W. Harding (1977) explores the phenomenon we casually refer to as "getting into the story." Initially the child develops an expectation of the book, based on appearance and the conditions under which he comes to read it. Then, Harding continues:

> Drawing on previous experience of comparable books, he has to decide whether the anticipated satisfactions are likely to outweigh the effort required to read it . . . The early part of the story is the difficulty. At first . . . the reader is in a confused position. He does not know the location, characters, or situation of the novel (though the pictures, blurb, and his previous experiences may have helped) . . . Then it all gradually becomes clear. This ambivalent period before "getting into the story" is critical in deciding whether to go on or put the book aside . . .
>
> It is the real test of a mature reader to see how long he can tolerate this ambivalent period of doubt. If the fantasy experience is not forthcoming quite soon he may lose faith in the novel. The inexperienced reader cannot defer his gratification for long. The expectation of pleasure must outweigh present dissatisfaction. (58–72)

Although I don't want to become an overbearing and unwelcome interruption of my students' experience, I can assist students in the difficult phase of assimilating the heaps of information thrown at them as they enter the virtual world of the novel. I can make the work of "getting into the novel" that much easier for certain students. I don't do this by providing summaries or guiding questions. Instead, I find ways for students to work together to bring aspects of the novel to life, making them more concrete.

In order to diagnose my students' needs as they are first getting into the novel, I visit with individuals during reading time, read their notes, and also check in with the whole class during meeting time. I look for patterns in the needs. These range from basic comprehension of plot, to understanding of the setting of the novel, to analysis of figurative language or the perspective in the text. (These are the sorts of things that students can be probing along the way—while I save deeper literary analysis for after students have completed the reading.) I then design complementary experiences to help them construct a clearer or deeper understanding of the

216

novels without taking the power of interpretation away from them or sending a message that their success in reading depends on the teacher's help.

DESIGNING GROUP MINIPROJECTS: LITERARY ELEMENTS AS KEY SUPPORTS

Most often I design group miniprojects that have students investigate a literary element in the text that I believe can unlock a layer of comprehension for them. I like to think of literary elements as the keys to investigating literature: together they form a kind of compass for literary exploration. Some literary elements, like character, plot, and setting, are more basic, more primary, than others. Figure 7.1 shows an example of instructions for a miniproject around the element of conflict. Other elements, like theme, style, and tone, are like secondary layers. They take a little more digging to uncover and are more appropriate once students have experience with the primary elements.

To introduce and illustrate the role of the different literary elements in stories, I pose to my students the task of creating "the shortest story in the world" using the fewest words possible. At each turn, I ask them, "What could you take out and it

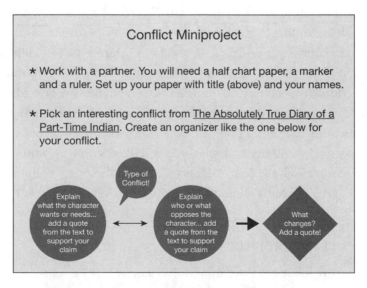

Figure 7.1 Instructions for a Collaborative Miniproject

217

would still be a story—though perhaps not a very good one!?" After much prodding, what is usually left in the end is a story where, at core, "somebody did something." This lesson shows the fundamental nature of character and plot to story creation. Students' inclinations to include more details point to the existence and importance of other elements. For example, students want to introduce obstacles, or something about how the story turns out, pointing to the importance of conflict and resolution. They want to add something about where the story takes place, pointing to the relevance of setting.

For example, it's early in the year and half of my class is reading *The Dream Bearer*, by Walter Dean Myers, about a boy who's dealing with his father's unstable mental health. I notice that a number of my students are having trouble getting into the story. In particular, I can see from their notes and brief check-in conversations that there is confusion about who's who. The story is told in the first person, but it's easy to miss the name of the main character, mostly referred to as "I." Several other characters are introduced early on. Some are family members; some are neighbors. Some are adults; others are children. I take notes on my clipboard about which students seem to have trouble with this. Rather than explaining or "correcting" these misunderstandings individually for each student, I design activities that create opportunities for students to work together to resolve confusion around characters' identities and relationships with each other. Figure 7.2 shows how students enjoy working together on these activities.

There are countless possibilities for these miniprojects. My colleagues and I have created a great assortment of activities over the years that respond to student needs in relation to specific texts. Some of these activities work particularly well with certain texts and not with others. Some can be transferred to any novel. Some work with any student, and others suit the needs of certain groups better than others. As you read about my examples, you will likely come up with ideas of your own that may work well for your students. Embrace these inclinations, and create new tools for your students along their reading journeys.

Differentiated Miniprojects

I've often used the following three miniproject assignments in one class at the same time to meet the needs of different learners.

Figure 7.2 Working on Collaborative Miniprojects

Facts and Figures

Based on my observations, I assign the students who have trouble identifying characters an activity I call facts and figures. I give them a large piece of chart paper, markers, and directions, and make sure each of them has a copy of the book for reference. The activity has them drawing the main character in the center of the paper, then listing facts about that character below him or her. Next to each fact, they must record the page number that holds their evidence for the fact.

Common Core Connection

The facts and figures activity and other miniprojects give students practice in CCRA.R.1: "Read closely to determine what the text says explicitly and to make logical inferences from it; cite specific textual evidence when writing or speaking to support conclusions drawn from the text."

219

This activity gives the students an occasion and method for going back to the text to reread for specific information that will lead to a better understanding of the story going forward. They are creating their own map, and they work together on this task. Students pool their knowledge to help each other to sort out who's who in the book.

Character Mapping

I notice in some other students' sticky notes a rarity of inferential responses. They seem to be grasping the plot and are sharing their reactions to the events and characters' actions. However, they are not recognizing the nuance the author has written into characters, interactions with one another, and what these interactions reveal about their relationships. For example, in a subplot of *The Dream Bearer*, the main character's mother is involved in a neighborhood action project that centers on a building owned by a minor character named Mr. Kerlin. Mr. Kerlin is also the man the main character's father works for, and the two parents have different feelings about him. Students easily overlook this subplot because it does not appear to be crucial to the main plot. However, all layers eventually become important to understanding this novel as a whole. I want to help students look more closely at the connections among and interactions between characters.

Character mapping gives small groups of students an opportunity to investigate the relationships among characters. Again, they receive chart paper, markers, a ruler, and directions, and they need their books. They write the main character's name in the center of the chart paper and other characters' names at the edges of the paper around it. They draw lines connecting all characters to the main character. They may also add lines connecting other characters to each other.

On the top of the line connecting two characters, the students describe the relationship in terms of the quality or tone of it. It's important that they get beyond writing mere facts, such as "Reuben is David's father," and then adding, "David doesn't know how to feel about his father, because his father acts strange and gets mad. David doesn't even call him Dad anymore." Below the line, they copy at least one quote that illustrates the statement they've made about this relationship. I encourage students to look for the quotes first and then create a statement that reflects the evidence they've collected.

The conversations that occur during this activity are fruitful as students share their varied impressions and memories of characters and challenge one another to find evidence for their claims. Though students take the literary journey of reading the book individually, they offer companionship for one another along the way through activities like this.

This and some other activities can be done on the computer using C-Map. C-Map Lite (http://cmap.ihmc.us/download/cmaplite .php) is free to download and provides a simple way for students to connect ideas neatly with lines that include descriptors.

Common Core Connection

Character mapping and the facts and figures activity help students practice the skills in CCRA. R.1: "Read closely to determine what the text says explicitly and to make logical inferences from it; cite specific textual evidence when writing or speaking to support conclusions drawn from the text." Character mapping also targets CCRA.R.3: "Analyze how and why individuals, events, and ideas develop and interact over the course of a text."

Literary Magnifying Glass

Some students demonstrate a high level of insight into characters and their relationships in their sticky notes, and I want to give them a chance to challenge themselves by holding a literary magnifying glass up to scenes that they identify as compelling. I want them to build consciousness of the author's craft choices as they read, observe them, and analyze their impact on the readers. This is the type of thinking that develops more naturally through the discussion seminars. However, this gives students who are ready a push in that direction.

I have students select several scenes—favorite scenes, least favorite scenes, or anything else. They draw a four-column table on chart paper (see Exhibit 7.1). In the left column they briefly describe the scene they have chosen and record its page number. In the next column, students give the scene a rating on a scale of 1 to 4 for intensity by answering the question, "How intense or interesting was this scene for you?" Students can also label a feeling the scene engendered in them as they read this section. In the third column, they record observations of the author's craft decisions in this scene. I provide a list of devices and craft elements to help them along:

- Dialogue
- First- or third-person narration
- Description of action
- Conflict
- Humor
- Suspense
- Uncertainty
- Interior monologue
- Description of setting
- Introduction of a new setting
- Imagery
- Introduction of new characters
- Surprise for the reader
- Confusion for the reader

- Flashbacks
- Background information
- Foreshadowing
- Symbolism
- Figurative language
- Satire
- Irony
- Anthropomorphism
- Double entendre
- Allusion
- Cliché
- Foil
- Juxtaposition
- Stream of consciousness

EXHIBIT 7.1 Format for a Literary Magnifying Glass

Description of scene	Intensity rating [1 = least compelling; 4 = most interesting] + mood	What craft elements and literary devices does the author use?	How do the author's craft decisions contribute to the impact of this scene on the reader?

I am aware that some devices on the list are familiar to the students and others are not. This is a chance for learners who are hungry for a challenge to research devices they don't yet know about, talk them over among themselves, and ask questions.

In the fourth column, the final step is for the students to talk over how the author's craft decisions in that particular scene created the intensity level and mood they identified in the second column.

The key aspect of this activity is that it begins with their choice of scenes and takes a closer look at their own responses to the scenes. The idea of this process mirrors that of the entire novel study: to experience the literature, respond, and then reflect on their own responses and analyze what the author has done to affect them in these ways. The activity also leads students to evaluate the author's craft. Some of the more interesting discussions occur when students choose to analyze scenes they found boring or frustrating. There is something empowering about developing language to critique literature effectively. Eventually the whole novels process arms all students with this skill, and I believe the skill transfers to other disciplines and areas of life.

Common Core Connection

In literary magnifying glass, students are practicing a number of aspects of CCRA. R.4: "Interpret words and phrases as they are used in a text, including determining technical, connotative, and figurative meanings, and analyze how specific word choices shape meaning or tone."

Depending on the direction of their analysis, they also have the opportunity to explore aspects of CCRA.R.5: "Analyze the structure of texts, including how specific sentences, paragraphs, and larger portions of the text (e.g., a section, chapter, scene, or stanza) relate to each other and the whole."

■■■

The previous three different miniprojects are happening all at the same time, in the same classroom, around one novel. The projects are tiered to help groups of students collaborate to take their understanding to the next level. In many cases, I don't tier the assignments. These projects are generally open enough to engage students with diverse readiness levels in meaningful learning, but the option of creating differentiated assignments is always there. I make the decision based on the nature of the text, my focus for the novel study, and my observations of the students' needs of the.

■■■

Miniprojects around Character

Tracking Character Traits

In getting to know characters at the beginning of the book, sometimes it's helpful to put students in pairs and have them come up with adjectives to describe the characters. I give seventh-grade students a paper with the outline of a person on the left-hand side and a similar outline on the right-hand side. I ask students to label the person on the left with the name of the main character in the story and then fill the space inside the outline (the body) with "strong adjectives" that describe the character. I talk to students about the difference between an adjective like *nice*, which is weak, because it's so general, and a strong adjective, like *compassionate*. This becomes a great vocabulary building exercise. We break out the thesaurus collection and students have a context in which to compare words like *spontaneous* and *hasty*.

Later in the study, as students near the end of the book, I have them revisit this activity to see how their character's traits have changed. They fill the second silhouette with adjectives to describe the character now. Some adjectives still apply, but others change. This activity is especially good for ELL students, as it helps them prepare language for the discussions, which come quickly thereafter. It also creates an opportunity to introduce the term *character development* and, in the case of some novels, *transformation*.

Character Complexity Rating

This activity is more appropriate for eighth graders or older who are exploring character traits. A student teacher, Finlay Logan, was working with me on a novel study in which students raised an important critique that some of the characters were stereotypes or clichés. Not to miss a teachable moment, Finlay and I added a twist to the character mapping we were planning to do. We had small groups of students pick a character from the book and encouraged them not to choose the main character. They wrote that character's name at the top of the chart paper. Then they brainstormed traits that applied to the character thus far in the book. They had to try to identify at least one positive and one negative trait. And for each trait, they had to find and record more than one scene in the book where the author showed the character with this trait. The conversations that emerged were interesting and intellectually rigorous, especially for characters that seemed to lack the depth of having positive and negative traits.

After completing the traits with evidence for the character, students rated the complexity of the character on a scale of 1 to 4. I introduced students to the notion of complex or round, developing characters versus flat, two-dimensional, unchanging characters. The group had to support their rating with an evidence-based paragraph. (Students write the paragraph collaboratively, using a format for a formal paragraph I've taught them previously.) This activity pushed students to think critically and critique the writing in a way that was grounded in the text.

Common Core Connection

The character complexity rating prepares students for CCSS.RL.9-10.3 in ninth and tenth grades: "Analyze how complex characters (e.g., those with multiple or conflicting motivations) develop over the course of a text, interact with other characters, and advance the plot or develop the theme."

Character Relationship Change

One year when students were reading *The Dream Bearer* and *Like Sisters on the Homefront*, by Rita Williams-Garcia, I noticed that the ELL students in my class seemed to grasp most aspects of the story, but the scenes with the elder characters (Great and Mr. Moses) seemed to lose them. I caught onto this when I noticed that

225

many students were skipping the scenes with these characters in their sticky notes. When I checked on this, asking a few students why they hadn't responded to these scenes, I got replies like, "I don't get that part." I'm comfortable with the reality that my students are not going to grasp every detail of the story. But these elder characters, and especially the relationships they develop with our protagonists, are important to the development of the story and its themes.

I determined that it was important for the students to note how the quality of these relationships changed over the course of the book. About halfway through the reading, I had students cut out faces from a magazine to represent the younger and the elder character and glue them on a half-sheet of chart paper. Then they drew thought bubbles for each character. In the thought bubbles they wrote what each character was probably thinking about the other toward the beginning of the book, including a page number where evidence that suggested this thought could be found. This required a fair amount of inferential thought.

The conversations around the task naturally required students to reread sections together and find evidence for their claims. In some cases, students asked for my help. I reread sections with them and helped them process the language that was giving them trouble. In some cases, this led me to the discovery that there was relevant historical context they did not know, which was keeping them from understanding some of the meaning of the dialogue.

> **Common Core Connection**
>
> Character change charts prepare students to progress on CCRA.R.3: "Analyze how and why individuals, events, and ideas develop and interact over the course of a text."

About a week later, I had them make an arrow, indicating change, and answer the question, "What changes?" This required students to look carefully at some later scenes between these two characters to understand what was changing between them. In most cases, an event or series of events provokes the change. Making sure students comprehended this thread of the story helped them discuss and find greater meaning in the work as a whole.

Miniproject around Conflict

Students often come to me with the notion that a story has to have a problem and a solution. This language is quite simplistic and by seventh or eighth grade, it's time to transition to more literary language. I hype it up, telling students that in life, we talk about problems we have, but in literature, the official term is *conflict*. And instead of talking about "a solution," which is more suitable for math, business, or other nonliterary subjects, in stories, we talk about "conflicts moving toward resolution," though not all conflicts resolve.

Next, I want to move on to the notion that the term *conflict* is synonymous with *problem*. While this is a convenient working definition, conflicts in literature, as in life, are multifaceted. A former colleague, Jane Willis, also a published playwright, defined conflict in literature as "a character wanting or needing something very badly, and someone or something stands in the way of him or her getting it." And instead of conflicts always leading to resolution, Jane pointed out that conflicts cause change. Jane created a tool for having students analyze conflicts according to three components: (1) the character wants or needs something badly, (2) someone or something acts to prevent the character getting this, and (3) something changes as a result.

Conflict analysis with partners works well for middle school students. In sixth grade, many teachers introduce the distinction between internal and external conflicts, which can be noted on the chart. In eighth grade, I want students to develop an awareness of the concept of society and the ways in which a character interacts with his or her environment and community, and vice versa. I find it extremely helpful to teach the classic four types of conflict. I replace the old-school, sexist *man* with *character* and teach (1) character versus character, (2) character versus self, (3) character versus society, and (4) character versus nature. I then have students identify a conflict in the text and analyze it using the tool, recording evidence for each component and labeling which type of conflict it is.

For students who complete the project quickly, I pose an extension challenge. For example, students have completed an analysis of a conflict in *The Absolutely True Diary of a Part-Time Indian*, by Sherman Alexie, that occurs between two characters. I ask the partners, "Is there another conflict that connects to this one? Does society play a role in this conflict? If so, can you analyze that layer of the conflict? Or does Junior also have a conflict with himself, connected to this conflict with Rowdy?" I tell students to create additional bubbles that show other levels of conflict.

> ### Common Core Connection
>
> Students become skilled at identifying intersecting layers of a conflict—for example, a conflict that occurs between a character and society, which provokes a conflict with another character and plays out in an internal conflict between the character and self. Students hash out these layers in discussions, which often lead to discoveries about the central idea of the text, or CCRA.R.3: "Determine central ideas or themes of a text and analyze their development; summarize the key supporting details and ideas."

Miniprojects around Setting

Setting Visualization

Sometimes we have to slow students down and give them a chance to examine the setting of the novel.

I have students work in small groups to find quotes that develop the look and feel of one setting within the book and copy them at the bottom of a large piece of chart paper. Then they must draw a picture of the setting according to what is stated or implied by the quotes.

This activity has two purposes. First, students take the time to look carefully at the details of the setting. Sometimes a closer look yields discoveries or the need for clarification about the setting itself. For example, in Nancy Farmer's *The Ear, the Eye, and the Arm*, set in Zimbabwe in the year 2194, the author introduces details that are so imaginative and foreign to us that they beg a closer look to fully comprehend them. Second, especially in novels with unusually vivid settings, like *Martian Chronicles*, by Ray Bradbury, or realistic settings described with unusual language as in Sandra Cisneros's *The House on Mango Street*, students need to understand the incredible work that good authors do to create a strong sense of setting—all with words. They can also appreciate what it takes for readers to receive these words and create pictures in the mind, while also following and responding to the characters and plot. Figure 7.3 shows a setting miniproject from *The Ear, The Eye, and the Arm*.

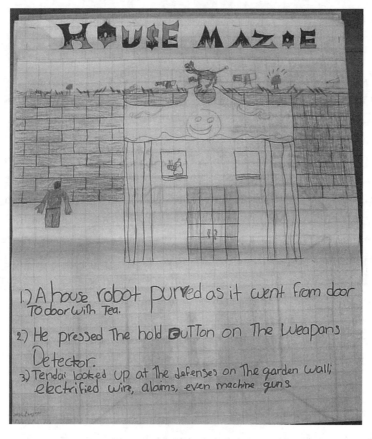

Figure 7.3 A Setting Miniproject

To add a layer to this activity, especially for older middle school students, introduce the element of tone. Have students reread the section in which they found strong quotes on setting and identify the tone of the scene. Since the tone may vary from scene to scene, have

Common Core Connection

The setting project and the focus on tone give students a chance to work on CCRA.R.4: "Interpret words and phrases as they are used in a text, including determining technical, connotative, and figurative meanings, and analyze how specific word choices shape meaning or tone."

them identify a tone that corresponds to the quotes they selected. This is another great opportunity for vocabulary building.

Multiple Settings Map

In a novel with multiple settings, a good variation is to have students work in groups to create a map of the settings of the story. They can begin toward the beginning of the book and use a corner of the chart paper, drawing the setting and recording quotes that support their visualization. A week later, they can return to the chart and add new settings. In some stories, these settings are simply different parts of a single environment. For example, in *The Jacob Ladder*, the map might include Tall T's home, his school, the shore where the banana boats are, the road to the shore, and the library. All of these locations are part of Tall T's regular life.

In a journey story, like *The Ear, the Eye, and the Arm*, the characters begin in their regular life, but soon that is disrupted as they embark on the journey. They move through several settings, distinct and separated geographically.

An extension of this activity is to note connections between these settings—not geographical ones—and any characters, history, or plot event that creates a connection between these distinct environments.

Levels of Setting

For a novel that takes place mostly in one setting, it can be helpful for students to note the levels of setting within which the characters' lives exist—as long as the novel is detailed enough so as to include some information about this. Students draw a set of concentric circles—usually about four. In the innermost circle, they describe the smallest, most intimate level of setting for their main characters. This is usually the character's home. In the next circle, students describe the main character's immediate community, which might include school or neighborhood. Next, they identify the larger setting, such as the city or region. Finally, the last circle includes the time period, the country, or world. In fantasy and science-fiction texts, this can get pretty interesting.

I'm always more interested in letting students grapple with the problem of determining the various levels than getting any kind of "right" answer for this activity. The purpose is to push them to think beyond the most familiar definitions of setting. In texts that act as social commentary, such as Harper Lee's *To Kill a*

Mockingbird, the time and place become especially important to understanding the significance of the story. Other times, the time period can help us understand details that seem strange to us now. For example in *The Hundred Dresses*, by Eleanor Estes, published in 1944, the class has a drawing contest: all of the boys must draw motorboats and the girls are assigned to draw dresses. In this case, the story is not about sexism, but this comes up as an issue for the students; understanding the setting of the story helps place this detail in context.

A Miniproject around Tone

Scene dramatization is a way to support students in their comprehension of the text and introduce the literary device of tone. In pairs or groups of three, they choose a scene from the book so far and reread it. I ask them to focus on what characters do and say in this scene, but also how they say and do them. How does the author describe their voices and actions? What is the tone of their words and actions?

It's helpful to take time to first practice dramatizing with tone. I create a situation, such as a character waiting for the bus. Then I ask for a student volunteer to play that character. I hand the student a card with a tone word written on it, such as *impatient* or *jovial*. He or she acts out the scene for about twenty seconds, and the class brainstorms words to name the tone the student used. We repeat this with different students and different tone words.

This exercise gives students a reference point from which to work in their groups to dramatize a scene and identify the tone of the scene. Finally, the groups play out their scenes for the class. We briefly discuss the tone of each scene and what the players did to convey the tone.

Miniprojects around Theme

Theme Scoring

When my eighth graders read *The House on Mango Street*, a book that is structured in short, poetic vignettes that can stand on their own, they are often a bit confused. Where is the traditional plot narrative they have grown so accustomed to

 Visit https://vimeo.com /61677458 for video 7.2: Theme Scoring.

in their reading and enjoyment of stories? How are the vignettes connected? As I described in Chapter 4, Daniel Brink-Washington, my coteacher, and I had the students track themes in each vignette in their sticky notes. As they did, they began to note that similar themes came up in many of the vignettes, but they still felt that the story was disjointed and strange.

We wanted to give them a way to investigate the common threads in the entire story, so that they might find patterns that would help them toward analyzing the meaning of the entire work. Dan came up with the analogy of a conductor looking at a score of music, seeing how all of the voices of the different instruments fit together.

In theme scoring, the whole class creates a visual score of the major and minor themes that run through *The House on Mango Street*. We came up with a color code for the themes we saw in the students' theme brainstorm sticky notes. Students work in partners to visually code the major and minor themes in each vignette. Students have learned the idea of major and minor themes in their theme brainstorm sticky notes. (In their notes, they brainstorm several themes for each vignette, but circle the one they believe is most significant, or major to the vignette.) Students also code the length of the vignette in order to represent how much time and space the author has devoted to developing this theme. For each half-page of the vignette, they use a half-sheet of white paper, taping together several pieces for longer vignettes.

As students complete their coding of the vignette, they arrange them in order in a long line across the front wall so that we can look at the thematic content of the entire novella (Figure 7.4).

Once we have all forty-four vignettes coded and sequenced on the wall, we meet in the front of the room. I give students a moment to look at the score and ask, "What do you notice now that you see all of the vignettes together coded by theme? Do you see any patterns in the themes? Any common threads, any clusters? Relationships between major and minor themes? Connections between the beginning and end?" I don't call on anyone right away, giving everyone time to think. Then we have a discussion.

There are many things for students to notice, and I am always surprised by what they end up saying. The idea I hope they walk away with is that although the story does not follow a traditional plot structure and may seem disjointed, the

Figure 7.4 Arranging the Theme Score

same handful of themes comes up throughout the story. Students always remark on this.

We begin to talk about the relationships of these themes. One student noticed, for example, that "oppression" or "feeling trapped" was a theme that came up in many vignettes. At the same time, in the same vignette or following a vignette with this theme, we would see "hope" and "freedom." Why would Sandra Cisneros do this? What's this pattern trying to tell us? We don't usually have time to fully investigate these questions after this activity, but it serves as a perfect precursor for our seminar discussions that follow.

Theme Analysis

Once students understand how to identify a theme in a novel, they need experience tracking its recurrence through the novel and work to interpret what the author is trying to say about this theme. One day I was working with students around theme analysis. I had them identify a theme in the film *Smoke Signals* and then find three scenes in the film where the theme came up. Students chose themes like tradition,

233

friendship, and forgiveness and worked to describe how their theme came up in three different parts of the movie.

On this day, a man who was working as a professional development consultant for our school happened to wander into my classroom. As is sometimes the case, I didn't know who he was or his purpose at our school. He observed for a while and spoke to students about what they were doing.

Later, the consultant asked me how I was defining theme for the students. I told him I was defining it as "an idea or topic that recurs throughout a piece of literature." He told me my definition was partly correct but it was missing some parts. First, the topic or idea needs to be one that recurs not just in this story but also in literature in general. In other words, even if bubble gum is a topic that comes up in this story several times, it might not qualify as a theme unless it also comes up in other works of literature. Although I'm not sure it's always so cut-and-dried, this definition is helpful for students because it suggests to them the connectedness of literature. Second, the consultant told me: "I used to be an English teacher, and I always told my students that a theme is an idea that recurs throughout a story, But," he continued, "that's not all. It's an idea that *the author has something to say about.*"

It had always bothered me when students came to my class with the notion that the theme is "the lesson" or moral of a story. From my classical musical background, I know theme as a melody that recurs and becomes recognizable within a longer piece of music. In my undergraduate studies in English, the key to discussing theme in literature seemed to be about looking for patterns. I had thought that repetition was the piece to focus on with students. But this classroom visitor pointed me toward the key to analyzing a theme: once we identify a theme, we've got to remember that it's intentionally being introduced and reintroduced. In fact, I knew that from my own literary studies, but I wasn't imparting it clearly in my teaching. The author is often not consciously trying to communicate a specific message about a theme, and there are themes that do not hold the central message of the book. Nevertheless, the author is trying to give readers something to think about in the development of a theme. It's our job to do the work of turning it over in our minds and interpreting its purpose in the text.

I never got to interact with this consultant again, but the quick wisdom he offered that day has stuck with me. My students now work together to identify a theme and write it at the top of their chart. Then they record three places in which the theme is introduced in the story in three bullet points. Finally, they draw a box at the bottom and explain what they think the author is trying to say about this theme. This last part can't be done effectively until students have completed the entire book or film. I often assign this miniproject after we watch the film *Smoke Signals*. Using the film to explore the author's message on a theme sets students up to apply the same thought process to the novel we read next, also by Sherman Alexie, with some similar themes. This project has the added benefit of being a good outline for an essay. Students can write the essay afterward or just store the experience in their memory, so when they do have to outline a thematic essay, they have this as a reference point.

> **Common Core Connection**
>
> The theme analysis miniproject is an opportunity for students to work on CCRA.R.4: "Determine central ideas or themes of a text and analyze their development; summarize the key supporting details and ideas."

USING PICTURE BOOKS TO STUDY PLOT STRUCTURE

When emergent readers work with longer novels, the question arises as to whether the book will continue to hold their attention. When my eighth-grade transitional ELL students started reading *The Ear, the Eye, and the Arm*, a dense, three-hundred-page novel with small print, I was justifiably nervous. In thinking about the book, I knew it wasn't the characters that would give them trouble. I therefore didn't choose to supplement the reading with character charts. It was the fact that it was so long and that they would have to push through descriptions, transition scenes, and many minor characters to feel the main thrust of the action.

For me, the reading was not difficult because I could detect the basic plot scheme for the book: the hero's journey. After the characters escaped from their sheltered home, made a fatal error in judgment, and were kidnapped, I knew the rest, at least abstractly. I knew they would encounter different kinds of trouble and strange characters. I knew that the main character would develop wisdom and strength to make it through, and I knew that when they finally made it home in the end, their relationships with their parents would be different and reflect the maturity they had gained through the experience. The interesting part in reading was to find out how the author would make this plot line believable and interesting in relation to the characters, setting, and imagery she had created. If my students could see the pattern, maybe they would be in a more relaxed state to enjoy the book.

I remembered studying two classic picture books in Madeleine Ray's Children's Literature course at Bank Street: *Where the Wild Things Are*, by Maurice Sendak, and *Sylvester and the Magic Pebble*, by William Steig. Both had stimulated high-level conversation in the course, and Madeleine had pointed out that both stories were versions of the hero's journey. I decided to supplement the process of reading *The Ear, the Eye, and the Arm* with studies of these two picture books. Students would practice looking at whole works of literary art, which would provide opportunities to study structure. It was an inspired experiment, and it worked.

To help students understand the classic plot arch of a story and apply that understanding to their reading of a full-length novel, my students and I study *Where the Wild Things Are*. As others have found, middle school students quite enjoy returning to beloved picture books, and this one has strong artistic merit. The story has a classic plot arch, and we also look at it as an example of a classic journey story. The lesson sequence for this picture book study provides a good example of the learning cycle (described in Chapter 5): exploration, discovery, term introduction, and concept application, a constructivist approach in which students make discoveries and the teacher introduces official terms that help name their discoveries.

Day 1: Exploring the Story

I begin by reading the story aloud to my students, followed by a brief, open discussion to share responses and pose questions. Then I ask them to take a closer look at the story in small groups, exploring aspects of it through one-word prompts, such as "Max" or "emotions" or "seasons." Each group receives a copy of the book and a notes sheet with the prompts. (See appendix C.) In this activity, I want students to explore everything they can: the characters and their relationships, the events of the story, conflicts, and illustrations. I'm hoping students will notice that as Max goes farther away from home and into the world of the wild things, the illustrations take up more space on the page. In the middle of the story, during the wild rumpus, there is a three-page complete spread of pictures, with no text at all. And as Max returns home, the pictures grow smaller and smaller, and the text returns, until the last page has text only. As I circulate, checking in with groups, I give students a nudge in this direction under the prompt "illustrations." We return to the whole group to discuss the story, its characters, conflicts, and events a bit more.

Day 2: EKG Chart

The next day, I tell the students we're going to use a tool to help us analyze the story further (see the directions in appendix D) in much the same way as a doctor first does a preliminary exam and talks to a patient to get basic information and develop some questions. But the doctor wouldn't stop there. She'd then do some lab tests on the patient to see what's going on.

I draw this symbol on the board:

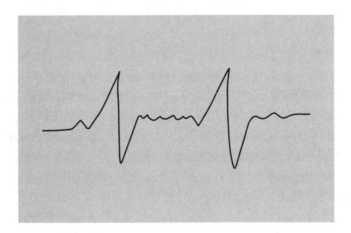

I ask the students, "Who has seen this symbol?"
Most raise their hands.
"What is it?" I ask.
"It's a sound wave."
"Great! What else could it be?"

"An earthquake! The thing that they use to measure it—a Richter scale!"

"A machine in the hospital that shows when the person is breathing!"

"So if we said it's a sound wave, what would this top part represent?" I ask, pointing to the top of the wave.

"Loud!"

"And this lowest part?"

"Quiet or silence," someone answers.

"Okay, what about the earthquake? What would this highest point represent?"

"A really strong earthquake."

"What about the machine in the hospital? What would this top point mean?"

"That's where the heart beats."

"And when it's flat?"

"The heart stops beating."

"So what do all these things have in common? What does the highest point always mean?"

"Something is strong!"

"Strength!"

"Intensity!"

"Great!" I say. "So we are now going to apply this idea of intensity to the experience of reading a story. What are the most intense parts of a story? This could include a book or a movie."

"The parts where you are dying to find out what happens next."

"Describe how that looks and feels."

"You're on the edge of your seat."

"You can't believe what's happening."

"What about the opposite? The parts that are not very intense?"

"Normal, boring."

"How do you feel?"

"Regular. Sleepy."

"Interested, but nothing special."

I draw an x- and y-axis on the board. I like to give the students a chance to show off their math skills, so I ask them what the axis labels are. I label the x-axis "Events of Story" and the y-axis "Intensity of Story."

"What is the first event in *Where the Wild Things Are*?" I ask, handing a student near me a copy of the book.

"Max makes mischief and gets in trouble," the student says. I make a dot on the *x*-axis, close to the origin. Then I write what the student has said underneath it, labeling the first event.

"Now, on a scale of 1 to 10 in storyland, how intense is this moment?" I ask. Students answer with varied ideas. Some go closer to 7 or 8, while others say 5, and some say 2 or 3.

"There's no right or wrong interpretation of the intensity of a scene, because each of us has our own experience of the story and our thresholds for intensity. For the sake of demonstration, let's average your answers and say 5."

I mark a big nickel-sized dot at the intersection of the first event on the *x*-axis and the number 5 on the *y*-axis. I instruct students to continue this process, interpreting each event with their groups. The result is a line graph showing a progression of intensity of the story. At the end, students write a paragraph collaboratively, explaining the trend of their line.

Day 3: Gallery Walk and Term Introduction

The next day, I put the large graphs around the room. I give students a template for noting similarities, differences, and patterns in the graphs. After the gallery walk, we have a meeting. I ask students to share observations. Especially, I ask, "What patterns did you notice in the various groups' graphs?"

"I notice that people felt really different about the beginning, but lots of people thought the middle was really intense."

"Which part was that in the middle that people thought was really intense?" I ask.

"I think it's when Max goes to the Wild Things."

"Okay," I say. "Can anyone be more specific?"

"It's when Max becomes king of the Wild Things!" someone says.

"It's when they tell him he can't leave, and then he stands up to them and says, 'Be still!'" another student offers. We establish some agreement that this part of the book is most intense.

"Why did everyone think this part was so intense?" I ask.

"Because it gets crazy, the, what's it called, the rumpus!" a student says.

"And Max becomes king."

"Did anyone notice anything about the pictures around this part?"

"Oh yeah! The pictures got bigger and bigger and then they took the whole page!" a student responds.

"Why would the author do that?" I probe.

"To, like, take you more into the setting. To make it more intense!" a student responds.

"Great idea," I say. "So actually, most of you seem to agree that the author created this scene in such a way as to make it most intense for readers, and most of your graphs show this same high point. There is an official name for this section in the world of literary studies. It's called the *climax of the story*." I pick up a piece of oaktag with the word *climax* written on it. I put a piece of tape on the back and affix it to the graph at the point of highest intensity. "What happens after the climax?" I ask.

"It kind of goes back to normal," a student says. We discuss how this happens in this story. I place the labels "Falling action," "Resolution," and also "Dénouement" on the lines between the climax and the final event of the graph. With younger kids, I might not use *dénouement*, but students get a kick out of esoteric words that are challenging to pronounce.

We then look at the earlier parts of the graph and label "Exposition," "Conflict," and "Rising Action" (Figure 7.5).

Day 4: Concept Application

As students return to their novels, I ask them to note on their sticky notes the stages of the story as they encounter them. For example, where does the rising action start? In *Where the Wild Things Are*, Sendak starts the rising action right away. In novels, however, sometimes there is a long section of exposition, where the author introduces readers to the setting, characters, and background information for the rest of the story. Helping students become aware of the general pattern of these stages can help them get through the exposition, where they might have been more frustrated before.

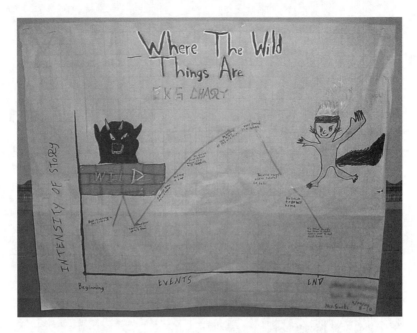

Figure 7.5 EKG Plot for *Where the Wild Things Are*

In addition to the plot stages introduced to students with the EKG chart, I want students to become familiar with the specific plot structure of a classic journey story so they can recognize and anticipate these events in the novels they are reading. We use William Steig's *Sylvester and the Magic Pebble* for this activity. We read together and examine the text in small groups as we did for *Where the Wild Things Are*. Then I ask students to work in groups to plot the main events of the story around a large circle on a chart paper, which we call the "journey cycle." This helps them notice that the journey begins where it ends—with Sylvester at home.

Students immediately draw connections between the story, where Sylvester goes missing and the parents get everyone they know to look for him, and *The Ear, the Eye, and the Arm*, where the main characters are kidnapped and the parents hire detectives to find them. Students also color-code each event on their diagram based on two factors: the

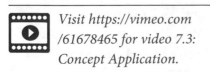

Visit https://vimeo.com /61678465 for video 7.3: Concept Application.

Figure 7.6 Journey Diagram

season during which the event took place (which represents another cycle) and the emotions that characterized each event. Later they label the stages of the plot: exposition, conflict, rising action, climax, and falling action (Figure 7.6).

This activity provides a visual representation and reference point for the journey cycle, so that students build an understanding of the patterns in structure of a journey story. These activities lead students to be able to apply their knowledge of plot and the journey cycle to their own fiction writing.

Common Core Connections

Analysis of the pieces of Sylvester's journey help students reach CCRA.R.5: "Analyze the structure of texts, including how specific sentences, paragraphs, and larger portions of the text (e.g., a section, chapter, scene, or stanza) relate to each other and the whole."

Comparisons of the journey and themes in *Sylvester and the Magic Pebble*, *Where the Wild Things Are*, and later the journey novels allow students to build toward mastery of CCRA.R.9: "Analyze how two or more texts address similar themes or topics in order to build knowledge or to compare the approaches the authors take."

USING SUPPLEMENTAL MATERIALS TO BUILD KNOWLEDGE BASES AND CRITICAL THINKING

Another way that I support the whole class in their reading during a whole novel study is by using supplemental materials, texts, and visual sources to help fill gaps in students' prior knowledge that may get in the way of comprehension. I also use supplemental texts to give students opportunities to be more critical of what they are reading by bringing them other perspectives on the text itself or the context in which the story takes place.

News Articles to Develop Background Knowledge

Articles can be helpful during the reading process to provide relevant background information that students might lack. For example, Sherman Alexie's *The Absolutely True Diary of a Part-Time Indian* depicts conditions on an Indian reservation in Idaho. My urban students living in the East have little or no knowledge of this setting, and they experienced some surprise and confusion at the alcoholism and depressed state of the reservation.

Lack of background knowledge can also interfere with students' ability to think critically about the author's depiction of a setting. They can't discern what is an attempt to be true to reality or what might represent hyperbole or an author's personal bias. I selected several articles that discussed issues related to reservation life today in different areas of the country to help students understand the context of the story. It helped that in their history class, they were studying westward expansion, including the Trail of Tears and the creation of reservations.

I've also had students read biographical articles about the author of the novel we're reading. For example, when we read *Nobody's Family Is Going to Change*, students found out several interesting facts when they read about the life of its author, Louise Fitzhugh. First, they were surprised that the author was white, when the characters in the novel are African American. Second, they found a significant similarity between the novel's main character, Emma, who yearns to be a lawyer like her father, and Fitzhugh, whose father is a lawyer. These bits of information about the author helped students think more critically about the story they were reading. Discussions of the book led to questions about the time period Fitzhugh was writing in—the prevalence of sexism in the workplace in the 1970s. I took the opportunity to find articles to support students in pursuing their questions.

With the emphasis on nonfiction in the Common Core Standards, English teachers are working to incorporate more nonfiction reading in their classes. We read fiction mostly for entertainment purposes, which is a natural hook for kids, and read nonfiction mostly to get information we need or to satisfy our curiosity. Curiosity is also a natural hook for kids, but we often fail to create conditions for curiosity to drive nonfiction reading. Questions that arise in fiction reading offer a perfect occasion for authentic interest in reading nonfiction.

Literary Criticism to Challenge Readers' Thinking

Once students have some baseline experience with a particular literary structure or element, I have found that they can benefit in several ways from exposure to small chunks of relevant literary criticism. After they have studied the picture books and begun to discover the structural pattern of the journey for themselves, I show them an excerpt of *The Power of Myth*, a six-episode 1988 PBS series in which Bill Moyers interviews Joseph Campbell, the expert in mythology and themes in storytelling from around the world. In the interview, which focuses on Campbell's book, *The Hero with a Thousand Faces* (1968), Campbell breaks down the pattern of the hero's journey and how he sees it repeated in stories and cultures around the world—from myths, to popular novels, to the *Star Wars* films, to world religions.

The clip we viewed is about five minutes. I pause the film frequently so that students can record the ideas in their notebooks. The language is much denser than what they are accustomed to, and each of Campbell's sentences requires significant processing for students to make meaning of them. The exercise pushes students to grapple with complex nonfiction texts, take notes while listening, and gain some general exposure to the work of literary and cultural critics. The exercise also points students to the connection between the plot events of the journey and the character development of a hero. They can then track the pieces of the literal hero's journey and the simultaneous transformation of the main character.

Another kind of literary criticism that I introduce to students in whole novel studies is the reviews and discourse that happen in newspapers and blogs about adolescent literature. It's a heated subject in many circles, and kids find this quite interesting. For example, before reading Robert Cormier's *The Chocolate War*, my coteacher, Marcia Stiman-Lavian, and I decided to give students an article about the banning of this book. This generated excitement about reading the book and also a sense that their very act of reading the book had significance beyond our classroom walls. Awareness of the debate around this book prompted students to ask themselves whether the concerns of book-banning organizations are valid by reflecting on the impact the book has on them as readers.

We also shared articles from newspapers and blog sites that revealed the more general debate around the content that appears in some young adult literature— violent, sexual, or otherwise controversial. It provided an opportunity for students to think critically about their own reading, as they found out that the majority of the novels we've read in English class are banned somewhere in the world. The nonfiction reading also provides exposure to current discourse that plays out in the world about works of fiction and a chance for students to weigh in with their own opinions.

Film to Build Relevant Experience

Sometimes literary works assume or require certain background knowledge about a location, a period in history, or a structural or thematic element. A thoughtfully selected film can provide a time and energy-efficient way to build students' experience in the area of need. The film supplements students' experience of the novel. Before reading Sherman Alexie's book, we watch the film he wrote, *Smoke*

Signals, which introduces students to the setting of the novel and gives them a mental picture of what the characters may look and sound like.

When my students, all from immigrant families, read *Like Sisters on the Homefront*, by Rita Williams-Garcia, and *Dream Bearer*, by Walter Dean Myers, I noticed that they lacked background knowledge of African American history, on which both novels draw significantly. Both novels feature African American protagonists who develop relationships with African American elders. The students responded well to the struggles and most of the relationships in which the protagonists were involved; however, they did not respond with understanding to key aspects of the relationships with the elders. After reading a chapter in which Gayle, from *Like Sisters on the Homefront*, talks to her great-grandmother, many students told me specifically, "I did not understand Chapter 10." When I looked back at the chapter, I saw that the character, Great, was telling stories from the family history, which assumed some knowledge of the post–Civil War South, and the Great Migration north. *Dream Bearer* draws on the same knowledge when the elder character, Mr. Moses, shares his dreams of slavery and the Jim Crow South with the main character, David.

I found a relevant movie: *Mama Flora's Family*. Much as in *Like Sisters on the Homefront*, a younger character travels to the South in the 1970s to stay with Grandmother Flora. Flora has a story to tell, and most of the movie is that story, conveyed through flashbacks. It spans the time of the sharecropping South, through World War II and segregation, the migration north to Chicago, the civil rights movement, and desegregation.

The students fervently watched the film, more so than I expected, and immediately connected it to the novels. I had them work together to make time lines of Flora's life and the conflicts they saw as connected to these events. This experience provided some factual background for the students, which allowed them to understand some of the references in the novels. On a more critical level, it helped students understand that some of the struggles of the characters in the novels were connected to struggles from the past, which the authors subtly impart in both the film and the novels.

Films can also be a powerful way to develop students' understanding of concepts in a novel. When my students study *The Chocolate War*, I want them to pick up on the theme of power relationships and structures at play. I showed the

In fictional works of literature that deal primarily with the coming of age of adolescent characters in the present time, some historical knowledge is important in understanding specific characters. The desire for the historical background came from the students themselves, who wanted to understand the characters. I emphasize this because of the trend to select novels to teach or correspond to a historical time and place, which the students usually have no voice in choosing. Literature can be helpful in a social studies classroom to look at historical bias and paint a picture of a time and place. I feel strongly, however, that historical fiction written for adolescents often does not achieve the literary greatness that would make it worthy of inclusion in a whole novels program. On an artistic level, many of these novels feel strained by underdeveloped characters who do not bring to life the settings the author has intended to create. It's crucial for teachers to read them thoroughly for themselves and decide if they are strong enough to make their students fall in love with literature in addition to teaching about the time period.

film *Swing Kids*, which takes place in Nazi Germany and presents an opportunity to discuss these relationships without entering into a discussion of the novel prior to students' finishing it. I introduce the archetypes of oppressor, victim, bystander, resister, and martyr, and students discuss these in relation to the film. I also introduce the term *moral dilemma* and have students explore the character's moral dilemma of a character in a creative writing project.

Students naturally make connections between the film and the novel, though they are related only thematically. They also naturally begin to apply the terms when we discuss the novel. Later, in a writing project, students draw from multiple sources to examine a theme, including *The Chocolate War*, *Swing Kids*, and "The Lottery" by Shirley Jackson, and a seeker opportunity, *The Book Thief* by Marcus Zusak. (More on seeker opportunities in the next chapter.)

THE POWER OF THE SIDE OF THE ROAD

There are myriad ways to assist students in developing a fruitful and successful experience through a novel without walking for them. The side of the road is a powerful place for learning. Miniprojects give students critical friends with whom to walk some of the way, express responses, and mull over ideas. The focus on one or two literary elements helps students comprehend the story on deeper levels. Supplemental readings and films create clearer and richer context for the novel study and parallel experiences from which to make conceptual connections.

The side-of-the-road experiences become their support network and tool kit. At the same time, students understand that the road itself is the whole novel. They know that they are going somewhere, and going independently.

PARTS OF THE WHOLE

Integrating Technology

New technologies are being introduced all the time, and students need experience, guidance, and instruction to be able to use them well. Depending on your school's resources, technology can easily become a part of the fabric of whole novel studies, providing another valuable layer of instructional opportunities for you and your students.

Here are a few ways I'm integrating technology into whole novel studies and others I want to try as soon as possible.

Online Discussion Platforms

Sites like Edmodo, designed specially for teachers, allow students to share reactions among themselves along the way in a protected online environment. I've started using the site for a variety of purposes:

- I have students post titles of their independent reading books, along with brief descriptions and recommendations for other students to read.
- During whole novel studies, students can make comments and post questions and replies related to the novels if they choose.
- Students reading seeker books can have discussions there online, since it's often difficult to schedule discussions during the school day.
- Students can post excerpts of their creative writing and get feedback.
- Teachers can create multiple-choice quizzes; Edmodo grades them on the spot and makes the score available to students and teacher. (You can create open response quizzes, but Edmodo obviously cannot grade those for you.) Teachers can put a time limit on the quiz. Although I'm not a big fan of multiple choice, there are times it can be useful, and the automatic grading is a big plus.

The site is well designed and compelling for students. (After we started using it, one of my students posted a comment there referring to "that awkward moment when we're all on Edmodo more than we're on Facebook.") My one caution is that teachers need to take moderation seriously. Talk to students about norms for the space, be present on the space, and follow up if norms are broken.

e-Readers

I allow students to read and write notes on their electronic readers and iPads as long as they don't take advantage of the privilege and use the technology for activities other than reading during reading time. Most e-readers have functions that allow readers to write notes in response to specific lines of the text. It's then possible to conveniently view all the notes at once on one page. I allow students to use this function in place of physical sticky notes. To assess their reading notes, I have to collect their e-reader and make sure I get it back to them quickly—usually that same day—or read and grade the notes during class. (I'm waiting for the function that allows students to e-mail their notes to teachers.)

Google Docs Reading Journals

My students all have a gmail account provided by my school, which is hugely convenient. I've used Google Docs in a couple of ways as reading journals. Students who demonstrate mastery of the basic sticky note annotation process have additional options for response to reading (described in Chapter 8), including keeping a reading journal on Google Docs. They must share it with me, and this allows me to easily comment on the notes (see Figure P7.1).

I've also had students read a book with a partner and keep a partner reading journal shared on Google Docs, which allows students to write back and forth to each other. Coteacher Daniel Brink-Washington and I created a format that asks students to write a response, identify literary elements they've commented on, and ask and answer one another's questions (see Figure P7.2). This made a great end-of-year project.

Author Sites

Many authors have websites that share biographical information and highlight their work. Jacqueline Woodson, graphic novelist Gene Luen Yang, and Sherman Alexie are a few whom students can explore in conjunction with a whole novel study.

However the only difference is that in Mango Street they don't keep talking about the characters in the next chapter, but in 'Parable of the Sower' the main character somehow finds a way to involve them in the next chapter.

So far the book hasn't been boring, but it hasn't been that interesting. The exposition has been okay, I think the way the author Octavia E. Bulter writes makes the story a bit more interesting to read.

Ariel Sacks
11:02 PM Today
Great comparison to setting and character in Mango Street! When you write "they," who do you mean?

Figure P7.1 Comment on Google Reading Journals

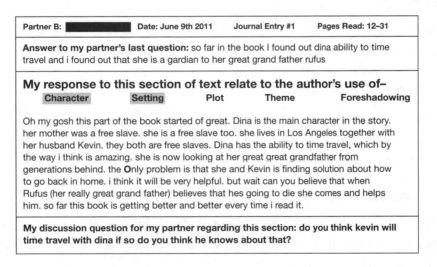

Partner B: ▮▮▮▮▮▮▮	Date: June 9th 2011	Journal Entry #1	Pages Read: 12–31

Answer to my partner's last question: so far in the book I found out dina ability to time travel and i found out that she is a gardian to her great grand father rufus

My response to this section of text relate to the author's use of–

     Character   Setting   Plot   Theme   Foreshadowing

Oh my gosh this part of the book started of great. Dina is the main character in the story. her mother was a free slave. she is a free slave too. she lives in Los Angeles together with her husband Kevin. they both are free slaves. Dina has the ability to time travel, which by the way i think is amazing. she is now looking at her great great grandfather from generations behind. the Only problem is that she and Kevin is finding solution about how to go back in home. i think it will be very helpful. but wait can you believe that when Rufus (her really great grand father) believes that hes going to die she comes and helps him. so far this book is getting better and better every time i read it.

My discussion question for my partner regarding this section: do you think kevin will time travel with dina if so do you think he knows about that?

Figure P7.2 Partner Reading Journal

Figment

Adolescent writers can create a profile, share their writing online with other writers and receive feedback, and participate in community events, such as contests and chances to talk to authors on Figment. The site now allows teachers to set up closed online classroom groups for their students.

251

e-Pals

This site allows classrooms in different regions or across the world to collaborate. Teachers can form a long-distance partnership with another teacher for students to read and discuss a whole novel together online.

Novel-Inspired Research

I encourage students to conduct Internet searches for additional background information on words or topics mentioned in a novel, about which students have questions. Sometimes I create an "Internet Search of the Day" as an optional part of homework.

Goodreads

Students can set up a Goodreads account and post reviews of books for a much wider community of readers than their classroom.

Moviemaking

Students can design their own movie projects related to the novel. Adapting scenes for film, interviewing a character on a talk show, or creating a trailer for an imaginary sequel for the book are some possibilities.

Book Soundtracks

Students can create a playlist that includes a song for each chapter of the book. Students who know how to use GarageBand can write original songs to go with a compelling part of the novel.

8

Differentiating for Diversity
Whole Novels for All Students

"Places to go, not places to stop . . ."

One of the reasons I continue to heed Madeleine's advice to let students read the whole novel and avoid prescribing questions and responses for students is that while we may think we are creating bars for students to rise to meet, we also send a message to students about where to stop. In other words, we often end up giving students an arbitrary or inappropriate place to stop exploring, pushing their thinking, asking questions, and taking risks. Whole novels and experience-based learning seeks to provide many places for students to go regardless of where they start.

253

I've had the pleasure and challenge of working in classrooms with a wide range of learners in New York City Public schools. Brooklyn Prospect Charter School, where I now work, serves a population diverse in student learning styles and special needs, as well as racial, ethnic, and socioeconomic diversity. In heterogeneous classes, I work with students whose reading levels span from second grade through first-year college. The challenge of providing places to go for each of my students has never been more interesting or rewarding.

In this chapter, I share the practices that my colleagues and I have developed and implemented that make whole novels an ideal framework for a diverse classroom. The whole novels program is a flexible structure that is ripe for problem solving in response to student needs. Through experimentation, support, and collaboration with coteachers and other colleagues, whole novels has become a robust program with adaptations to suit the diversity of learners who walk through my classroom door each year.

Many teachers I've talked to about the method share concerns over how whole novels could work for struggling readers, since students must read the whole book and delay discussions until they have completed the reading. In fact, this very practice has some benefits for struggling readers, as well as advanced students, because it allows us to differentiate the support for individuals during the reading portion of the study instead of moving through a novel in lockstep. Learning specialist Marcia Stiman-Lavian, who has cotaught an inclusion class with me for two years, has this to say:

> I think the whole novel study is a great opportunity for diverse learners. It allows kids, especially with learning disabilities, to go at their own pace and access the book in a way that works for them, without the pressure of feeling like their peers are ahead or understanding the book better or differently than they do. I have been in classes where we read a book as a class, stop to answer comprehension questions, and talk about them as a class. In these instances I have often found students who struggle not participating in these discussions, because for one reason or another they didn't feel connected or weren't able to understand the material in that format.
>
> In whole novel studies, by not discussing fully until the end, we allow all students to access the book their way, and then feel really ready when

the book is over. Especially since they know the discussion is coming, and they know the date, they can get really ready to be involved. Since all kids must participate, students know they have to be ready with something. This often motivates kids, who are normally not prepared to share their responses, to get ready. Then they can participate fully in the group discussion, often times for the first time in a while.

I also have academically gifted students in my class who can read more than one book in a day. In whole novel studies, I don't hold these students back to match the slower pace of the majority of the class or separate them from the class with an entirely different assignment. I create places for them to go to augment their learning within the context of each whole novel study.

CREATING AN ATMOSPHERE OF GROWTH

One of my desires as a teacher of English is to help my students develop reading lives of their own. Through the whole novels program, I offer them a series of occasions and a community in which to do this. That said, I have to come clean about something: I do not particularly think of myself as a reading teacher. I think of myself as a leader of a group of readers. I position myself more as a remover of barriers between students and literary worlds. I imagine my students and me bushwhacking through a jungle. Sometimes I might be in the lead clearing the path; sometimes I might show students how to chop brush or avoid poisonous snakes along the way. Ultimately I'd like to be alongside them and, eventually, watching them lead the way. I want to help them use compasses, maps, and landmarks to figure out which way to go and facilitate their strategizing with one another about how best to do it.

My work with individual students in whole novels is about figuring out who they are as readers, what's going on for them, and helping each of them access the novel study as fully as possible. To this end, I begin by developing relationships with them around their personal reading habits, interests, and needs. There are many different kinds of readers, and the intricacies intrigue me. Identifying reading levels is just one way of filtering these differences.

I emphasize to the class during the reading portion of the novel study that we each have our own process for reading and responding. I have students openly share their process in whole class meetings, which sends a message that these differences are interesting and worthy of our attention. Sometimes these check-ins focus on the content and experience of reading the story itself. (I wrote about this in Chapter 4.) At other times, student comments revolve around the process of writing sticky notes. I've found this to be highly productive to discuss.

Some students like to write lots of stickies. "I've been writing, like, a sticky on every page," says Yvonne in meeting.

"Wow," I say, encouraging the conversation. "What makes you do that?"

"They help me understand and remember," she says.

Three hands go up and wave passionately. I call on Jake, who tells us, "I don't like to write them at all. I just wanna read and read. When I have to stop and write a note, I lose that feeling of reading. Then I don't want to read."

"Oh, no!" I respond. "Does anyone have any advice for Jake? How could he work this out?"

"Well, what I do," a student offers, "is I read as much as I want that night, and when I read, I put a note where I find something interesting. But I don't write anything. I go back another time to write the notes."

"That's pretty cool! Do you think that might help Jake keep the feeling of enjoyment?" I ask.

"Yeah, because you can read as much as you want and not worry about notes, but also you don't forget the interesting parts. I usually do the actual notes in class," the student offers.

Another student adds, "I read a chapter. At the end of the chapter, I stop and go back and find a few things to write about."

Another hand goes up. "I read really fast. I read this whole book in two days. I couldn't stop. So now I'm just going back and rereading it and doing the notes."

I ask, "Do you get anything new from this second reading? Or is it just a drag?"

"At first I thought it was a drag, but now I'm finding more and more to write," the student answers.

"When I'm home reading," Choron says, "I feel like there's this dude sitting on my shoulder whispering in my ear telling me not to write the sticky notes, like, 'Don't do it!' And I sometimes listen to the little dude." We have a laugh.

Another student chimes in, "I feel like it's the opposite! I feel like the little dude is telling me to stop and write a note! At first I didn't listen. Then about halfway through the book, I started listening to the little dude. I wrote one note, and then I just couldn't stop writing them! I had so much to say!"

"What I do," Logan shares, "is I read in school and at home. Then during class, I work on the notes. I have to write notes for another class I'm in, too, so I have time to write there. That's how I get it all done and keep on schedule." Logan is talking about the intensive reading class he takes in addition to English class. He's been assigned to the class because his reading skills have been significantly below grade level. The fact that he was comfortable sharing this part of his process with his classmates showed me that he saw diversity as a normal and valuable part of our learning community.

My goal is that each student becomes aware of his or her own process and discovers what works. As students read during class, I circulate around the room and have quick conversations with them about their reading. During the reading process, a student's ability to decode and comprehend the text is of primary importance, so I am first looking at how this is going, diagnosing issues when I see them, and trying to figure out best next steps.

I begin by peeking at their sticky notes, the main place they record their thoughts, questions, and responses to the text as they read, and assess comprehension through these notes first.

My general rule during the reading process is that if students basically comprehend the text and respond authentically to it, I don't want to intrude. And if I can see that they are on a path toward these types of responses, I just want to encourage them in the right direction rather than interrupt progress. I'm interested in talking to them about their process, as I'm doing in Figure 8.1, so that they might develop metacognitive skills, but I don't want to teach reading strategies when students are making good progress on their current path.

Experience is a great teacher, and reading literature is virtual experience. I'm interested in pushing their thinking about the content in the novels, but I think they can gain more from making discoveries on their own and with classmates. Under the right conditions, students develop tremendously through the experience of interacting authentically with a literary text and in a literary community.

Figure 8.1 Informal Assessment of Individual Students

DIAGNOSING AND INTERVENING WITH INDIVIDUAL STUDENTS

Depending on what I observe in students' notes, I make decisions about how to respond. Table 8.1 sets out some of the common situations I encounter as I engage with students around their notes and my thinking about next steps. Some students need some instruction through conferring, but in whole novels, conferring is not the main mode of instruction. Experience is. So the focus of my work in conversations with students about their reading is figuring out who needs some individual instruction through conferences, who might benefit from small group support or assistive technology, and who doesn't need anything at this point other than the individual and group experiences that the basic curriculum provides. In other words, some students are headed in the right direction, and I don't want to attempt to control that even if they are not excelling in all areas. Others are heading off in a direction that may not work without intervention, so I want to adjust their focus and method a bit.

Table 8.1 Diagnosing the Needs of Individual Readers

Observation	Objective	What I Might Say	Next Steps
Joe's notes are too vague or too few to tell if he is struggling with comprehension	I want to know if Joe is having trouble comprehending or with note taking and get him the support he needs.	"Hm. What did you mean when you wrote this note? Can you explain it to me?"	If Joe shows that he comprehends, discuss note-taking expectations; if not, get more information and consider special supports.
Ilana shows strong comprehension in literal and inferential responses, but her notes are mostly about character; she writes virtually no critical responses.	I want Ilana to strengthen critical response, or at least become aware that this is an area for her to develop further this year.	"Great job recording what's happening and observing characters' motivations! I want to push you on critical thinking. What do you think about the world the author is creating? How do these characters compare to people or places you know?"	I feel confident the curriculum this year will provide Ilana with tools and opportunities to develop more critical responses. This is not something I need to teach her through conferencing.

(*continued*)

Table 8.1 *continued*

Observation	Objective	What I Might Say	Next Steps
Marcus's notes show opinion and suggest critical thinking, but lack detail; it's unclear what he is responding to.	I want Marcus to write more detailed notes that reveal more of his thinking and engage more explicitly with the text.	"Can you explain this note to me?" Then, "What you just said is really interesting, but I can't tell any of that from this note! Can you elaborate like that on your notes?"	Check back later that period to look for more detail and again daily. Use peer feedback to reinforce the message. If the problem persists, get more information; find out if there's a skill deficit, a motivational issue, or both.
Shantia's notes are predominantly summary and questions; they lack inferential thinking.	I want Shantia to begin using clues in the text to attempt to answer some of the questions she has.	"I see that you are recording what's happening in the story. And you're asking a lot of questions, which is great! Now when you ask a question, I want you to take your best guess at answering it using clues from the story. Try one now, and I'll be back in a moment."	Check back quickly. Talk to her about the guesswork she tried to answer the question. Have Shantia name which type of thinking this represents (inferential). Have her talk to a partner about her questions.

(continued)

Table 8.1 *continued*

Observation	Objective	What I Might Say	Next Steps
Porfirio is writing a good variety of literal, inferential, and critical notes.	I want Porfirio to know that I recognize his good work and use it to fuel discussions; I want him to expand his literary life over the course of the year.	"Great observations! You're using a variety of types of thinking." Then pointing to one interesting note about a theme, "I'll be curious to hear more about this in discussions!" or I write a comment or question back to him on a sticky note to push his thinking.	Get out of the way! The curriculum is designed to guide Porfirio to develop deeper levels of literary skills and understandings through discussions and a series of rich reading experiences throughout the year. Let him do the work.

Note: My actual notes on student conferences are not this organized. For effective ways to organize observations and notes from reading conferences, see Nancy Atwell's *In the Middle* (1998).

DO YOU RECOGNIZE THIS READER?

Some types of readers have presented challenges for me and taken me longer to figure out how to provide support. In these cases, the conversations we have are key to setting them on a path toward authentic reading. In some cases, I failed in the past by forgetting to build the relationship and coming down too strong or too quickly. Struggling readers have often built up so much insecurity and masking of the problem that it can be challenging to have a genuine conversation about reading with them. In other cases, I responded too casually, thinking they would eventually make progress on their own, but they didn't.

I've created a few composite characters, based on certain types of readers I encounter early in the year and how I begin working with them.

The Summarizer

As I look at Valerie's book during an independent reading cycle at the beginning of the year, I see that she has a note or two on nearly every page. "Wow!" I say to her, flipping through the first twenty or so pages of the book. "You have written so many notes!" She beams. "How do you like this book?" I ask.

"It's really good," she says, smiling. As I begin reading her notes, I notice that in almost every note, she is summarizing the main events of the story. I haven't read this book, but with some quick reading of the text behind the notes, I can tell she is doing a good job of recording the key events as she reads, though none of the notes show critical or inferential thinking.

I'm careful how I phrase my suggestion so as not to devalue what she's doing. If I'm not thoughtful, my feedback could easily suggest that she's doing only one of the three things she should be doing. To focus on the deficits would show a misunderstanding of who she is as a reader at this point. Although it may seem like a waste of time for her to summarize everything she reads—and for many of us, it would be—I've found that this is an effective comprehension tool for many struggling readers. Some readers feel that if they stop summarizing, they'll lose their footing in the text and forget what they've read.

Reading requires holding many things in the working memory at once. Avid readers decode most text unconsciously, so the brain can focus on experiencing the elements of the story as they unfold, assimilating new information with what has come before it. (We can approximate this experience for struggling readers with storytelling or reading aloud so they can exercise their working memory as they access the narrative auditorily.) When the brain is working actively to decode text, experiencing the story becomes more difficult. Recording the main points of each page or so of text is an important step in comprehending not just the words but also the story. The notes also become a reference tool for the student. As she moves on to the next section and again fills her working memory with double the load of an avid reader, she can easily look back to the previous note to keep it in mind as she assimilates the new information.

I've already noticed that Valerie's English language arts (ELA) test scores from the year before are quite low; she has no diagnosed learning disability, but I suspect she struggles with reading comprehension. At the same time, she's working hard and succeeding in this area.

I begin, "Valerie, you're doing an excellent job of writing down what is happening in the book. I can tell you're really understanding what you're reading! Now I have a question for you. Do you think that writing these notes as you read is helping you to understand better?"

She nods. This confirms for me that Valerie has devised a system that is working for her for the moment and will help her strengthen her reading muscles. (If she had responded negatively to that question, I would want to know whether she had mistakenly thought she was supposed to write down all of the events, which happens sometimes.) I know Valerie will be reading a great deal in my classroom over the year, and I'm confident that over time, she'll rely on this strategy less. I don't think it would be productive to interrupt this process that's working. At the same time, I don't want Valerie to miss out on responding to the text personally and thinking critically about characters and themes.

"Great! I'm so glad you've found this tool helpful," I say. "One thing I notice is that almost all of your responses explain what is actually happening in the text. If we were to categorize your notes using the three ways of thinking, what kind of responses would most of these be?"

She looks at the poster in the front of the room that we've been using in the lessons and responds, "Literal?"

"You got it," I say. "Almost all of your notes are literal . . . except one," I say smiling. She looks both pleased and puzzled. "I want you to look back through your notes and see if you can find the one that is *not* literal. Raise your hand when you find it, and I'll be back."

Leaving at a moment like this is strategic so that I don't put her on the spot. I give Valerie the time she needs, while I go back to circulating around the room. I check in with a few more students, most of whom are getting the hang of responding with the three kinds of thinking, appreciate a bit of encouragement, and just want to keep reading. Then Valerie's hand shoots up, and I return to her table.

"I found it," she says, pointing to a note that is much shorter than the rest.

I smile. "Interesting! How did you decide it was this note?"

"Because this one says what I think."

She shouldn't have done that.

"What were you writing this one about?" I ask.

"Well, I meant that Alicia shouldn't have lied to her mother about getting in trouble at school, because the school could call her house and then she could be in worse trouble."

With another student, I might have encouraged her to write out the entire thought—with names and details and no vague pronouns. However, I want to stick to one piece of critical feedback at a time, so I don't mention that right now. It's enough that she speaks the complete thought to me.

"I see what you mean! And what kind of response is that?"

She looks back at the poster, and I give her as much wait time as she needs. About ten seconds later, she says, "Critical."

"How do you know?"

"It's my opinion," she says.

"That's it!" I say. "So keep on doing what you've been doing, but try pausing sometimes to write down your opinions or questions about the story. I know you have them! You can look at the chart of 'Things to Write on a Sticky' if that helps."

"Okay," she says, nodding.

I don't expect a huge change all at once, but I know that our conversation has created a place to go for her and that we'll be able to check in about her progress throughout the novel study and year.

The Nonreading Note Taker

Juan Carlos has spent the past ten minutes of reading time attempting to chat with the other students at his table. Every time I look his way or start to say something to him about it, he quickly returns to his reading. And every time I turn my focus to another student, he is chatting with his neighbor again. Finally I ask him to talk to me privately in the meeting area.

"Juan Carlos, you seem to be having a lot of trouble focusing today. What's going on?"

"It's that I don't like the book," he says. It's a book about baseball, his favorite topic.

"Oh! You were so excited when you picked it out yesterday and started reading. It's not meeting your expectations?"

Just yesterday he was bragging to the class about how "This is my *book*! This book is the *bomb*."

"I don't know," he says. "It's not as good as I thought it would be."

"What's not as good?" I ask.

"I don't know. It's not really, you know, pulling me in. I'm not really reading it."

"Do you want to pick a different book?" I ask, knowing that is the only baseball book I currently have on hand.

"No, this is the book I want to read," he insists. "I'm going to do my work. I'll stop talking now."

"Well, I'll be back to check on you soon," I say, unsure that we've gotten to the heart of the problem. He returns to his seat. He works quietly for a good ten minutes and seems to be writing lots of sticky notes.

Then I hear, "Ms. Sacks!" It's Juan Carlos with his hand up. When I arrive at his table, he proudly flips through his book, showing me many sticky notes. I'm still unsure how much progress has been made. I begin reading the notes.

The notes go on like this for many pages, responding to exactly one sentence on each page. Each note begins with a phrase that seems to come from the "Suggestions for Sticky Notes" poster. I marvel at the fact that out of the minimal structure I've suggested for the free-form notes, Juan Carlos has interpreted a place to stop in the assignment: a way to stop reading and learning and just get the assignment done.

Approaching him about the notes is tricky. One thing I know about him is that he seems to care about meeting external expectations, about things looking the way

> page 1: I think this book is going to be about baseball.

> page 2: Why does she have her green purse over her arm?

> page 3: I'm confused about why he says fat chance.

> page 4: I can connect to this because Juan is part of my name too.

they are supposed to look. That's why he bragged about the book he was going to read, why he stopped talking every time I looked his way, why he wrote the sticky notes, and why he used the suggestions poster to phrase his notes. But he's missing the meaning in these actions—and *the reading*! I decide to use his attention to external expectations as a way in to the discussion.

"So, I see that you are asking questions, making connections, and stating opinions—all things we've been talking about in class," I point out, giving him some credit for his attention to these aspects of the work. "And I see that after we spoke, you stopped talking and focused on your work."

He smiled tentatively. "I told you I was going to do my work," he said.

I would like for him to admit that he hadn't actually been reading so that we might have a conversation about what could help him read more actively and critically. This might prove challenging.

"As I read your notes, I don't see evidence of your literal comprehension of the story or that you're making inferences as you read. Are you understanding what you read?" I ask.

There is a pause before he answers. "Yeah, some of it," he says, deflating a bit.

I am pretty certain Juan Carlos doesn't have trouble decoding most text, and I'm almost as sure that he wouldn't have much trouble comprehending the story if he put his mind to it. A hint of the challenge he is facing is that his reading scores, though lower than they should be, are by no means failing—very difficult to achieve without reading the passages. Like many young people who don't have much reading experience but do play video games and are used to that immediately interactive nature of the game, Juan Carlos would rather not spend the energy it takes him to truly pay attention to a story, especially in the long form of a novel, long enough to "get into it." At the same time, he doesn't want to be seen as lacking the skills to do so, and he's motivated in a general sense to do his schoolwork. It's highly possible that in previous years, teachers have mostly read books aloud to him, or in some other way he's been able to not actually read books.

I need to find a way to trick him, if you will, into relaxing his usual attention receptors—the ones that are constantly jumping from stimulus to stimulus—long enough to truly enter the world of a novel. I'm confident that if he can have that experience a few times, he'll become awakened to the interactive nature of reading, and he'll find places to go.

"Okay," I ask, "so what do you understand about this story so far? What's going on?"

"I can't think of it right now."

We've hit a wall. "Is the book perhaps too difficult for you?" I ask with no judgment.

"No," he says. "I only read a little bit of it." Truth. Finally.

"I see. Let me guess. You read a little bit and then wrote a sticky?"

"Yeah," he says, averting his eyes with a little guilty smile.

"One problem with doing that is that you don't end up understanding enough about the story. You don't demonstrate your literal comprehension or your ability to make inferences, which I know you can do!" Juan Carlos is a great contributor to whole-group response sessions.

"I just don't like reading that much," he reveals.

"I'm sorry you feel that way right now. But I think a big part of that has to do with the little bits and pieces you're reading. Imagine watching a movie by playing just thirty seconds and then forwarding to the next scene. Would you understand what was going on in that movie?" I ask.

"No."

"Would you enjoy watching movies that way?"

"No, I guess not," he admits.

"Well, that's what you've been doing with reading," I say. "Here's what I want you to do now. First, take your book into the meeting area and find a place where you can at least imagine that you're by yourself. Then I want you to read just a page, a whole page. Write down on a sticky note what you know so far about the story: who's there and what is happening. That's it. Don't worry about anything else for the moment. Then go on to the next page and do the same."

He nods his head with a hint of relief. The task would sound exceptionally dull to many readers, but Juan Carlos liked the fact that (1) it was in small chunks, because his attention controls couldn't handle much more, yet, (2) it was something he knew he could be good at, and (3) it recognized where he was failing himself without shaming or punishing him for it. Instead it provided him a way to go forward.

Soon he's waving his hand for me to come over to see his first sticky note: it explains exactly what's going on. I know he is on his way to reading and authentically responding to literature.

The Speedy Reader

In the independent reading cycle at the beginning of the year, I also take special note of students like Emma who read extremely quickly. Emma has proven to me through conversations and my observations of her reading habits that she enjoys reading quite a lot (she can sometimes be found reading while walking down the hallway) and she doesn't have trouble with comprehension or response. But she'd rather not write down any responses at all. She's accustomed to breezing through book after book and just enjoying it.

"I feel like writing sticky notes is holding me back," she says. *Hmm*, I think. I want to investigate whether the sticky notes could be helpful to her.

"Why do you think I've asked you to record your thoughts as you read?" I ask.

Emma stalls for a moment, then replies uncomfortably: "To see if we read the book?"

I chuckle a little, shaking my head.

"Well, that is a part of it. I like to see what students are thinking as they read; it helps me understand how I can help students. But that's not all of it," I add. "Any other ideas about why I might want you to do this?"

"Maybe it's so that we remember important things later?"

"Yeah, that's right. Soon we'll start a whole novel study, and you'll read the novel by yourself and then discuss with the class at the end of the study. I want you and the other kids to get in the habit of collecting interesting thoughts about the story for discussions. The notes can help you easily refer back to parts of the book."

"Okay," she says. "But what about now? I'm the only one reading this book."

"Well, there's one more reason I want you to practice what's called text annotation—recording your thoughts about the text in the margins or on sticky notes on the pages of the book. This is a valuable skill. I used it all the time in college to collect my thoughts about complicated texts. Some of the stuff I had to read was really hard to understand, and I had to record things as I figured them out, as well as questions I had and comments. This was the only way I could truly make meaning out of difficult texts. Then I got into the habit of it. I realized I noticed more about the story when I was writing down the little thoughts I had along the way. My reading was deeper."

Emma looks interested but still unconvinced that she wants to embark on a journey of deeper reading. She's happy right where she is.

"Let me ask you: Are the books you've been reading challenging for you?"

"No, not really," she admits. She's reading books that are at the upper level of an eighth-grade reading library, but not beyond—a book like *I Capture the Castle*, by Dodie Smith, for example. There's plenty to take notes on in that book, but it didn't present a challenge for her.

"If you read a book that was more challenging for you, you might have more to say in your notes. I want you to try and practice that."

We decide that she would have two books at all times. One she would read slowly and annotate, going for deeper meaning. The other would be for fast, fun reading.

This seemed to work for her. When I check in with her a day or two later, she has finished one fun book already and is taking her time with Robert Cormier's *I Am the Cheese*, We both agree it is not a difficult book to decode, but it is a challenge to understand what in the world is going on. She's keeping sticky notes on everything she notices and wonders as she reads it.

I have a similar conversation with another speedy reader, Benny. He's wanted to take on the challenge of reading Melville's *Moby-Dick*, and our conversation is a catalyst for it. He is, in fact, capable of reading this book, but it slows down his usual pace considerably. The day after our conversation about his choice, he bounds into class and announces, "Guess what, everybody? I like writing stickies now! I'm reading *Moby-Dick*!" He relishes the snickers, which can be heard from classmates at his mention of the title.

"Ms. Sacks, now I read every page twice!" he continues. "The first time I just read it. The second time I write sticky notes—like three on each page!" he says. Benny is having a similar experience with *Moby-Dick* that some struggling readers have with eighth-grade-level texts.

The Code Breaker

Hector's story takes place over a longer period of time. Hector came to our school in the sixth grade as a nonreader. In the sixth grade, he had a lot of trouble

269

following basic procedures and maintaining good behavior. He had developed so many ways of distracting himself and others from his inability to read, including whistling through the plastic clasps on his backpack during class and cracking jokes in Spanish, while opting out of work. This affected his performance in almost every class, except physical education and, to some extent, math.

I met him as a seventh grader, and I was also his advisor. In conversations, it was clear he was bright, capable of critical thinking, and socially on par with his peers. He did any work he was able to do, such as copying notes and completing checklists. But he was lost most of the time in class and too ashamed to seek or accept help. I waited until I had gotten to know him a bit and begun to gain his trust to talk to him about the reality of his reading skills. (The fact that I understood all his Spanish slang helped my cause.)

I assessed his reading using leveled reading passages and methodology from the Reading and Writing Project at Columbia University's Teachers College. He was able to recognize many one-syllable words, but he had trouble comprehending even third-grade-level texts because there were many words that he didn't know. I suspected he had so little experience reading that there were other gaps as well, but the main issue was that he could not break the code of the written word. I did notice that he was able to sound out short words. Hector understood the sounds of the letters when they followed regular rules, but he didn't know how to pronounce a word like *through*. This gave me great hope.

"Hector, you seem to know how to read some words, but the ones you don't know are getting in the way for you. Can you understand what's going on in this story?"

"Not really," he said quietly.

"That must be very frustrating for you when you read," I said, attempting to validate his feelings. He was quiet.

"I can help you this year," I said, with a very serious look on my face. It was important that I meant it. I can recall making a claim like that earlier in my career but having no idea how to help him. I felt confident that with two experienced teachers in his ELA CTT class, and an intensive reading class, we would indeed be able to help him progress. "But it's going to take a lot of work. Do you want to work on your reading this year?" I asked soberly, indicating that I wanted an honest answer and was not sure which way he felt. Hector nodded.

We came up with a plan for a buddy system in each class—someone he would sit near who could explain directions to him. We also came up with a hand signal he would discreetly show teachers when he wanted help.

Daniel Brink-Washington, my coteacher, and I began offering him and other struggling readers audio recordings of most of the whole novels we read as a class. For independent reading, we helped students choose books they could read on their own. We initially offered this in class only through a set of wireless headphones that connected to a listening station, and we allowed any student to use it during class. Students at all levels responded enthusiastically to the option, and it took away the stigma around needing additional support. Then Danny, who is chair of the special education department, got school funds to purchase a collection of pocket-sized MP3 players with ear-bud headphones. We loaded them with the audio recordings of our whole novel selections and created an official sign-out process. Students could then follow along with the audio recording in class and at home. We gave priority to students who needed this help the most, and the MP3s were a huge success.

Hector began using the audio support for novel studies during seventh grade, and had what I believe was his first positive experience reading a chapter book. He participated in discussions with the rest of the class and seemed to get enjoyment from the experience. He also received instruction in decoding through the Wilson program. He made huge progress that year. He still did not pass his statewide ELA test and many of his classes, but he met his individualized education program (IEP) goals and became a participating member of our classroom learning community.

Now Hector is an eighth grader, and I get to keep working with him. In our first novel study, *The House on Mango Street*, he used audio and wrote some sticky notes on his own. He participated in partner reading, reading aloud with a classmate and working on notes together. His stickies, though incomplete, showed some personal responses to the vignettes, and he was able to identify themes. He did not do language notes.

Today we've launched our second novel study, Sherman Alexie's *The Absolutely True Diary of a Part-Time Indian*, and students are excitedly beginning to read the first chapter. They quickly realize that there are curse words and cartoons in this book and begin remarking excitedly about it. Hector's interest is piqued, and he opens his book, looking around to see who else is already reading. Danny walks around to offer MP3 players to students who might need one. For the first time, Hector declines the MP3. I'm not sure why and am slightly concerned that it's because he's embarrassed by it. But Hector proves me wrong. He sits reading and runs his finger across the lines of text on the page as he reads. At one point he elbows Noah next to him, and they whisper about something in the book. He keeps reading for the rest of the period. Danny and I exchange curious glances, but we don't bother Hector.

The next day, Hector reads in class again, running his finger across each line. At this moment, I realize his victory: he has broken the code of the written word!

Hector does not read the whole book in the three weeks the class has to complete it, but he reads half of it, which is over one hundred pages. He writes stickies only when he's working with a partner or in tutorial, a small extra-help group that Danny runs three times a week. His writing is still quite labored, and it seems he doesn't yet feel that the effort it takes to write responses pays off for him.

We let him participate in discussions even though he hadn't finished the book. Afterward, while the rest of the class moves into an independent reading cycle, he continues reading *The Absolutely True Diary*. He finishes all 232 pages a few weeks later.

From Hector, I learned to see and appreciate my students' relative progress across a year. Hector's progress, which probably represented a jump from first-grade to a third-grade reading level, does not show on his eighth-grade state test. However, the tremendous effort it takes for students to catch up with their peers must be acknowledged and celebrated. No matter how he measures up to his peers, Hector has fought to get on a path that can lead him almost anywhere. He can read now, and he's learned from his experience that his efforts to improve do pay off.

Danny reflected on Hector's story:

I think of Hector as a student who really benefited from whole novels. He came to us as a nonreader. It wasn't successful for him 100 percent of the time, but the program got him interested in literature and language in a way I'm not sure anything else would have. He'd been through a lot of skills boot camps before, and these didn't work. This method really compelled him to want to read and respond to the other forms of help that were available to him.

For code breakers who come to us in middle school in need of serious remediation, a multipronged approach is necessary. I'm convinced from Hector's case and other students I've worked with and achieved similar results that whole novels studies is an essential element of an overall plan, despite how counter-intuitive this may seem.

SPECIAL SUPPORTS FOR STRUGGLING READERS

For many students, the experiences of interacting authentically with novels, along with the whole class supports described in Chapters 4 and 5, are sufficient to propel them forward as readers and thinkers. For other students, and for Hector, these experiences alone are often not enough. For these students, my coteachers and I have designed supports for the students who need them. In accordance with the principles of universal design, much of the work that we've done to help struggling readers grow in whole novel studies has ended up benefiting all students.

Danny shares his thinking about our collaborative planning process:

Whole novels present a set of challenges. A variety of strategies need to be employed in order to facilitate an entire grade-appropriate novel for a kid who's not even reading two-page articles at a lower level. At first it was daunting. I hadn't tried to do that before. I had tried taking the attitude of, "Well, just read it, and it'll be an experience." That's a common strategy that sometimes leaves special needs kids out. They will have an experience, but it's not addressing their specific needs. In planning a novel study, I think, *How will I leverage the text to make sure that by using it, we're addressing the goals in their IEP and the foundational skills that will help them most?*

So a lot of the structures we worked on came out of that need. Part of the approach was to attack the volume of reading by finding ways to share that reading, read sections aloud, offer audio books, allow them to keep up with a class that was working otherwise much faster than they could. We see that in the partner reading strategies and in the stickies— especially the specific formats for sticky notes we designed.

We would look at the novel and ask, "What opportunities does this text provide for all students? Based on the nature of this text, what are things that we're going to be talking about?" Once we identified these elements, I'd think, *Let's create a system for kids to start thinking about those things on a regular basis.* The theme and conflict stickies were especially helpful for kids in our special education population. [See Chapter 3 for details on formats for sticky notes.]

Kids got better at them. They don't start out good at them. As folks got better at those things, it focused their thinking on what we were leading up to as a discussion on the content of the book. In discussions, students with special needs had tended to talk less about author's craft and focus more on what was happening—finding ways to figure this out, even when the author doesn't say it directly. We would do a lot of picking out a place where the plot or a character's actions were confusing and rereading and talking about it. The stickies allowed them to take their thinking further. With the specific formats for stickies, they would bring things they noticed to discussion. That wasn't stuff that they were pulling out on their own before. Observing the whole inclusive class, some kids were already doing it and naturally did it. The formats helped other kids learn to do it.

At the same time, for the students who were commenting on literary elements and author's craft more naturally, the formats had a benefit as well: it helped them practice using literary terms to name their observations, something only a few students were doing on their own.

Partner Reading

One of the ways that we help struggling readers to access the novels is by pairing them strategically with a classmate and giving them class time to share the reading and response experience (Figure 8.2). Pairing students who have similar reading abilities tends to be most helpful, and motivation and productivity are highest this way. A pair of students who struggle with similar things can problem-solve together, which is relieving and empowering. Pairing two highly able readers together allows them to push each other's thinking in powerful ways as well. With homogeneous groupings for this activity, we avoid the frustration a more

Figure 8.2 Partner Reading

confident reader feels when held back by a more struggling reader, and the embarrassment a struggling reader may feel when paired with a highly able reader.

Visit https://vimeo.com /60983679 for video 8.1: Partner Reading.

Occasionally I partner two students who read on very different levels. When the two students get along (the stronger reader is patient and the weaker reader is interested and open to working together and receiving help), this can be a fruitful and enjoyable experience. The stronger reader is able to help the struggling reader understand, but both students contribute to responding to the content and end up having interesting conversations they might not have had otherwise.

This activity can be helpful in any whole novel study, but certain books lend themselves to being read out loud. The language of Sandra Cisneros's *The House on Mango Street*, for example, has a special musical quality that comes out when it is

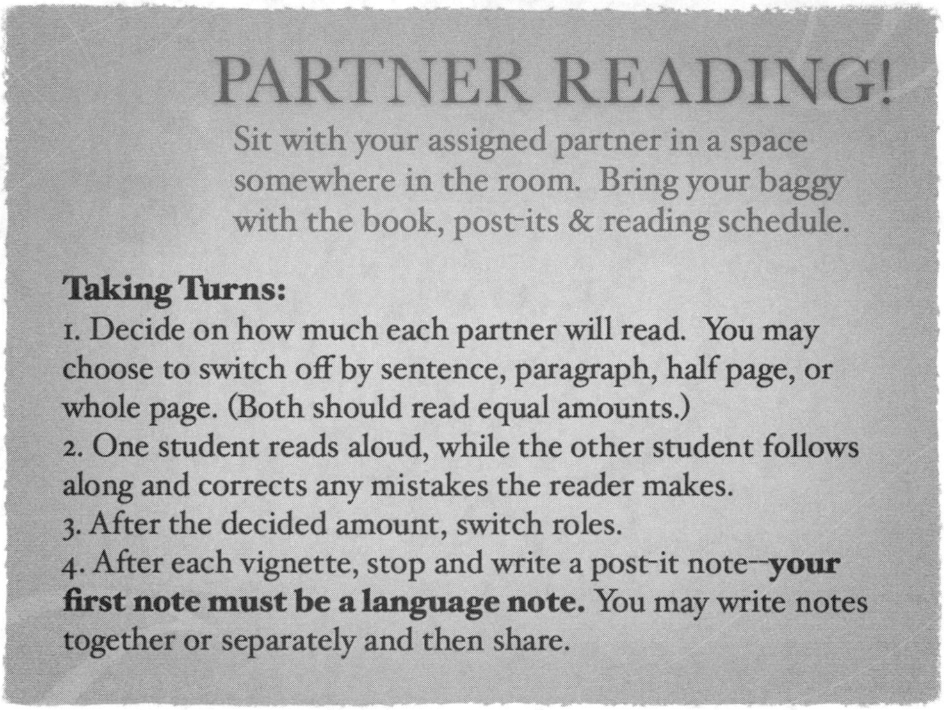

PARTNER READING!

Sit with your assigned partner in a space somewhere in the room. Bring your baggy with the book, post-its & reading schedule.

Taking Turns:

1. Decide on how much each partner will read. You may choose to switch off by sentence, paragraph, half page, or whole page. (Both should read equal amounts.)
2. One student reads aloud, while the other student follows along and corrects any mistakes the reader makes.
3. After the decided amount, switch roles.
4. After each vignette, stop and write a post-it note--**your first note must be a language note.** You may write notes together or separately and then share.

Figure 8.3 Directions for Partner Reading

read aloud. I have students work on language notes together in this study and love observing the conversations.

Other texts may not be so musical but have a lot of subtext, as in *The Chocolate War* by Robert Cormier. Students can benefit from reading sections with a partner and talking through the layers of what's going on.

Early in the year, I establish a procedure for partner reading. I select pairs and post the names on the board. Students find a space in the room and take turns reading aloud to each other. The directions for the students for partner reading are in Figure 8.3.

Informal Partner Reading

Once we've established and practiced the procedure for partner reading and kids begin to see the benefits, I allow them the option of reading with a partner during regular independent reading time. They move to the meeting area and read aloud to each other, pausing to work on sticky notes. I have seen caring, productive relationships develop around this reading, where one friend helps another and both gain from the experience. Occasionally students try to take advantage of the opportunity and socialize instead of read. This is easy to spot, since most of the rest of the class is reading silently. I have a quick word with them and send them back to their seats if they don't use the time productively.

Strategic Rereading of Complex Texts

When the class was reading *The Chocolate War*, it became clear that it would not be a good idea to have to wait until the discussions to reread sections of the text. So much of the plot of the novel is implied through Cormier's layered narrative that a good number of students were missing key events. Instead of giving up on the whole novel structure and giving students comprehension questions or telling them what's going on, I wanted to take the opportunity to teach the strategy of rereading, which I had to do a lot of in my college literature courses to understand the plot of some stories and is an essential skill for reading complex texts.

We came at it in two ways. First, in a whole class meeting, I'd ask students, "Which part from last night's reading was confusing?" When students identified sections, I'd pick the one that I knew was most important to their understanding of the overall plot. We'd read it aloud together and talk through what was happening. Usually I would just ask, "What's happening here? What do you notice?" Students were generally able to clear up confusion as a result of the rereading and opportunity to process. We practiced this skill and discussed how rereading changed their experience.

After a few days of this, I began giving them a warm-up activity at the beginning of class that drew from the previous night's reading. My students love to just read at the beginning of class, and I adjusted this to use the time for *rereading*. I gave each student a long, lined sticky note (five by eight inches) and left directions on each student's table to reread a specific page from last night's reading and then answer the 5 Ws and 1 H about the passage on their sticky note:

Who is in this scene?
What is happening?

Where are they?

When is this?

Why is it happening?

How do you know?

Then students would share what they found with others at their table, and we'd debrief in the whole class meeting. Students found this remarkably helpful. It taught them a strategy they could apply to any difficult text and showed them that there was a specific way they needed to read *The Chocolate War* in order to understand it. They had to constantly be asking themselves, "What's going on, and how do I know?" in a way that more straightforward narratives don't require.

Audio Support

The special education department at my school has purchased a collection of pocket-sized MP3 players. We load audio files for each whole novel study, often with the author reading his or her own novel, and make them available to all students. Students can listen on headphones in class, following along in the book, and pause the recording to write sticky notes (Figure 8.4). Some students listen with a partner, one ear bud for each.

Marcia Stiman-Lavian describes how she uses audio books to help students in our class:

> I offer all students with IEPs the use of an audio device, and anyone else I think might benefit from it in a novel study. For students who I know are auditory learners, where hearing text is just processed easier, I try to encourage them to utilize it. I find it especially helpful for students who have trouble processing text while reading. For example, many of our students aren't at an eighth-grade reading level. Students who struggle with decoding can be so consumed with decoding that they aren't able to comprehend the text, even if they are successful at decoding. The effort it takes to decode takes all their energy, so they don't really experience the story. The audio device takes that struggle away, and they are able to

Figure 8.4 Audio Support

access just the content. This also helps students who are intimidated by text and students with various other reading disabilities. Having the audio takes that struggle away. I have presented it to our students as a really cool chance for students. They seem to really enjoy getting to break the rules in class by listening to a device that is normally banned.

When I ask her what she thinks of the notion that this is a crutch for students and not "real reading," Marcia replies:

I think it is important to always keep in mind what the goal is for our students at any given time. Are we trying to teach them decoding skills at this moment or comprehension of the text? In a whole novel study we prioritize the comprehension and the student getting a deeper and more meaningful understanding of a literary text. If decoding is an issue, then taking that issue away allows the student to be on the same level as their peers when it comes to discussing story elements.

279

Daniel Brink-Washington adds:

I get why people might think it's a crutch, but I think the experience of being included in discussions is important for all students. Oftentimes kids who need audio and need help decoding are entirely capable of participating in rich discussions about content of a book. When you don't allow them to read intricate, complex texts, what happens is that they don't get to have those conversations because the stuff they can read on their own isn't that interesting or complex.

In the end, I don't think crutches are good, but I see this more as assistance. You have to look at it as a means to an end. This is an experience the whole class is having. Take Hector, for instance. You could say, "He just won't read what the other kids read." But that would be an unnecessary loss for him. Will he get the practice he needs in decoding through whole novel studies? Not if you don't structure the kids' use of the text. We've begun doing that.

Looking forward, I think there's a really amazing curriculum that could evolve when you have differentiated minilessons on the same piece of text. Audio-supported reading can't be the only reading instruction that kids get, but vilifying audio books suggests that that's all that's happening, which isn't the case.

In my own mind, students who make use of the audio device are simulating the experience I had as a child when my parents read me chapter books. It's common for parents to read picture books to their toddlers and young children, but far fewer parents read whole chapter books to school-age kids. Listening to the entire *Narnia* and *Lord of the Rings* series gave me a strong ability to picture things just from language and move with it in my imagination until it took no effort and I got lost in the world of the book. Listening to full novels builds patience and an ability to absorb large amounts of language in readers. Children then bring this skill to their own reading once they learn to decode.

 Visit https://vimeo.com /61677461 for video 8.2: Student Voices on Audio Support.

Small Group Support

My school schedules a study hall period twice a week. During this time, we schedule small group tutorials for students who need extra help. Three teachers run ELA tutorials for eighth graders, and I coordinate with those teachers about supporting students in reading and responding to novels. Marcia and Danny have both run small reading groups during class time while most of the class is reading independently. Marcia likes to pull a group of three to five students into the hallway to read together. "This way the students have a chance to read and hear the text out loud. They also get to process what is going on in the story out loud with their peers. This helps many students increase their comprehension," she says. Marcia also runs small group sessions before and after school. She connects with parents of struggling students and requests that students come in the morning or afternoon for extra help if they are having trouble or falling behind.

In my previous school, I also worked with a wonderful CTT teacher, Alicia Thacker. One year we had a class that had a great deal of trouble calming down and focusing on their work. Individually every student seemed to want to learn and make thoughtful contributions to the class, but the mix of personalities and learning needs was not working. We became overwhelmed by the amount of "performing" behavior we were seeing from certain students, who seemed to be trying to impress each other while avoiding deeper learning issues.

In planning the next novel study, we decided that Alicia would work with a small group of about five students who all had IEPs and struggled with reading comprehension. We found that when we split the large class, both smaller groups settled down immensely and formed a more positive group dynamic. Alicia was able to focus on her students' reading needs instead of managing their behavior, and I was able to focus more intensely on the needs, interests, and group behavioral dynamics of the rest of the class (which still included students with IEPs but who were able to read a novel with less support). Sometimes we would begin class all together, and then Alicia would move to the other classroom when it was time to read. Other times we would be separate the whole period.

We continued this for about six weeks. When we returned together for the next unit, the improvement in the whole group was noticeable. The small group support had increased Alicia's students' confidence and focus, and my group had gotten a chance to develop a more functional group dynamic that created more space for academic thinking and risk taking. We still split for certain activities and it never became a perfect situation, but the flexible small group experiences were a powerful tool.

Targeted Questioning Conferences

My coteacher this year in CTT classes, Yusuf Ali, is experienced in reading intervention and has begun experimenting with how to use remediation strategies within the whole novel studies for students in need of intervention. We talked about how he might confer with specific students who struggle with comprehension during reading time, in a way that would help them access the text without putting them on an entirely different path from the rest of the class. Yusuf explains the need he wants to address:

> I wanted to be able to ask some of our struggling readers in the class targeted literal, inferential, and critical questions that would point them to important parts of the text to help them get the meaning, but also help them formulate more personal, critical responses to the text. What was happening was that struggling readers are focusing so much on compre-hending the literal story that they often miss out on the opportunity to dive deeper into the richness of the text. This is one of the challenges of having them read something that is not necessarily on their independent reading level. I also wanted to be able to collect data on what I was doing and track my students' progress.

In our weekly collaborative planning meeting, we employed a technique I learned from a blog post by Bill Ferriter at The Tempered Radical, featured by the Center for Teaching Quality (http://www.teachingquality.org/blogs /billferriter). Bill, my virtual colleague on the Teacher Leaders Network, shared his practice of creating Google Live forms to collect data from classroom observations and conferences with students using an iPad. Yusuf and I created the fiction question tracking form, a Google Live form that he could use on his iPad during class. (We created a separate form for nonfiction texts.) The form includes the student's name, grade, and the text he or she is reading (Figure 8.5).

Text Title?

○ The Absolutely True Diary of a Part-Time Indian

○ The Chocolate Wars

○ Other: [ ]

What kind of thinking is being asked?

○ Literal

● Inferential

○ Critical

Was the question answered correctly?

○ 0--The answer was not correct.

○ 1--The answer was almost correct and supported with weak evidence from the text.

○ 2--The answer was correct and supported with weak evidence from the text.

○ 3--The answer was correct and supported with evidence from the text.

Quick Note about Response.

[ ]

What kind of Literal?

☐ Solving Words--Using a range of strategies to take words apart and understand what words mean.z

☐ Monitoring and Correcting--Checking whether reading sounds right, looks right, and makes sense, working to solve problems.

☐ Searching and Using Information--Searching for and using all kinds of information in a text.

☐ Summarizing--Putting together and remembering important information and disregarding irrelevant Information while reading.

What kind of Inferential?

☐ Expections--Using what is know to think about what will follow while reading continuous text.

☐ Making Connections--Searching for and using connections to knowledge gained through personal experiences, learning about the world, and reading other texts.

☐ Inferring--Going beyond the literal meaning of a text to think about what is not stated but is implied by the writer.

☐ Synthesizing--Putting together information from the text and from the reader's own background knowledge in order to create new understandings.

What kind of Critical?

☐ Analyzing--Examining elements of a text to know more about how it is constructed and noticing aspects of the writer's craft.

☐ Critiquing--Evaluating a text based on the reader's personal, world, or text knowledge and thinking critically about the ideas in it.

☑ Send me a copy of my responses.

( )

Figure 8.5 Targeted Questioning Conference Form

It has a space for the teacher to record notes on his or her interaction with the student, a category for the question (literal, inferential or critical), and a scale from 0 to 3 for how well the student answered the question and used evidence. That rating system is aligned to sequences Irene Fountas and Gay Su Pinnell use in their assessments. For each kind of thinking, there are subcategories, shown below. "I'm using Fountas and Pinnell as a resource, because that's what I'm trained in. Moving forward, I'm interested in incorporating Bloom's system as well," Yusuf says.

Yusuf creates questions ahead of time, reviewing sections of the novel and using question stems from the *Fountas & Pinnelle Prompting Guide Part 2 for Comprehension* (2012) in literal, inferential, and critical categories that he writes on note cards. He phrases them generally, so that they can be reused with a different text—for example, "How do you think the main character feels about himself or herself at the end of this chapter?"

"I drop a question I've chosen off to a student and ask him or her to write a sticky note about it. If they are in partner reading, I'll have both partners work on it. Then I'll confer with another student and circle back to check after a few minutes," Yusuf explains.

When Yusuf returns, he talks to them about their response, and fills out the Google form, and holds onto the question card to use in other conferences. He explains, "The Google form is really informal. Bringing the kids into the technology of it has been exciting for them. The students see what I'm writing, and that what they say is important—I take notes on what they say. We talk about their answers, and I suggest a next step for the student. *They* press Submit on the form when we're done. Everything happens on the spot."

I'm struck by the immediate feedback students are getting on their work in this process. They seem to like it and appreciate that they are getting extra attention they need.

This practice is still in the pilot stages, and Yusuf is working out his next steps. "Later, I do an error analysis. I'm figuring out what things I need to teach as a group to the most struggling readers. Some things I can teach in the moment, like how to pronounce a certain sound, but other things need to be returned to in a different format."

Differentiated Novel Studies

In whole novels, the whole class does not always read the same book, so students can choose from different books that connect thematically. The novels also range in difficulty, and students nearly always choose the book that is most appropriate for them in terms of reading level. During our journey novel study, one group reads *Somewhere in Darkness*, by Walter Dean Myers, while another group reads *The Ear, the Eye and the Arm*, by Nancy Farmer, and another reads *The Alchemist*, by Paulo Coelho. All three follow the classic journey structure, but Myers's book is much more readable for eighth graders with lower reading skills. The differentiated novel studies provide teachers a chance to tailor the miniprojects and other assignments to the needs of the specific group.

If this is the case, I like to alternate a differentiated group experience like this with a whole class story experience. That might be a novel everyone can access, or it could be a graphic novel, film, folktale, or short story that builds on the literary focus of the whole novel studies.

Parallel Programming

At my first school, I had classes of mostly transitional English Language Learners. There were no special education accommodations for these students, and I had no collaborative team teachers. It was just a wide range of learners and me. Every class was different. Sometimes the whole class could decode well enough that with my support and the right book selections, the whole class could make progress with one novel or with two whole novel groups.

There were also classes where I had several students who were not ready to read novels. In some whole novel studies, I did my best to facilitate their inclusion in the reading of a specific book. In other novel studies, like the journey study, they formed their own group, and I created picture books series that followed the journey structure. They moved from picture books to reading the text of folktales that also involved journeys. They worked on sticky note responses, and we held discussions at the end to discuss multiple stories. The picture book study came as a relief for them. They got to work on decoding skills and building their English vocabularies. They also, like the rest of the class, gained story experience and analyzed literary elements and discovered a lot about the classic journey story.

Using Outside Supports

Clearly I'm fortunate to work with wonderful special education coteachers who contribute a great deal to the success of the class and individual students. There are other partners I've connected with to help support students in general, but especially in whole novel studies.

Speech Pathologist

The speech pathologist at my school has a number of my struggling readers on her caseload. In the past and at previous schools, she has pulled students out of regular classes to work with them on their speech and language skills. This year, she's been doing a mix of pulling students out and pushing into classes, and she's been able to use the novels as a context within which to support students' language development. Now when she pulls students out of my class, she checks with me first about what they're working on and helps them with their reading, responses, or preparation for discussions alongside the goals of her therapy. When she pushes into class, she works with them on the class work, but adapts the activities to help her meet her objectives in her role as speech pathologist.

Our collaboration has effectively made us both stronger, and our students as well. Instead of coming at many of the same skills separately, working together creates a more unified, productive experience for kids.

Wilson Teacher or Reading Specialist

In a previous school, many of my students received pullout support from the Wilson program, designed to teach decoding and fluency skills specifically to middle school struggling readers. Since my seventh- and eighth-grade classes were not designed to teach decoding to students, Wilson provided invaluable support to those who needed it. I watched students jump up many levels in their reading throughout the year, finishing the year with the ability to read grade-level texts on their own.

The Wilson teacher remarked to me that my students seemed especially motivated in her class. We found that students who were in my English class and working with whole novels made significantly more growth on average than the rest of the school population who received Wilson reading instruction. I believe that whole novels and the community the program provides students around reading creates a compelling reason for struggling readers to want to improve—to accept the help and do the hard work of catching up.

Social Studies Teachers

I talk with social studies teachers—humanities teachers, as they're called in my school—about the content and concepts they are teaching and try to select and schedule novels so that they can offer students opportunities to make thematic or historical connections to their learning in social studies class. This helps create a richer, more cohesive experience for middle school kids as they develop critical-thinking skills. When they see an idea in more than one place, the process of crystallization happens more quickly and more fully for them.

For example, we read *The Absolutely True Diary of a Part-Time Indian*. I give students nonfiction articles about the conditions on reservations today to help them understand the setting of this story and place it in a larger context. At the same time, students are learning about Westward expansion and the creation of reservations in humanities class with teacher Andre Theisen. Andre and I wondered if students were able to connect some of the issues our country faces today, especially with poverty, with the history they learn. It's a big concept and not something I want to present to a diverse group of middle school kids with a heavy hand. Like clockwork, though, in discussions of the novel, students began to connect the historical oppression of Native Americans in this country to the conditions our characters from the novel face on the reservations. This connection helped them gain deeper insight into the characters and conflicts in the novel, as well as the relevance of the history they were learning to life today.

During this discussion, one student had this moment of crystallization:

GINA: There's this part when Junior's at the basketball game. He's describing the basketball team. Not Reardon, but the Rez team, Welpinit. He says all of those kids are not going to college; seven have alcoholics as parents. Two of them their dads are drug addicts. The way he describes it, it just stayed with me. Man, these kids are almost set up for failure. The houses they are living in . . . the really sad thing is that Junior knows they are not gonna have a future. Basketball, the sport, and winning, is really the only thing they have going for them.

ALLIYAH: Junior—he gained more friends. Respect, because of the way he plays basketball. All the times he got hurt playing, he wanted to try again. Staying in the game made him want to stay strong. Junior and Victor both liked playing basketball.

JAMES: Also going back to Gina's point. After the final game, he said that he felt really bad. Probably when the kids go home the dads that are alcoholics are probably going to punish them really bad because they lost. He wanted to lose so they won't get hurt when they go home.

KAREN: I'm not sure if it was Junior or his grandmother or both. They said that they never drank alcohol. The grandma. That reminds me in *Smoke Signals* when the officer accuses them of being drunk and he says he's never had a drop. Some don't drink.

CANDICE: I don't think they were set up for failure. I think they just had to try. I don't think they were trying too hard. Junior tried and got into Reardon and did well. You have to try. Can't just be drunk all your life.

COURTNEY: I agree with Candice. I don't think they were set up for failure. All these people had a choice to stop drinking, but didn't.

MANNY: I agree with Gina that they are set up for failure. If your role models are your parents—if you're looking up to people who are drug addicts and drug dealers, who's going to tell you have to try to get an education and have a better life?

SAMUEL: I'm going to connect this to history. We just learned that Native Americans have been pushed into reservations, totally disrespected throughout history. They've gone from a large population to so few people living on horrible reservations. This connects to them being set up for failure. It's hard to get out of that position. Junior was an exception, and he was lucky because he had Mr. P telling him to go.

CANDICE: I was gonna bring up his sister. She tried, and she left. As long as you see the future for yourself, you don't have to follow your parents or anyone.

KAREN: When Junior tried to leave, people picked on him, so that makes it harder.

The level of synthesis of ideas here is something students are able to do because they've built up prior knowledge through their humanities class. They're taking that historical knowledge to another level by applying it to literature and the human condition in a way that's literary and distinct from the discipline of history. Also, students in every single one of my classes made this connection—those who achieve in the top third of their class and those in the bottom third. The common background knowledge clearly benefited all students.

Parents

Parents are a big piece of the puzzle that is every child's learning. They are the other teachers in kids' lives. By working together, teachers and parents can make a tremendous difference for students. In Chapter 6, I discussed how I work with parents to help hold students accountable for reading outside school. Though it takes work, parents can also become even more involved partners in their child's learning in and out of school.

Collaborating with parents means having the same sorts of open-ended conversations about learning I try to have with my students. We're both trying to figure out who the child is as a learner and what he or she needs and wants. We have different pieces of information, which is why conversation between us is so essential.

Here's a story about Jamar, where my persistent phone calls to his mother about her son's lack of reading led to a real partnership between us that neither of us had any idea would happen. I wrote this about him in an *EdWeek* article in 2010:

> Last year I had a student I'll call Jamar. Jamar was a sweet, very sociable kid, who always expressed a desire to do well in school, but who, in reality, was pretty disengaged with his school work. He had a lot of trouble focusing and following through on assignments. His grades in most classes, including mine, regularly hovered between a D+ and a F. His skills more or less matched those grades . . .
>
> Jamar was reading very little, especially at home. I had made a few phone calls to his mother. As it turned out, she was out of work on disability and so she had plenty of time to spend with Jamar in the evenings. This time I was calling about a novel—*The Dream Bearer* by Walter Dean Myers—that the whole class was reading. The deadline to complete the book was two days away, and Jamar needed to finish it in order to

participate in seminar-style discussions. "That's it," his mother told me. "He's gonna read this book."

The next day, Jamar skipped into school early. "Ms. Sacks, you're not going to believe it. I am SO tired. I was up til 2 a.m. reading that book with my mother! But you know what? The book is really GOOD! And you're gonna love reading my sticky notes!"

The following day the book was due, and Jamar came in boasting to everyone that he'd finished. His participation in discussions that week was exemplary. His insights into the book were deep and well evidenced. A new voice—both knowledgeable and inquisitive—emerged in our classroom that day.

I called Jamar's mother to tell her how wonderfully he'd done and thanked her for her help. She said, "You know, I'm home with him every day. I always ask him what homework he has and he says he already did it. This is the first time I got to really work with him on anything." She also told me how much she'd enjoyed reading the book with him and asked me what other books I had that might be similar so they could read some more together . . .

The amazing thing was that Jamar was not the same student after that moment. Something had clicked. He became much more engaged with his work, not just the reading, and not just in English class. He had benefited from the real intellectual experience of reading and was able to speak from that experience in an academic context. The power that came from that work of the mind, and the deepening of his relationship with his mother, was great enough to turn him on to learning.

This experience taught me that you never know when a parent can become a teacher's greatest ally. It's worth it to reach out often and not give up on the collaboration.

MODIFICATIONS FOR ACADEMICALLY ADVANCED STUDENTS

I always struggled to find ways to challenge my most academically able students. At Brooklyn Prospect, that challenge became even more pronounced. I constantly had ideas for how students could expand their learning, and sometimes I said them out loud, but I didn't have a system for communicating these opportunities or accounting for work students did by choice. After teaching seventh grade for one year at Brooklyn Prospect, I was looking forward to working with the same group of students as eighth graders the following year, and I was determined to create a system for my especially curious and quick students who easily blazed through a novel in a couple of days.

Seeker Opportunities

When the seventh graders had read Rebecca Stead's *When You Reach Me*, which builds significantly on plot and concepts from Madeleine L'Engle's *A Wrinkle in Time*, I ordered copies of the entire *Wrinkle in Time* series. I made these available to students who finished *When You Reach Me* early and were looking for their next book. At the same time, Danny thought it would be interesting to give students a chance to read something related to the idea of time travel, which figures prominently in these fiction selections. Danny found *How to Build a Time Machine*, by Paul Davies, about the theoretical possibility of time travel. He created a forum through our school's Google website, and interested students could read the book and participate in online discussions.

And did they! The discussions were lively, and there was a buzz throughout the grade about time travel and wormholes! Moreover, the energy students gained from these opportunities to expand on concepts within the novel study fueled their discussions of *When You Reach Me* with the rest of the class.

Over the summer, I looked at each whole novel study and selected related texts for students to explore after reading the main novel. I imagined students extending their learning in various directions originating from a common point. The image of a door came to mind. The door is the whole novel. Everyone has to open that door and step through to the other side. We explore together through discussions and in writing. But students who are able to take the learning further should have pathways for doing so. I wanted a name for this curricular structure. My colleague and frequent thought partner, humanities teacher Rachel Beerman, offered the name of her mother's longtime book club: The Seekers. It conjured up the right image for me.

Now, for each unit, I offer seeker opportunities, usually in the form of a text or film that connects thematically or formally to the "door" novel. I offer students a lot of choice in how they respond to these texts, whether it's participation in an

> ### Common Core Connection
>
> Seeker opportunities allow students to push themselves as readers toward CCRA.R.10: "Read and comprehend complex literary and informational texts independently and proficiently."

online discussion, an artistic response through sculpture or in iMovie, or a thoughtful book review. (See appendix E for an example of a seeker opportunity assignment sheet.)

Seeker opportunities are offered for credit as part of the ELA course, but not as extra credit. The way I handle this is by creating an assignment in my online grade book. I enter grades for those who choose to complete it. For those who don't, I enter nothing, and it has no effect on their grade. I count seeker opportunities on a pass or no-credit basis. Students who take on the opportunity receive full credit in the grade book. In this way, the work can only help their grade, because they receive either 100 percent or no grade at all. In the rare case that a student turns in a seeker assignment that doesn't warrant credit, I simply hand it back and explain the reason I haven't given any credit. In this case, the student may choose to redo the assignment. I post these assignments on my online teacher page, so parents can see them as well.

A good range of students takes up seeker opportunities—they are not always the most academically advanced students—which is encouraging to me. It shows that students are engaged and curious about the ideas of the curriculum and interested in spending more time exploring through reading. Now the practice is spreading with teachers in other classes who are offering seeker opportunities, expanding the amount of reading opportunities students have at a given time, especially in nonfiction. For example, about thirty students have chosen to read *The Immortal Life of Henrietta Lacks*, by Rebecca Skloot, in conjunction with study of DNA in science class. The book offers many chances for students to make interdisciplinary connections. Students can receive credit for both science and English class for participation in this project.

Alternative Formats for Response

For advanced readers, annotating texts, especially complex ones, with sticky notes as they read helps them extend their learning. Some really get into the process and find an expressive outlet in these responses. For others, especially when the text may not present much challenge for them, it weighs on their experience. I don't cater to this complaint much at the beginning of the year, because text annotation is an important skill for all readers.

However, based on conversations with students I had taught for over a year (as seventh graders and then eighth graders), I decided to experiment with more options for students who had proven that they had mastered the skill of text annotation and who read voraciously. There had to be a transparent system, though. I couldn't just go on a hunch, since adolescents are very concerned with fairness.

In coming up with alternative response formats, I thought about what was most important to me about the notes once the questions of basic reading skills and accountability were answered unequivocally. What I came up with was that the notes were valuable because they helped students collect thoughts about specific parts of the book that they could share in discussions and refer back to in writing.

We began by striking this deal: students who prove in two consecutive grade-appropriate (or above) novels that they can record their thought processes with evidence of literal, inferential and critical thinking and comments on specific literary elements have additional options for response. To prove this, they need to earn a grade of 95 percent or higher for two novels. This can include one whole novel and one independent reading book or two whole novels. They need to identify just ten specific places in the book to comment on in writing. In particular, I want them to record ideas they think would be interesting or important to bring up in discussions. They can do this as they read or later as a rereading activity. If we are focusing on a specific literary element or in the novel study, they need to incorporate that element into at least a couple of their responses.

I encourage using a longer sticky notes (five by eight inches) for these ten responses, because they are about the right size for a slightly longer response than a regular-sized sticky allows. I also allow them to record responses in journal form, either on a Google Doc that they share with or on paper, making sure to record a page number for each response. We started calling them "long notes."

At the right is an example of one in response to *Absolutely True Diary of a Part-Time Indian.*

Some students who earn the freedom to write long notes choose to keep writing more consistent shorter notes. Later in the year, some readers proposed new options. One reader who loves to sketch proposed a combination response journal and sketchbook. It was beautiful and more than met all the objectives I had for the assignment.

So. This is a big change for Junior. He realizes he's not alone and that he *does* fit in. He is part of a bunch of different "tribes." There are so many people in the world who belong to the tribes that Junior does, some of them, I'm a member also ☺. Junior went from being a shy guy who thought he didn't really fit in anywhere and he didn't really know who he was to a more confident, happier Junior who knows where he belongs and thinks he knows who he is.

The alternative requirements for responses have prompted some students to ask more questions about how they can improve the quality of their notes, which has led to some interesting and seemingly productive conversations. At the same time, I'm somewhat uncomfortable with students striving for grades connected to what is supposed to be their authentic response to reading. I want them to develop in a natural way, motivated by intellectual engagement. Some educational thinkers, like Alfie Kohn (2007), argue that external reward structures are not helpful for students to develop critical thinking. Ideally, I would want to help students decide when they have mastered the skill of text annotation—but I have yet to figure out how to do that.

Letting Students Lead the Way

Damian, an advanced reader, made a strong case for writing a book review for our final novel study of the year. At first I objected, because I find students' understanding of what a book review is tends to be superficial. He asked me to be specific about why a book review wouldn't be acceptable. I told him I worried that the book review would be too general, not rooted in specific sections of the text, and not interacting with literary elements.

"My book review would do all of those things," Damian claimed. I was impressed by his persistence.

"Okay," I said. "Write a quick proposal, an outline, of what your book review would include." The next day he brought me an outline that included grading and analyzing the author's use of each literary element. I was sold. Damian's book review far exceeded my expectations. (See appendix F for his complete book review.) By getting out of my own comfort zone, I had allowed Damian to discover a new place to go with his response.

WHOLE NOVELS FOR ALL

An atmosphere of growth in the whole novels program becomes contagious. All students benefit from the understanding that we are all different as thinkers and learners. There are infinite places to go with our learning, and many different ways to get there. Because of the simultaneous flexibility and cohesiveness of the whole novels program, it is an ideal approach for a diverse classroom.

Daniel Brink-Washington has this to say: "When I observe the whole inclusion class, and the specific students I work with, I can't imagine anything more appropriate for this group than reading a whole novel. Some of our students have serious learning disabilities, but they are capable of this experience. It's totally possible to think about how to accommodate them through the novel. It's about thinking—Who are the kids? What are their needs? How am I going to give that help they need and also all the range of learning experiences they deserve?"

9

Analyzing the Results
What We Know and Where We Can Go

"Will your book become a classic?"

This week, I had a conversation with my students about writing this book. They've known all year that I've been writing a book, and when I told them I was almost finished, they had a lot of questions. "What's it really about? What's it going to be called?" and so forth.

"The book is about the way we study literature in this class—the whole novels method—where you all read the entire book and then we come together to discuss and analyze it," I say. "Does that sound to you like what we do?" Nods all around.

"The book is for teachers, about why I believe in studying novels in this way and how to do it." They looked puzzled, as if they hadn't considered this idea from a teacher's perspective, and the wheels were turning. "There are other ways students study novels," I offer. "For example, some teachers don't believe we should all read the same book, because students don't all have the same reading interests and they should be able to choose what they read. Has anyone ever been in a class before where you always choose what you read and never do whole class novel studies?"

A bunch of students raise their hands and I see looks of recognition and puzzlement on their faces. The reading workshop method is prominent in New York City public elementary schools, so most students have experienced it in pure form at least once. In my imagination, my students are trying to remember back to those classes and assess whether they would prefer only choosing their own books at this point. "We do some independent reading in this class, but we also study whole novels together," I clarify.

"Many teachers do teach whole class novels, though," I continue. "But usually students read a chapter at a time, answer questions, and talk about the chapter." Many students nod and a few groan. "You've done this before?" I ask.

"Yes!" many students cry.

"In my perspective," I continue, "there's not one right way to teach, and different methods work well for different teachers, but I think there's something special about whole novels, and I want people to know about it."

James, an academically advanced student, raises his hand. "Well, I think it's good that we do it this way, you know, reading the whole book, because in fourth grade I used to get pulled out of class with a couple other students and we would read the book together, and talk about each chapter," James says in an even tone. "But we would start to run out of things to say because it was only a chapter, and I would get bored. This way we get to, kind of, read the book in our way, and then we have a lot more to say in discussions."

"Wow, that's really interesting, James! That's actually a point I try to make in the book," I say. I do my best to hide my delight that he's articulated my central argument.

Yvonne, a student who struggles with comprehension but has come a long way in just three months this year, raises her hand. "When we talk about each chapter, sometimes I forget what's happening in the story. It takes such a long time," she says. A few other students nod.

I take a few other questions from students, including, "Are we going to be in the book?!" and, "Will we get autographed copies?!" and we move on to the day's work. We've just finished our study of *The Absolutely True Diary of a Part-Time Indian* and we're moving into a new unit.

"We're moving into new territory today," I announce. "Everyone put your arms to the left side of your body, and now pretend you're turning a huge page from left to right, to signal the transition." I always think of curriculum as a big story or pathway, and I want students to understand the metaphor by making it three-dimensional.

"What book are we reading next?" a student asks.

"Actually, in our next unit, we're not going to be studying a novel," I answer. Students look surprised, given our earlier conversation.

"We're going to be studying the neighborhood." I see some excited looks on students' faces. The neighborhood study is a journalism project that begins with observations and inquiry into the neighborhood. (I've written previously about this project. See Sacks, 2011.)

"Cool!" a few students call out.

At this moment, something clicks for me. The neighborhood is our text in this upcoming study. And because of their intense work with whole novels, not only do my students know how to read novels, but they've also gained understanding of how to study something. They know how to record their thinking along the way, ask questions, check back to resources to help them answer questions, and draw conclusions. They know how to look at something from a variety of perspectives, as a whole and taking it apart. I can see my students poised to apply these skills to a new context—from the novel to the world around us.

THE TRANSFERABILITY OF FICTION SKILLS

Sometimes teachers question why I spend so much time working with students on teaching fiction, given the emphasis on nonfiction in the Common Core State Standards. It's not that I don't appreciate nonfiction. In my own reading life, I read more nonfiction than fiction these days, but that didn't start to be true until my later years of college. As a middle school student, I loved reading novels but had no trouble understanding nonfiction texts in my social studies and science classes. In working with adolescent readers, I find that fiction, because of the rich virtual experience stories provide, is what compels them most to read. It's the right place to start. And given the types of reading students are likely to do in other core subjects, English class is often the only place where kids get to read fiction and poetry.

Can students learn the skills they need to read nonfiction by reading mostly fiction? I believe the answer is yes, as long as they have chances to apply their skills to nonfiction texts across disciplines. First, kids who read a great deal of fiction generally become strong readers and strong students. They perform well in English classes, as well as other disciplines that require mostly nonfiction reading and on tests of their fiction and nonfiction reading skills. It seems the skills of nonfiction develop easily for students who are voracious readers of fiction. For students who have trouble comprehending and responding to nonfiction, I would prescribe a heavy diet of fiction, through which they can strengthen their decoding skills, reading stamina, vocabularies, and response habits.

Some data from my seventh graders in 2010 corroborate my claim that fiction skills transfer to nonfiction. The way I collected and organized the data that year, as well as my exclusive focus on novels that year, make it easy to make the argument. In subsequent years, I've collected data differently and included more nonfiction alongside novel studies, making it more difficult to present this argument using hard data.

In September 2010, I gave my seventh-grade students a reading diagnostic test using the reading passages and multiple-choice questions from a previous year's New York State eighth-grade ELA test which included a balance of fiction and nonfiction texts; 47 percent of my students scored proficient on the exam. During that fall, we worked pretty much exclusively on whole novel studies and student-selected independent reading novels in English class. In January 2011, I gave my students an interim assessment that consisted of two fictional passages and a poem from a different previous New York State ELA test and the corresponding multiple-choice questions; 83 percent of my students scored proficient on this test. I was pleased with the results, but I logically wondered how they would do on the rest of the test, which would include as much nonfiction as fiction and poetry. Three weeks later, with no addition of nonfiction texts or instruction in my class, my school gave students a complete reading portion of another previous year's New York State Eighth-Grade ELA test; 80 percent of my students scored proficient on this test, which included more than 50 percent nonfiction texts and was more than double the length of the interim assessment.

My 2010 data collection does not prove anything unequivocally, and I haven't concluded that I have no responsibility to help my students read nonfiction. However, it is at least an example of one diverse group of students that was able to transfer fiction-reading skills they gained over about five months to nonfiction texts with no explicit instruction. And it's an example that doesn't surprise me.

THE BENEFITS OF FICTION IN THE REAL WORLD

The tendency to downplay the real-world benefits of reading and studying fiction is sorely misguided. The study of fiction is academically rigorous and has many benefits. Reading fiction has been shown to help individuals develop empathy, which is important for anyone who needs to get along with others and understand people's motivations—which basically means all of us. In the *Harvard Business Review*, Anne Kreamer (2012) writes, "Academic researchers such as Oatley and Raymond Mar from York University have gathered data indicating that fiction-reading activates neuronal pathways in the brain that measurably help the reader better understand real human emotion—improving his or her overall social skillfulness." She goes on to argue the applicability of fiction skills in our daily lives: "Think about how many different people you interact with . . . Then think about how much effort you devoted to thinking about their emotional state or the emotional quality of your interaction. It's when we read fiction that we have the time and opportunity to think deeply about the feelings of others, really imagining the shape and flavor of alternate worlds of experience."

In *A Whole New Mind: Why Right-Brainers Will Rule the Future*, author Daniel Pink (2006) writes about the shifting skills necessary for success in the twentieth-century world, given that machines and cheap labor sources overseas can take over so many rote tasks for us. Whole novels help students strengthen many of the six senses Pink introduces in the book. Empathy is one of them—it's something that machines don't possess, and it's hard to employ at a distance. Play, which comes up in the fiction-writing exercises in whole novel studies, is another one. Symphony, which is the ability to see the big picture or the whole as well as the intricate parts, is another one. Finally, in addition to the capacities to design and make meaning of experiences, Pink devotes an entire chapter to the "sense" of story. The ability to understand and create stories is an essential skill in law, where lawyers create persuasive stories about their clients based on evidence. Increasingly, story ability is being emphasized in the medical profession, where doctors need to listen to the history and all evidence and create a narrative that frames a patient's unique health condition. Literature studies have been added to the course work at a number of cutting-edge medical schools. Finally, in today's marketplace, the story behind a business or product is as important as the product itself to selling.

Even teachers need the sense of story, argues cognitive scientist Dan Willingham in his book *Why Don't Students Like School?* (2010). Willingham suggests that through narrative storytelling, great teachers create compelling lessons that keep students actively thinking about the content, making it stick in their memories.

THE STORY THE DATA TELL

The data I am most interested in are the long-term data, which I hope will show how students of whole novels gain skills that have value in their personal and professional lives. However, in the short term, I have some data suggesting on a small scale that the whole novels program has some immediate benefits on student achievement levels as measured by the standardized tests. I had the opportunity to work with the same group of one hundred students for two years in a row as their seventh- and then eighth-grade teacher.

The data in Figure 9.1 tell a story of a group of students in which the number of kids who met increasingly demanding proficiency criteria grew steadily each year

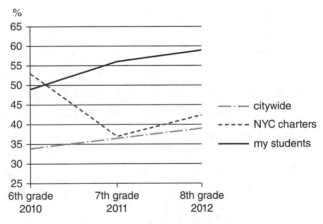

Note: The "My Students" line represents the seventh- and eighth-grade students I taught using the whole novels program.

Figure 9.1 Proficiency Rates on the New York State ELA Test, 2010–2012

they worked with me and studied whole novels. (New York State has been making the tests more challenging each year since 2009, when it faced criticisms that the tests had been "dumbed down.") The growth in proficiency rates is greater over this two-year period than that of citywide public or charter schools. In 2012, Brooklyn Prospect Charter School was ranked twenty-fourth among New York City Charter Schools in overall performance across grades on the state ELA Tests; the eighth-grade class, however, was ranked ninth against other charter schools in overall performance on the same test. (All data have been made public by the NYC Charter School Center at nyccharterschools.org)

I do not offer these results to make the claim that whole novels is the way to raise students' test scores. I believe standardized tests do not allow students to demonstrate learning that is complex and layered, and I'm skeptical that they ever could. I offer these results instead to make the case that in teaching whole novels, we don't throw our students or ourselves under the bus in today's test-driven educational climate. If anything, we may be at a slight advantage.

My friend and colleague Nancy Toes Tangel, who also studied at Bank Street with Madeleine Ray, taught whole novels to a high-need population of students in Newark, New Jersey, for years. Her students' standardized test scores consistently showed slightly over two grade levels of growth each academic year. This reality would shock some, because Nancy spends considerable class time working with students on artistic expressions of the literature they read, a practice I've heard belittled lately for supposed lack of rigor. When I ask Nancy to share her reasons for building out the connections between literature and visual art, she writes, "I can make a case for the long-term value of a sophisticated learning of visual thinking, the building of collaborative skills, the development of qualitative thought, but maybe it is because it brings an element of play into my classroom. And it is in that moment of spontaneity that the relational art between teacher and student, that I work to establish in my classroom, reveals itself. Providing both the adolescent and myself with an understanding of the beauty of making art." Her response reminds me of another of Daniel Pink's six essential senses for the twenty-first-century workplace: design.

Nancy adds, "And for struggling readers who often identify themselves as visual learners, the visual arts allow for the seeing of the who, what, when, where, and why. This often helps to establish a framework for knowledge that can then

Figure 9.2 Literary Elements Quilt

be reassembled in new ways, allowing for original ideas from these students." Figure 9.2 shows Nancy's students' visual interpretation of the literary elements in *The Outsiders*, by S. E. Hinton.

To be sure, Nancy does not focus on short-term, skill-based achievement goals for her students when she designs learning experiences for them. She prioritizes on getting to know her students and helping each of them to engage deeply in the reading of literature, writing, and artistic creation they do in their own way. When forces seem to pull me away from allowing my students the deep learning they deserve in favor of more easily measurable outcomes, I often think of Nancy's example.

WHAT BECOMES OF STUDENTS OF WHOLE NOVELS?

Another result that I look at is how my eighth-grade students of whole novels manage when they enter high school. Though I'm in touch with a number of my former middle school students (some of them in college now), it's generally been difficult to get more than a general sense of how my students fare in high school—that is, until now. My eighth graders last year, whom I taught for two years, moved on to become ninth graders at my current school. My colleague, Meredith Byers, now teaches some of them in her ninth-grade Literary Studies class. Of the twenty-six students in the class, fourteen are my former eighth graders, and twelve students are new to our school.

Meredith is familiar with the work I did with the students because she observed me a number of times last year and we've talked about whole novels before. Once I asked her if she noticed anything about her students that she might connect to their participation in the whole novels program for two years. This is her reply:

> The best word to describe the students you had last year is *patient*. We recently spent two days listening to an audio version of Athol Fugard's *Master Harold . . . and the Boys*. This is a play, which can sometimes pose difficulties for even the strongest readers. Reading drama is a very different experience. The whole novel veterans were able to sit with the entire text. They weren't intimidated by it. They weren't afraid of it. They were able to listen to the text for the full two days. We didn't really discuss the play until we had listened to it, and we aren't going to launch our whole class discussions until we have done some background work on the play and talked about the historical context. The whole novel students can handle this. They have posted and written thoughtfully about the action that happens in the play, but they are able to hold on to these thoughts until we are ready for a discussion.

The chance to study novels deeply in middle school sets students up to be patient, as Meredith describes. They also have enough experience and maturity to be able to anticipate and comprehend the shape of longer texts and unfamiliar forms of literature, which is so important in high school.

Meredith, in her second year of teaching, shared with me her plans to have students go back through the play and visually mark the appearance of specific symbols throughout the story to help them analyze their significance. "I've worked really hard on this plan, and I'm curious what you think. Will it work?" she asked me.

"I think it sounds great! I might want to steal that and try it in the eighth grade!" I said. "One thing, though. Who came up with the symbols?"

Meredith smiled knowingly. "I did," she said. "But I think I see where you're going with this."

"Well, that would be the only part of it I'd do differently. I'd want the students to come up with the symbols," I said.

"That's great. How would you do it?" she asked.

"I'd have them start discussing the play openly, and then I'd ask them, 'Did anyone notice any images or symbols that kept popping up in this play?' and just see what happens," I answered. "The worst thing that can happen is that you discover they haven't identified symbols and then you can still give them the ones you prepared."

"That's awesome, Ariel. Exactly the feedback I was looking for. I'm going to try it that way," Meredith said.

The next day, she sent me this message:

> I gave them a chance to identify the images and symbols at the start of class. Your students were able to identify ALL of the important images. Solange and Jean, especially, picked up on the symbolism of dancing and were eager to begin going back to the text and piecing together the different references. I can tell that this is from the work they did in your class last year. They can go through an entire text and process what's going on. They can think about these images and then ask a question like, "Why are there so many references to dancing in this play, and what does that mean?"
>
> It is awesome that your students can ask questions like that, so I don't have to. It makes for much stronger readers and it sets them up for success at the college level. I know all of my college classes had us read a novel per week and then we would discuss it in class. I really believe that your program prepares students for the demands of college-level literature classes.

When it was time for her ninth graders to discuss the play, Meredith also decided to put her prepared discussion questions aside and try an open, whole novels–style discussion. Later that day, I heard not from her but from the high school principal, Kim Raccio, who happened to observe that class and told me about it at lunch: "The kids were so engaged in this discussion—it was really great to see. Some of our more unruly students were getting really worked up, but it was about all the right things! It was all about this play, arguing their points. I loved it!"

Meredith's work with ninth graders makes me excited about what the results would be for students who participate in whole novel studies over several years. I have seen the approach work at the elementary school, middle school, and high school levels, but I have never seen students work consistently in this way for more than two consecutive years. I don't mean that I would like to see students do nothing but whole novel studies in their ELA classes. I hope I've made it clear that the whole novels program is meant to be one component of an entire curriculum. Still, I've seen the approach applied in only short spurts throughout students' education. How would we stretch this from grades 3 through 12? How would the work change over time? What would we discover about the development of readers if we tried this? What would the effect of consistent participation in whole novel studies be on students' reading and writing in other contexts over time? These are questions I hope to be able to answer in time.

The whole novel approach, as I've noted throughout this book, is a flexible framework; anyone can adapt it to suit the needs of their students and the literary works they've selected to study. Teachers can meld whole novels studies in dynamic ways with other approaches to teaching literature and writing. How could we include whole novels experience in different ways throughout a child's education? As we make the transition to the Common Core Standards, I believe now is the time to have this discussion.

IT'S NOT ABOUT ME; ANYONE CAN LEARN TO TEACH WHOLE NOVELS

Sometimes teachers hear me talk about whole novels and say, "That may work for you, but I could never pull that off." This sentiment doesn't match my experiences, though. Having worked with many different coteachers, student teachers, and now other colleagues, I've seen many teachers with different styles quickly pick up the whole novels approach and techniques to support it. For example, since I coteach three out of four classes this year, I tend to hold two discussion groups at once. Since there's one class I teach by myself, I need another teacher to help run discussions if I don't want to throw off the pacing of this class. I've started calling on a colleague, Juliana Garofalo, who teaches ninth grade and has extra time in her schedule to support other English teachers when needed. Juliana taught English for several years before coming to our school, and she never used a whole novel approach.

I explained to Juliana the general format for discussions and my reasons for leading in this way. Juliana led discussions beautifully. I was impressed with the notes she took on the students' comments, which she sent me afterward. I asked the students who had been in her group, "How did it go?" They all had positive things to say.

One boy said, "It was pretty much like how it goes when it's with you."

"You know why?" I responded, smiling. "Because it's not about what I say or do or what Ms. G. says or does. It's about you guys and what you say!" He smiled, as if I had given him a big compliment.

The point here is that I am not special. I'm just committed to making this approach work. Juliana had never led a discussion this way before, and she was successful right away. Something about this method works for kids. After she'd led several rounds of discussions for two different novels, I asked Juliana for her impression of the method, and she wrote the following message:

> The whole novel approach seems to allow students to build confidence and create their own individual opinions . . . Even with very minimal teacher facilitation, every student contributes to the discussion in a meaningful way, and many students build upon each other's ideas. The students feel ownership of their ideas, and it is clear that many of these thoughts have been developing while the students were reading the book. So many of the students refer back to the text and make connections between various events, characters, themes, and other novels.
>
> While reading *The Absolutely True Diary of a Part-Time Indian* I know that the students had learned about conflict in class, and, in their independent reading of the novel, the students explored various conflicts. During the discussion students were ready to talk about these conflicts in a specific way by using evidence from the text. Overall I feel that this is a very successful model for teaching literature and for building a lifelong love of reading and learning.

ADVOCATING FOR SPACE TO TRY WHOLE NOVELS

The response I've gotten to the whole novels program from colleagues and administration at Brooklyn Prospect Charter School has been supportive and affirming. That hasn't always been the case for me. In my first school, a different partially scripted method for teaching reading was being mandated in the district, and I had to fight for the space to teach whole novels. I developed a way of communicating only part of what I was doing to my supervisors and maintaining my own practices behind my closed door. I also found ways to learn from and incorporate some of the mandated techniques into the whole novels framework so that I could always explain how I was doing what I was supposed to be doing.

Was it ideal to keep so much of my teaching to myself and pretend to be doing something I wasn't? No. But I spent three years developing my practice without compromising my beliefs much at all. During this time, it was crucial that I had people to talk openly to about my teaching. Madeleine Ray, Renata Robinson-Glenn, Jane Willis, and some other colleagues became my sounding board. Without them, I could have lost my way and started teaching according to someone else's beliefs and ideas.

I've learned that there's not one right way to teach. At the same time, each of us needs to be able to follow our convictions and find the ways that best create learning among our students and us, even if that means changing course unexpectedly. In my case, I've stayed on the same course I started on, but I've developed confidence and awareness of what I'm doing, why I'm doing it, and its impact on students. At this point, I doubt I'd ever feel the need to hide my teaching practices. If I interview for a teaching position at a new school, I've learned to ask up front if I'll be able to teach whole class novels, and whether there are any requirements around text choices and methodology. If I'm told in an interview I'm not going to be able to teach whole novels, that's a deal breaker for me. Luckily, principals have a lot of autonomy in New York City schools, so encountering scripted curricula or rigid instructional methods is not that common.

The landscape of English language arts instruction is shifting a lot due to the adoption of Common Core State Standards. The reader's workshop model has been the progressive alternative to traditional whole class novel studies for several decades. Now teachers are being challenged to try different methods, an opportunity to propose whole novels to a team or administrator.

If you plan to try a whole novel study at your school, you must get enough copies of the novel to allow students to take their copy home. Otherwise you're stuck reading only in class. This will take too long, and the experience for you and your students will suffer. (One workaround is to start with a quality graphic novel.) When I started teaching, I had only twenty students in a class, and I'd buy twenty books with my own money. My school did have money for books, but ordering through the school meant I might not see my books until the next year, and I needed them right away. The school I teach in now has a clear and reliable process for ordering materials, and books orders are always approved. And I no longer spend my own money on novels! (Ziplock bags are a different story, though.) If ordering your books through your school isn't an option, try posting on DonorsChoose (donorschoose.org). Funding is almost guaranteed for something as essential and relatively low cost as books.

Once you have books, ziplock bags, and sticky notes, here are a few things to mentally prepare for so that you'll be able to respond to any questions from colleagues and supervisors; in parentheses I identify the chapters in this book that discuss this:

- A quick explanation of your book choice—why you think it's a good match for your students and why it's a strong piece of literature, and what literary element students will focus on (Chapter 2)
- A quick explanation of the opportunities the novel provides for students to practice specific state or other standards (Chapters 3, 4, 5, and 7)
- A quick explanation as to why students will wait to discuss the novel until they have finished it (Chapter 1)
- A quick explanation of what students will do during the reading portion of the novel study (Chapters 3, 6, and 7)
- A quick explanation of how you will track students' progress as they read and support students with varying levels of readiness (Chapters 6 and 8)
- An idea for a writing project connected to the book, even if your idea changes later (Chapter 5)
- Some thoughts on how to connect to content, themes, or skills your students are encountering in other subjects if collaboration or interdisciplinary connections, or both, are emphasized at your school (Chapters 2, 7, and 8)

- A few ways to use technology in the novel study if technology is a focus at your school (See Parts of the Whole: Integrating Technology in Chapter 7)

If students are likely to need a lot of support in reading the novel on their own, reach out to colleagues at your school who can help, parents, older students, or other volunteers who can help read with students. Consider purchasing audio books and allowing students to load the files on their phones or MP3 players. Listening stations also provide in-class audio support. Many schools have funds set aside for technology or special education supports and might be able to purchase a listening station for your classroom or department, even if purchasing a class set of books is not possible.

WHOLE NOVELS FOR THE WHOLE CLASS: A HOPEFUL FUTURE

Sometimes I forget how unusual the whole novels method is in K–12 schools. It has become second nature to me and a reality for my students, but the approach is not a common idea or anywhere close to a household name in education.

After a year of student teaching at Bank Street, I was applying for teaching positions. I felt quite prepared to get into my own classroom, but I had no idea how challenging interviews would be. Principals asked me questions for which I had only vague answers (more like guesses). I have no idea how I responded to many of those questions. But I do remember one interview in which a principal asked me to describe how I would teach literature. The interview had been going very well, and I was feeling confident. I had already developed an interest in whole novel studies and had tried it out at Bank Street's School for Children. I started describing how I would conduct a whole novel study by giving each student a copy of the book, sticky notes, and a reading schedule. I explained that they would read the book on their own and when they had finished, we would discuss the book together. In the discussions, students could say anything they want, and I would write down what they said.

I could see the uncertainty building on the principal's face as I described my method. "How would you support students in reading the book?" she asked. There it was: a question for which I had only a vague answer.

"I would work with students individually on whatever they needed," I tried.

"How?" she asked. I don't remember what I said next, but she looked disappointed, and understandably so. I knew then that I probably would not be getting that job. I was right.

Nine years later, I've written the first book I know of on the whole novels method. When I talked to my classes about it, one student, Kimberly, who struggles with reading but has an especially good auditory memory, asked, "Do you think your book will become a classic?"

I laughed at first, surprised at the question. At the beginning of the year, when we started reading *The Hundred Dresses,* by Eleanor Estes, I had told the students that the book, published in 1944 and still in print all over the world, was considered a classic. We had discussed what made a classic and whether newer, widely popular books, like *Harry Potter,* could be considered classics. We agreed that we'd have to wait and see if a book like *Harry Potter* stands the test of time. If people are still interested in it years later, it can become a modern classic.

Initially I was inclined to dismiss Kimberly's question without answering it. Do I think my book will become a classic? It was a cute and clever question, but this book doesn't fall into the genre that I think of as producing classics. (Students were more excited when they thought I might be writing a novel.) Then I remembered that there are classics in education—books that say something important about teaching, something that needs to be said at that moment in time, in the right words, and that continues to be important.

Madeleine Ray has been encouraging the whole novels approach to her students for decades. Many teachers have tried it in their student teaching, as I did, and a large handful of teachers is experimenting with it across New York City today. When people ask me to tell them what I'm writing my book about, it sounds like such a simple idea: let students read the whole book first, before beginning discussions and analysis. They nod and say, "Oh yes, that makes sense," and then there's a pause, followed by one of three questions: "So how do you make sure they read the book?" or, "So what do you do for students who have trouble reading?" or, "So what do you do in class before they finish the book?"

Then I pause. "Well," I usually say, "it would take a book to explain that."

The answers to these questions are not simple or obvious. They've taken time and skill to figure out. But as Madeleine reminded me on the phone recently, "What you are writing could really change the way children read in school—revolutionize it really."

At this moment, I believe that the need for a radical new way of working with the whole class novel is on the tip of the collective tongue of English educators. I hope that in writing this book, I have articulated an answer to that need. I've done a lot of figuring out how to make whole novels work in the classroom. Now it's yours to adapt, innovate, develop with your students, and share with others.

I hope that if this book does not become a classic, at least it will make it possible for a new teacher to go into an interview, and when the principal asks, "How will you teach literature?" the teacher may respond, "I will use the whole novel approach," and see a flash of recognition in the principal's eyes and be able to explain what whole novels is in a convincing way. And get the job.

Appendices

Appendix A

Transcription of Whole Novel Discussion Notes

The following is an exact transcript of eighth graders' discussion of Sherman Alexie's *The Absolutely True Diary of a Part-Time Indian*.

DAY 1, ROUND 1

CARL: It was really interesting book. At the same time funny and serious.

ANICA: I think its got a lot of dark humor in it. Its weird. Like you're laughing and really depressed.

MICHAEL: I didn't like how some of the bad things happen really quickly. Like when the grandmother died it happened really quickly. Talked about pow wows and then out of nowhere struck and killed by drunk driver.

PETER: I want something better to happen than what happened in the end. It was like, they just played ball together. Other than that, it was pretty good. And I think if him and Penelope don't work out he's gonna go after Rowdy.

CANDIDO: I thought it was good. I had a lot of connections w the book. Main theme had to do with struggle of minorities. He lived on the rez with many native americans. Lots of racism in the book and I encounter that a lot. Not every day but often to other people. Also he seemed really happy in the beg. Before he went to Reardon. Somewhere in the middle a giant mess was occurring when he transferred. Whole rez disliked him and he punched Roger. It could have been better.

HASSAN: I liked the book but the part I didn't get was when his grandma died and Eugene died and Mary died. Those were part of his life, and he felt miserable.

ADELITA: I thought that there was a lot of denial in the book. After everybody died it seemed really different. Kind of weird. Felt awkward that he didn't know what to say or do. Always had this haunting him. He didn't have so much experience with the ones who died. It hit a lot of emotion.

KENDRICK: I thought this was one of the most realistic books I've read. Not that a lot of people have his problems, but the whole atmosphere including the vulgarity does make it so realistic. And it's a good book.

SAM: I liked how our main character Junior wasn't a perfect person. He had faults. Kind of crazy and the scene when he flips out when his sister died and d was like, "Son you're freaking me out." Lots of bad things that happen to Jr weren't his fault. But he did some things that brought on bad luck.

LUKE: I like the cartoons. They helped with the story but also helped better understanding what Junior was thinking. In the bk you can only understand so much. And with pics it helps you picture it all in your mind.

ADAM: Toward the end the scene where he and Rowdy climbing the tree. It's a metaphor for him overcoming the challenges he had.

NAIMA: Overall I really liked the book bc it was realistic. One of my favs now. I don't really like how it ended bc I really thought it was going to be different. I wanted to see what would happen with the rest of his family. It was like everyting happened and the solution to his problem with Rowdy only mattered. Didn't show Penelope, or others . . .

ALEX: I liked the book. I liked the part when he switched schools and got to meet people all over again. That were not his race. It was different for him to fit in with everyone else.

ADAM: the tree is 220.

MS. SACKS: Let's save that part for later.

ALEX: Blurb says events were inspired by author's experiences. That must have been hard.

NAIMA: I asked Mr. Ali [Yusuf, co teacher]and he said he didn't.

MICHAEL: The grandmother's death was on p. 159 [Here students are finding evidence for points that students brought up earlier. We need to pick a thread to explore.]

ALEX: Why did the author put things in here that didn't have to do with the book? Like small little chunks of information. One was about scientists. I'm an invisible scientist.

HASSAN: At the end of the book—usually I read the back before I read the book—but with this I decided not to. But the end wasn't that interesting.

KENDRICK: I want to figure out why so many people say it's a great ending. Mr. Ali kept saying he likes the ending. It's like an ending of most fiction stories. The main character.

PETER: It seemed like the type of book where it wouldn't end up all good again where him and Rowdy are friends, but it kind of did, which is why I didn't like it. I thought he was gnna beat Rowdy by a point.

LUKE: I agree w Peter. I thought they were gonna become friends but realized they weren't. after the bball game, Rowdy elbowed Junior in the head, he got a concussion I realized they weren't going to become friends. After the sister died Rowdy was crying and tried to beat up Junior. But right after the basketball part at the very end I think they will become friends

CANDIDO: I sort of agree and sort of disagree w/Peter and Luke. Even Rowdy threatened to beat up Junior. Thought he was joking when he wasn't. even with the best of friends there are arguments

MS. SACKS: whats the big conflict w him and rowdy?

NAIMA: The big conflict wasn't even about Reardon. In some way Rowdy thought that Junior thinks hes better than him. Rowdy says, "You always thought you were better than me." Junior even suggests that R goes to school with him

ALEX: Now that I reread the end, I think I realy like it now, Its not really an ending of the book, but more to it. The book is finished but could still go on to be longer. That's why some don't like it bc it feels unfinished.

KENDRICK: I agree w Naima's idea that its not him moving to Reardon. Its him just leaving Rowdy. He could have been going anywhere. This maybe made it a little harder, because it was the white school.

SAM: I thought it was int. how Junior used to sort of fit in the rez before he left. Once he left, he didn't fit in anywhere. That was interesting.

CANDIDO: I remember Mr Ali telling me this—the separation between one world and another—two cultures. Mr Theisen [their social studies teacher] said that assimilation had to do with fitting in and forgetting about his old culture. He even said that he felt more white than Indian. Sounds like he really assimilated and forgot about his heritage.

CARL: I remember Mr Theisen said that many native am's were forced to the rez and it got smaller and smaller. Rowdy thought that Junior was "better" cuz he . . . [lost track of conversation in notes here]

HASSAN: I think when he got to Reardon it was like a curse bc when he got there half of his family died. When he was at the rez it was normal.

JENNIFER: I notice that Eugene is kind of like a rebel but not what you would think of as a rebel with no heart. He said that Jr has a lot of courage. Even though Jr says he is a wuss. Eugene never really fulfilled his dreams.

SAM: when we found out Eugene was really good at bball but didn't make it to college but couldn't read—told me a lot about the schools on the reservations if someone could get to high school not reading.

ADELITA: Eugene reminds me of Rowdy in a way. Rowdy's trying to be like his dad. Rowdys more of a bully type and Eugene's more of a rebel. Rowdy might go down the same path as Euegene. Might go down the path himself. Might get a motorcycle, get drunk . . . something could happen.

MS. S: you imagine R's future might not end well?

ANICA: Francesca sad he doesn't think he has potential. In one chap, Jrs telling him how hes gonna play bball for seattle. Then R says, no I'm not. He doesn't believe in himself.

PETER: I think as the book progressed, Jr.'s confidence in himself grows. In the beg hes talking about how he has this horrible disease . . . if you only read the back part you would never know has ths thing. Stops feeling sorry for himself; does well in bball.

318

KENDRICK: I also think its int. how in the beg he tells us about his brain/head injury. Since its in the beg you think its going to affect his life, but then you never hear about it . . . nothing happens because he has this.

ALEX: Overall think when he made that decision to go to the school he had to change his life to fit in. You would have to be more like a white kid than an Indian.

NAIMA: I wonder if the people on the rez are sort of jealous of Jr. They probly know hes going to make it far and do something good for himself. Feel jealous bc never had the courage to do it themselves.

SAM: In this bk I read, theres ths guy in jail and trying to get on parole. Everyone fights with him bc they think he can make it out and don't want to be left behind. They want to hold him back.

JENNIFER: I agree. I notice that in this bk its hard to fit in when you're different in a way, and when you care about your future (and others don't). I read this book about picking cotton, about this guy accise of rape, but not guilty. When his time was up, this guy who was guilty got mad and tried to kill him.

CANDIDO: agree. Honestly if our whole generation was like being on a rez, and only one of us were really smart and intelligent and the rest knows hes gonna success, we'd try to stop it bc then the rest of us would be done for . . .

SAM: at the beg we first meet Roger, hes a really bad person, says racist joke, but then after Jr punches him in the face, he respects him and then gets really nice. Lends him 40$ rides him home, ect.

NAIMA: I think the reason Roger suddenly changes is bc he was intimidated by Jr from the start bc they made it seem like Indians were scary.

MS. S: could they be? Sterotypes or real?

NAIMA: at grandmas funeral, said he wanted to return the grandma's costume but mom said it didn't belong to them so they couldn't return it.

ADELITA: in the beg. All of the authors usually have dedications. He says "for Wellpinit and Reardon, my home towns." He had this experience and maybe changed some things. Also a weird quote: "There is another world but it is in this one" by W.B. Yeats

ADAM: back to Naimi's idea—I think Ted the rich guy, when he gave the powwow costiume to Jr's mom. I think she lied when she said it wasn't there. a way to make him feel embarrassed for being rich

ANICA: The quote: I think it means the rez is within this community of white people and sort of like the world of the rez to the world of white people. The world in the world. The rez sounds like totally different country. Completely

KENDRICK: why did you want us to read this book?

LUKE: I think that were a lot of metaphors in this book. Esp toward the end. The stupid horse one was a metaphor for not getting into things that are over your head. The way the dad described it, I don't think it's a very good metaphor but not a good lesson. Dad is basically telling him to not try for anything.

NAIMA: disagree w Luke. I don't think father meant that. He was just telling him not to try anything stupid.

MS. S: playing with fire?

JENNIFER: I disagree too. Think about how they said tried to kill horse and went back. If something gets u down don't quote.

Student Writing Questions

Here, I asked students to share some questions they'd like to investigate further. (This was a double-block period, which happens once a week, so these questions were in place of our usual homework questions.) Students then had about eight minutes to write freely in response to any of the questions. When the writing time was up, I asked students to share which question they chose for their writing. I put their names next to the questions and had them meet in small groups to share their ideas and continue discussing:

1. Why did the author use curses? (Carl, Michael, Peter, Carl, Hassan)
2. "There is another world, but it is within this one" (Yeats). What are your thoughts about this quote? (Adelita)
3. Why did Ms. Sacks want us to read this? (Alex, Candido, Adam)
4. What is the significance of the drawings? Is this part based on his life? (Luke, Sam)
5. Which parts of the story resolve? What's left? How would you end it differently? (Anica)
6. What do you think Junior's future is going to be like (based on the text so far)? (Naima, Jennifer)

DAY 1, ROUND 2: SHARING OUT

For the second period of our block, we came back together as a group and started by sharing our new thoughts that emerged from the small group conversations.

ADAM: In our group we discussed why you want us to read this book. I thought it might relate to our theme of 2 worlds. Switiching btwn life on the rez and reardon—hence the name part time Indian—and same with other things we read and saw—smoke signals, ABC, Mango st. author. Switching between life then and npw. Fits the main theme.

CANDIDO: also its our year before high schoo. You want us to know how fitting in.

SAM: Luke and me did question #4 about cartoon.s Lucas said maybe its to get inside Junior's mind. Seems like a good idea.

LUKE: Also decided it wasn't part of Alexie's life. Cartoons. We thought that if he could draw that well, he wouldn't need an artist.

NAIMA: but he does write—bc he says "diary" of a part-time Indian.

SAM: if it's a diary then maybe this dedication is not actually by the author, but by Arnold/Junior's dedication.

ADELITA: I'm confused about if Arnold's mom is his grandmother's daughter. But his dad's last name is spirit.

KENDRICK: we pretty much said that curses added realism to the book. Really isn't a part of most books. Not that realistic, at least in modern days.

HASSAN: I said that he tried to express his feelings by cursing.

ALEX: I disagree. I don't think cursing expresses anything. Even though I sometimes do it when im frustrated. I think its just a nasty way to talk.

SAM: I agree with Alex. I think its an easy way to make the book funny. In a lot of books that Ive read and are moderns they have a lot of curses. Made it seem more lifelike.

PETER: I agree w Kendrick bc all kids books don't have cursing even though a lot of kids curse. They are trying to shield us from this language but we know it all.

KENDRICK: I think one reason we thinks its more funny is cuz we're reading this book in school. If I just picked it in the book store I wouldn't think its that funny, but when you're in school its different

MICHAEL: I thought it made the book more relatable when he cursed bc theres a lot of cursing in the real world. Not a day you can just walk to school and not hear a curse.

ANICA: Nothing has been resolved completely in the book. It's life. In the last chapter everything just doesn't come together

JENNIFER: I think that Jr's future can be bright. Reminds me of freedom writers, how the kids are living in poverty. In gangs. Urban LA.

DAY 2

We begin by reading over printed copies of notes from the previous day's discussion. Then we continue with open discussion.

LUKE: it was int. that Jr fit in more at Reardon than he did at the rez bc he had more than 1 friend, a girlfriend and ev seemed to like him. back at the rez people seemed to fight him.

KENDRICK: wondering why it was like that. Just cuz he punched roger in the face? Did that pretty much gain him respect of the whole school? Or in his own kind of world where he was born he didn't have the same amount of respect as he did in the place where they're not "supposed to" give you respect?

MS. SACKS: Sup[posed to?

KENDRICK: the stereotypical view of whites

PETER: only native am that wasn't always mad. Wanted to take his anger out on other people. Wanted to take his anger out on other people kind of mean to each other.

CANDIDO: I have to add on to what Peter and Kendrick had said. Maybe he became popular and more not bc he punched roger I his face but bc he started liking Penelope and she started saying positive things about him to the community. Ntil they started dating, continuing to show affection fr one anotger. Maybe that's why roger and the team liked him.

ADELITA: I disagree with that. Reason why he had a better time is that he had a more positive attitude. Everybody knew each other and about him on the rez. At Rear he had a chance to show out, not all his flaws. Different setting

ADAM: Adding onto Candido's point, Jr wasn't very popular and everybody was being racist towards him, but as soon as he started dating penny everybody became nice to him.

NAIMA: back at the part where Jr found out that Penny was bulemic. I think reason they started dating and whatever relationship formed was bc he was the only one who tried to see how she felt bc she said that everyone expects me to be pop and pretty and intelligent.

LUKE: I think it was the part where he punched roger in the face. I think the part where they started to like him was when he started to darte penny. Respected him.

SAM: I thought it was really annoying how much power Penelope had over the school. It worked out for Jr but annoying. He showed up at the dance and she said he looked good and everybody liked the pants.

KENDRICK: the page where he punched Roger is 65.

CANDIDO: Adding onto what Sam said, besides Luke, when he first came to Reardon and his dad started dropping him off on his motorcycle to school, Roger started liking him after he had punched him in the face-he was like, oh, that's a nice bike. Maybe that's why he got more respect. Just assuming.

JENNIFER: adding onto Sam's idea bout the dance. At the dance he liked being popular and being w penny was a moment he treasured a lot. Best night of his life.

NATE: (absent Day 1) I think maybe the motocycle wasn't why. It added onto the respect that he was getting

ADAM: There are a number of things—when he punched roger, got on the motorcycle, dating penelope, dance. All of those things together got him respect.

ANICA: Im wondering if the motorcycle and punching that guy sort of speeded up how fast they started to respect him. there was the stereoptypical image of the Indian as tough. When he did those things he lived up to that stereotype.

NAIMA: I agree w Adam bc in the bk where he started to get respect after punching roger and dating P, these things revolved around each other, if he had just punched roger, people would be afraid. If he only dated penny, hed only talk to her.

    We read p. 65

    We discuss "chief"

    —Way of commenting on him being Indian

    —Pointing out that he's different

    Could be form of respect but depends on how he says it.

    Depends on your relationship with that person. Could sound different.

    Also shows they don't pay attention to the society—they don't really know about it; just using whatever little that they know

    Eye contact, body signals matter too

    We read the fight p. 65

SAM: its weird that he thinks of those rules as rules.

JENNIFER: if you look at the rules p61

KENDRICK: interesting—if you think somebody is thinking about insulting you then you have to fight them . . .

ADAM: they must get into a lot of fights.

LUKE: I think some are pretty presumptuous. "You must always pick fights with the daughters or sons of white people living on the rez". Presumes they will be racist . . .

NATE: "freaky alien and no way to get home"

NAIMA: Where he comes from, people understand how he acts and fights that way.

MS. SACKS: Does this factor into why it's so hard to leave the rez?

CANDIDO: We talked about him getting a better life and getting rich and others on the rez not liking that. He got popular because he was smart . . .

This is close to the end of the discussion, but I often lose track of the ends of discussions, because I get so interested that I stop taking notes.

Appendix B
Spanish Translation of the
Parent Letter

Háblele a su hijo/a sobre sus lecturas

Los estudiantes de Brooklyn Prospect Charter School tienen tarea asignada todas las tardes, con la única excepción de los miércoles por la tarde. Háblele todos los días a su hijo sobre su progreso académico, así se asegura del triunfo en sus tareas diarias.

Prepare un momento y lugar tranquilos para la lectura

Consiga un lugar tranquilo donde pueda leer sin ninguna distracción provocada por la televisión, computadora, radio, o videojuegos.

Converse sobre sus tareas y sus lecturas

Pregúntele qué lee? Cuál es el libro y de qué trata?

- Si puede, no le pregunte "Si terminó la tarea."
- Sustituya la clásica pregunta con una parecida, "De que trata el libro?"
- Muestre interés haciendo más preguntas sobre la historia, los protagonistas, y sus conflictos.

Esta es una buena forma de comunicarse neutralmente con el adolescente y su nueva independencia. Sepa que su conversación puede darse en cualquier idioma.

Cree una nueva relación basada en los libros

Los siguientes patrones le ayudarán a crear ricas actividades motivacionales de lectura en torno a su hijo:

- Descubra los libros favoritos de su hijo.
- Vaya a la librería y escoja libros fascinantes que puedan leer!
- Lean los dos juntos en silencio o léanse el uno al otro capítulos en voz alta, después tengan una buena conversación sobre el libro.

Appendix C

Notes Worksheet for Picture Book Study

Name_____ Date_____

Studying *Where the Wild Things Are* by Maurice Sendak

Look closely through the book with the other students at your table. Write down your thoughts on the following prompts.

Max . . . _____

_____

_____

Feelings in this story . . . _____

_____

_____

Setting . . . _____

_____

_____

Illustrations . . . _____

_____

_____

Mother . . . _____

_____

_____

Conflicts . . . _____

_____

_____

Changes . . . _____

_____

_____

Questions/Comments . . . _____

_____

_____

Appendix D
Directions for Plot Charting Activity

EKG Charting for *Where the Wild Things Are* By Maurice Sendak

1. Title: EKG chart for *Where the Wild Things Are* by Maurice Sendak. Write names of students.
2. Create an *x*- and *y*-axis on your chart paper.
3. Label the *x*-axis "Events in Story."
4. Label the *y*-axis "Intensity of Story."
5. At the bottom of the *y*-axis, write "0." At the top, write "10."
6. Write in the key events of the story on the *x*-axis.
7. For each event, decide how intense it is on a scale of 1 to 10. Make a point for the intensity of each event above it, using the *y*-axis.
8. Connect the points for each event to make a line.
9. On a large index card, work together to write a paragraph that describes your line. What does it show about the story?
10. If you have time, copy at least one illustration from the book into free space on your chart paper.

Appendix E
Seeker Opportunity Assignment Choices

ELA08 Seeker Opportunity!

1. Read *Martian Chronicles* by Ray Bradbury.

2. Pick **one** assignment to do. These need not be lengthy. One page is sufficient for written assignments; however, you are free to do more.

   - Letter correspondence with a character: Write a letter to a character in the book. Or pretend to be a character and write a letter to another character in the book, or a historical figure.
   - Newspaper article: Write a brief news article reporting an event from the book. Make sure to give it a catchy headline.
   - Create a sequel for the book: Write the first chapter of the sequel, or make a dust cover for the sequel.
   - Literary analysis: Write an essay (at least 3 paragraphs) about an aspect of the book—for example, the author's use of language, symbolism, the development of a particular character, theme, or your guess as to the author's purpose.
   - Visual representation: Create a visual representation of a key scene or element of the book. For example, draw the setting in detail, sculpt the main character, or make a diorama.
   - Rewrite a scene: Pick a scene and rewrite it from another character's perspective or in a different tone.
   - iMovie dramatization: Use iMovie to dramatize a scene from the book, or create a movie trailer for the book.
   - Other: Design your own. Check your idea with me first.

   DUE: Wednesday, November 2. Discussions will be held after Thanksgiving break.

Appendix F
Student-Designed "Book Report"

After almost two years of studying whole novels, Damian proposed this book report as a substitute for sticky notes, and he rose to the occasion. I describe the interaction in detail in Chapter 8.

The Alchemist

A Book Review by Damian Barros

The Alchemist is a novel by Paulo Coelho. Originally written in 1988, it was written in Portuguese, and it has been translated into 71 languages as of 2011. It is an international bestseller, selling over 65 million copies, and holding the record for most languages a book was translated into for any author alive today. It is a book enjoyed by many, but to understand and truly indulge yourself in it, you have to dig deeper in, analyzing things like literary elements, plot structure, and levels of thinking throughout the story.

Literary Elements

Setting

The Alchemist is a book that shows many settings through the story. It is structured (setting-wise) like a journey story, because the main character leaves his home, and travels to many places on his journey before returning home. He starts in Andalusia, where he is a shepard. Then he travels to Tarifa (reason in plot analysis), where he stays for a while. Then, the second part begins, and it is taken up mostly describing his trek across the desert, arriving and staying in Faiyum (The Oasis), and finally, his travel to The Pyramids and back home.

Setting Grade: B+ Setting is key in any adventure book, and is used well in The Alchemist, because different settings should co-assign with rising and falling action in the plot, and it is practiced well in The Alchemist.

Characters and Character Development

There are too many characters that are introduced to remember, or for each one to have a large effect on the story, but that is the case with most books in general. Their are only six characters you really notice however, as most just come and go.

Santiago: Santiago is the main character, and is the character making the journey. He is a shepherd in the beginning, and after going to a fortune teller and being visited by Melchizedek, realizes his personal legend is to go to the Pyramids in Egypt and get his treasure. A strange part of the story is that it says Santiago's name once in the beginning, and then calls him "The Boy"

Melchizedek: Melchizedek is the king who appears in the town square, and informs Santiago about the Pyramids, his personal legend, and the world around him. He gives Santiago Urim and Thummim, which re-occur many times in the story, as well as the idea of the king and the things he said to Santiago re-occur many times throughout the story in Santiago's mind. Though he is only physically in the story for maybe 10 pages, to some people he is a more important character than Santiago.

The Shopkeeper: The Shopkeeper gives Santiago a job in Tarifa after he has been robbed. Santiago takes the job at the crystal shop and learns much about the shopkeeper's attitude toward life and the importance of dreaming. The

(*continued*)

(continued)

shopkeeper, while generally afraid to take risks, is a very kind man and understands Santiago's quest—sometimes more than Santiago himself. An example of this is when the shopkeeper tells Santiago that he will not return to Spain, since it is not his fate.

The Englishman: The Englishman introduces Santiago to the aspect of Alchemy when they are in the caravan together to Al-Fayoum, and as the Shopkeeper does as well, introduces Santiago to his attitude on life, and spends time comparing and trying out the other person's ways.

Fatima: When they get to Al-Fayoum, Santiago befriends a beautiful woman named Fatima. They talk everyday, until Santiago asks her to marry him. She insists that he finish his personal legend before marrying her. This angers and confuses Santiago, until The Alchemist explains to him that true love never gets in the way of fulfilling one's dreams, and if it does, then it is not true love.

The Alchemist: He is a very powerful alchemist who lives at the Al-Fayoum oasis in Egypt. Initially, Santiago hears about him through the Englishman, but eventually Santiago reveals himself to be the Alchemist's true disciple. The Alchemist teaches Santiago ways of life and the language of the world and many other things. The Alchemist is probably the most influential character in the story.

Character Grade: A+ Characters are beautifully crafted and put together, and is probably the best part of the story.

Character Development Grade: B— There is really only one character throughout the entire story, as all of the other characters stay in mind, but aren't actually in the story, And that character develops new outlooks on everything, but the other characters don't really change or develop besides The Shopkeeper.

Conflict and Side-Conflicts

There isn't much of a main conflict in The Alchemist, more just a journey with many side tracks and roadblocks that maybe could be considered Side-Conflicts. Some of these are being captured by a tribe, getting his money stolen, and getting beat up when he finds his "treasure"

Conflict Grade: N/A It's hard to grade how an author writes a conflict if there isn't one.

Side-Conflicts Grade: C— They weren't side-conflicts as much as obstacles.

Theme

In The Alchemist, Santiago revisits things that have happened in the book many times, remembering things like his conversation with the king, conversations with the englishman, things he learned from the shopkeeper, and many others, developing not a theme, because then there would be too many themes to revisit and evaluate, but a theme that the characters in the book often go back and think about things they have experienced. For example, many times during the trek across the desert Santiago thinks about things the englishman and the king have said, and often when he is under stress about a decision or a decision he or someone else has to make, he revisits things the king has said and the alchemist has said. If a theme had to be pinpointed, it would probably be the theme that there is a "Wise Old Man", or in this book's case a few wise old men (shopkeeper, the king, the alchemist) whose advice has altered the way he thinks or makes decisions. The book as a whole revisits ideas that have come up in the book beforehand, but that is probably more of a style of writing than a theme.

Theme Grade: **B** A theme is revisited throughout the story, and the story sticks with the theme the whole time, and does it well too!

Writing

Flow

Ok. The book was written in Portuguese. Translated 72 times . . . you can't get angry that the flow of the story and writing isn't perfect. It is good, but if it weren't translated, I don't think this would be published. That's how bad the flow of the story is. Time flies by, one point Santiago says he is returning to Spain, and $\frac{1}{3}$ of a page later, he says he will go on with his journey to Egypt, that he has had a crazy change of heart. It takes way too long to describe some parts, and too short description for things that need longer descriptions. But again, the word of the day is *translated*.

Flow Grade: **N/A** It is a translated book, and I don't read Portuguese, so I cannot grade this. Just know that at some points, the flow of the writing is so bad, that I have no doubt that if Paulo Coelho had written this book in English the same way it is written in the translated to English version, we wouldn't have a book called The Alchemist by Paulo Coelho to review. It's that bad.

(*continued*)

(continued)

Levels of Thinking

The Alchemist is a very un-detailed book, and even when you can tell Paulo Coelho is trying to be more descriptive, it isn't very descriptive. You have to re-read often. You only do critical thinking most of the time. For someone who doesn't like processing and thinking deeply about a book, this is 150% not a book for you. Enough said.

Primary Level of Thinking: Critical Inferential Thinking

Everything is put in the book, you just have to do all the thinking. The book is like MAD-LIBS. You are given all of the words in the outline, you just have to think of the main things.

Plot

Review

There are several stages of The Alchemist, all pretty well defined by the switching of the 5 main side characters' being with Santiago, and also defined pretty well by the switching of the setting and environment they are in. A typical adventure story; Start, realizes quest or journey, starts journey, rising action, more rising action, climax point, goes home. These can all be matched with a setting and 1–2 characters besides Santiago. See chart below:

Section of Story	Setting	Character(s)	Description & anything else
Start, Beginning	Andalusia (Santiago's hometown	Santiago	He is a shepherd, has no idea about his journey yet
Journey is introduced	Tarifa Market	Santiago, Melchizedek	The king tells Santiago about his journey
Journey Starts	Tarifa	Santiago	Santiago gets all of his money stolen

Rising action	Tarifa	Santiago, The Shopkeeper	Santiago works in the shop so he can get money to go to the pyramids and learns many things from the shopkeeper
Rising action	Tangier and numerous places in the desert	Santiago, The Englishman	Santiago goes on the caravan across the desert and meets the englishman who introduces many ideas and thoughts into his head, including alchemy
Rising action	Al-Faiyum	Santiago, The Englishman, Fatima	Santiago meets Fatima and she teaches him many things about life and he asks her to marry him.
Rising to climax	Al-Faiyum and other places in the desert	Santiago, The Alchemist	Santiago meets the Alchemist and they leave the Oasis to get Santiago's treasure and so Santiago can be taught by the Alchemist
Climax	Tribe military camp in the desert	Santiago, The Alchemist	Santiago and the Alchemist are arrested, the Alchemist says Santiago is the Alchemist and he can perform miracles, and they give him 3 days to destroy their camp with a wind, and he speaks to the world and does it
Climax peak	The Pyramids	Santiago	Santiago finds the treasure, only to find out his true treasure isn't there after the bag of gold he finds is stolen by a thief
Goes Home	Andalusia	Santiago	Santiago finds his treasure

(continued)

(continued)

Final Evaluation

Literary Element Use: B

Writing of Story: N/A

Main Level of Thinking: Critical

Plot: B+

Final Grade: 83 out of 100

Re-Read Factor: Medium, Depends if you like going back into books a second and even third time to really envelope yourself in it.

Yes or No: Yes. 100% read this book. It's boring in the beginning, but it gets real good. Real good.

Fin

Appendix G
Variations on a Theme Assignment

Variations on a Theme: *The House on Mango Street* Project

As you have seen, *The House on Mango Street* is a novel composed of a series of vignettes, or snapshots from Esperanza's perspective. You've now identified major *themes* that run through the whole work. A theme is an idea, topic, or feeling that occurs over and over again in different situations throughout a story.

Your task: Pick one of the themes that is present in *The House on Mango Street* (you are not limited to the list we used in class this week). Explore this theme by writing vignettes of your own, from your own perspective.

The Project

- Write three "vignettes" that deal with your *theme*. Each one needs a title.
- Write in the first person. The narrator should be the same for all 3 vignettes.
- Your vignettes can be realistic, but they should sound like fiction. Make-up names for your characters.
- You must think of a title for your project that includes your "theme word" in it.
- Be creative with language! Use descriptive language. *At least* one vignette needs to have figurative language, i.e., similes, metaphors, and/or personification. Try for more!
- Each vignette should be about one page, handwritten (or more).

Suggestions

- Pick a vignette from *The House on Mango Street*, and rewrite it from your own perspective. For example, rewrite "Hairs" about your family. Or write a vignette called "The House on _____ Street," using your own street name.
- Try looking back at the vignette you wrote in class last week. Can you adapt this to deal with your theme?

Due dates: Your choice of theme is due at the end of class *today*.
You will have *2* days in class next week to write (while discussions are happening).

Appendix H
Hero's Journey Cycle Activity

The Cycle of the Hero's Journey

Use your notes from Joseph Campbell's interview and your knowledge of the stories to create a chart of the hero's journey. Do not use details from specific stories—just refer to a "character."

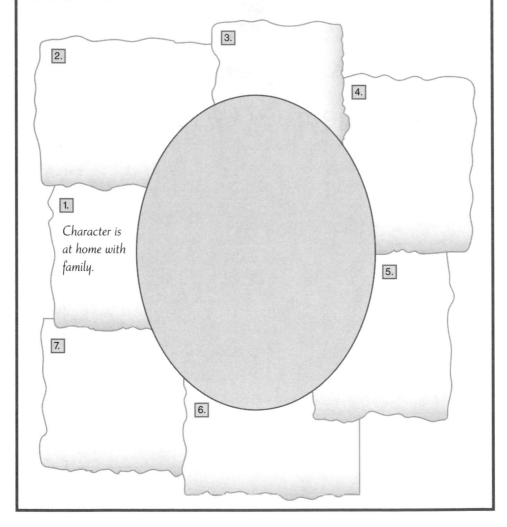

1.

Character is at home with family.

2.

3.

4.

5.

6.

7.

References

"Achievement and Testing." http://www.nyccharterschools.org/content/achievement-testing

Appleyard, J. A. *Becoming a Reader: The Experience of Fiction from Childhood to Adulthood.* Cambridge: Cambridge University Press, 1991.

Atwell, N. *In the Middle.* Portsmouth, NH: Heinemann, 1998.

Beers, K. *When Kids Can't Read: What Teachers Can Do.* Portsmouth, NH: Heinemann, 2002.

Campbell, J. *The Hero with a Thousand Faces.* Princeton, NJ: Princeton University Press, 1968.

Elkind, D. *A Sympathetic Understanding of the Child: Birth to Sixteen.* Boston: Allyn & Bacon, 1995.

Ferlazzo, L. "An Effective Lesson on Metacognition." October 2011. http://larryferlazzo.edublogs.org /2011/10/31/an-effective-five-minute-lesson-on-metacognition/

Fountas, I., and G. S. Pinnelle. *Fountas & Pinnelle Prompting Guide Part 2 for Comprehension: Thinking, Talking and Writing.* Portsmouth, NH: Heinemann, 2012.

Gallagher, K. *Readicide.* Portland, ME: Stenhouse, 2009.

Gottschall, J. *The Storytelling Animal: How Stories Make Us Human.* New York: Houghton Mifflin Harcourt, 2012.

Harding, D. W. "What Happens When We Read?" in *The Cool Web: The Pattern of Children's Reading,* edited by M. Meek, A. Warlow, and G. Barton, 58–72. London: Bodley Head, 1977.

Jairrels, V. *African Americans and Standardized Tests: The Real Reason for Low Test Scores.* Chicago: African American Images, 2009.

Joseph Campbell and the Power of Myth with Bill Moyers. PBS, 2001.

Kohn, A. *The Homework Myth: Why Our Kids Get Too Much of a Bad Thing.* Philadelphia: Da Capo Press, 2007.

Kreamer, A. "A Business Case for Reading Fiction." 2012. http://blogs.hbr.org/cs/2012/01/the _business_case_for_reading.html.

Lawson, A. E., M. R. Abraham, and J. W. Renner. *A Theory of Instruction: Using the Learning Cycle to Teach Science Concepts and Thinking Skills*. Manhattan: Kansas State University, National Association for Research in Science Teaching, 1989.

Lesesne, T. *Reading Ladders*. Portsmouth, NH: Heinemann, 2010.

Lesser, S. *Fiction and the Unconscious*. New York: Vintage, 1962.

Lobel, A. *Mouse Tales*. New York: HarperCollins, 1972.

Meek, M., A. Warlow, and G. Barton, eds. *The Cool Web: The Pattern of Children's Reading*. London: Bodley Head, 1977.

Miller, D. *The Book Whisperer*. San Francisco: Jossey-Bass, 2009.

National Endowment for the Arts. *"To Read or Not to Read: A Question of National Consequence."* Washington, DC: National Endowment for the Arts, 2007. http://www.nea.gov/research/ToRead .pdf.

Pink, D. *A Whole New Mind: Why Right-Brainers Will Rule the Future*. New York: Penguin, 2006.

Pink, D. *Drive: The Surprising Truth about What Motivates Us*. New York: Riverhead Books, 2009.

Ray, M. "Building a Literature Program." Course materials for Children's Literature in a Balanced Literacy Curriculum, Bank Street College, 2003.

Rosenblatt, L. "Literature: The Reader's Role." *English Journal* 49:5(1960):5–39.

Sacks, A. "Getting Real Reading to Work." *EdWeek*, March 10, 2010, http://www.edweek.org/tm /articles/2010/03/10/tln_sacks_reading.html.

Sacks, A. "Writing the Neighborhood." *Edweek Teacher*, April 4, 2011, http://www.edweek.org/tsb /articles/2011/04/04/02sacks.h04.html.

Style, E. "Mirrors and Windows." 1988. http://www.randolphschool.org/media/uploads /CurriculumWindowMirror.pdf

"Theory and Practice." 2010. http://bankstreet.edu/theory-practice/

Wakefield, D., ed. *Kurt Vonnegut: Letters*. New York: Delacorte Press, 2012.

Willingham, D. *Why Don't Students Like School? A Cognitive Scientist Answers Questions about How the Mind Works and What It Means for the Classroom*. San Francisco: Jossey-Bass, 2010.

Witter, M. *Reading without Limits: Teaching Strategies to Build Independent Reading for Life*. San Francisco: Jossey-Bass, 2013.

Worthy, J. "'On Every Page Someone Gets Killed!' Book Discussions You Don't Hear in School." *Journal of Adolescent and Adult Literacy* 41(1998):508–517.

Index

e represents exhibit; *f* represents figure; *t* represents table.